# Paul Celan

*Judaic Traditions in Literature, Music, and Art*
Harold Bloom and Ken Frieden, *Series Editors*

Select Titles in Judaic Traditions in Literature, Music, and Art

*Benjamin Fondane's "Ulysses,"* bilingual edition
Nathaniel Rudavsky-Brody, trans.

*The Implacable Urge to Defame: Cartoon Jews in the American Press, 1877–1935*
Matthew Baigell

*Literary Hasidism: The Life and Works of Michael Levi Rodkinson*
Jonatan Meir; Jeffrey G. Amshalem, trans.

*The People of Godlbozhits*
Leyb Rashkin; Jordan Finkin, trans.

*Petty Business*
Yirmi Pinkus; Evan Fallenberg and Yardenne Greenspan, trans.

*Pioneers: The First Breach*
S. An-sky; Rose Waldman, trans.

*Red Shoes for Rachel: Three Novellas*
Boris Sandler; Barnett Zumoff, trans.

*With Rake in Hand: Memoirs of a Yiddish Poet*
Joseph Rolnik; Gerald Marcus, trans.

# *Paul Celan*

## THE ROMANIAN DIMENSION

Petre Solomon

*Translated from the Romanian by* Emanuela Tegla

*With an Introductory Essay by* J. M. Coetzee

Syracuse University Press

Syracuse University Press
Syracuse, New York 13244-5290



First Edition 2019

19 20 21 22 23 24 6 5 4 3 2 1

Originally published in Romanian as *Paul Celan. Dimensiunea românească* (Bucharest: Editura Art, 2008).

∞ The paper used in this publication meets the minimum requirements of the American National Standard for Information Sciences—Permanence of Paper for Printed Library Materials, ANSI Z39.48-1992.

For a listing of books published and distributed by Syracuse University Press, visit www.SyracuseUniversityPress.syr.edu.

ISBN: 978-0-8156-3594-9 (hardcover)
978-0-8156-3602-1 (paperback)
978-0-8156-5450-6 (e-book)

**Library of Congress Cataloging-in-Publication Data**

Names: Solomon, Petre, 1923–1991, author. | Tegla, Emanuela, translator.
Title: Paul Celan : the Romanian dimension / Petre Solomon ; translated from the Romanian by Emanuela Tegla. Other titles: Paul Celan. English
Description: First edition. | Syracuse, New York : Syracuse University Press, 2019. | Series: Select titles in Judaic traditions in literature, music, and art | "Originally published in Romanian as Paul Celan: dimensiunea românească (Bucharest: Editura Art, 2008)." | Includes bibliographical references and index.
Identifiers: LCCN 2018053984 (print) | LCCN 2018058782 (ebook) | ISBN 9780815654506 (E-book) | ISBN 9780815635949 | ISBN 9780815635949 (hardcover : alk. paper) | ISBN 9780815636021 (paperback : alk. paper) | ISBN 9780815654506 (e-book)
Subjects: LCSH: Celan, Paul—Criticism and interpretation. | Celan, Paul—Friends and associates. | Celan, Paul—Correspondence. | Solomon, Petre, 1923–1991—Correspondence. | Margul-Sperber, Alfred, 1898–1967—Correspondence.
Classification: LCC PT2605.E4 (ebook) | LCC PT2605.E4 Z82713 2019 (print) | DDC 831/.914—dc23
LC record available at https://lccn.loc.gov/2018053984

*Manufactured in the United States of America*

# Contents

# Note to the Present Edition

Petre Solomon's book was first published in 1987 by Kriterion Publishing, Bucharest. In 1990, a shorter version of it was published in France under the title *Paul Celan—L'adolescence d'un adieu* (Éditions Climats). In Romania, the revised edition was published in 2008 by Editura Art, Bucharest. The present translation is of the 2008 text.

In the 1987 edition, addenda included the lyric and prose poems written by Paul Celan in Romanian, a sample of the game Questions and Answers, and the four texts by Kafka that Celan had translated into Romanian. These texts could not form part of the present edition.

The same first edition contained the entire correspondence between Paul Celan and Petre Solomon, as well as manuscript images of some of them. The photos and several letters could not be included in the present edition either.

All the translations of Celan's Romanian (prose) poems and letter fragments are mine. Unless otherwise indicated, all the other translations of quoted material are mine, as well. Original endnotes written by the author are followed by the abbreviation [A.N.]; new endnotes that I have added are followed by the abbreviation [T.N.], indicating translator's note.

—Emanuela Tegla

# Acknowledgments

*I* would like to express my gratitude to Gordon Collier for his cooperation throughout the process of translating the book. He has been of invaluable help, in terms of thorough revisions, encouragement, and guidance. I also owe sincerest thanks to Charles Armstrong (University of Agder) for his help and enthusiastic support, and to Mirela Dredeţianu, for her kind assistance with the French texts.

My editor from Syracuse University Press, Deborah Manion, deserves my thanks as well, for her support, patience, and understanding.

I would also like to extend my special thanks to Alexandru Solomon, for allowing me to translate his father's book of memoirs into English, and to J. M. Coetzee, for his kind permission to reprint his essay on Celan as the introduction to the present translation.

—Emanuela Tegla

# On Paul Celan

*J. M. Coetzee*

Paul Antschel was born in 1920 in Czernowitz in the territory of Bukovina, which after the break-up of the Austro-Hungarian Empire in 1918 had become part of Romania. Czernowitz was in those days an intellectually lively city with a sizeable minority of German-speaking Jews. Antschel was brought up speaking High German; his education, partly in German, partly in Romanian, included a spell in a Hebrew school. As a youth he wrote verse and revered Rilke.

After a year (1938–39) at medical school in France, where he encountered the Surrealists, he came home on vacation and was trapped there by the outbreak of war. Under the Hitler-Stalin pact, Bukovina was absorbed into the Ukraine: for a brief while he was a Soviet subject.

In June of 1941 Hitler invaded the USSR. The Jews of Czernowitz were driven into a ghetto; soon the deportations commenced. Apparently forewarned, Antschel sought hiding the night his parents were taken. The parents were shipped to labor camps in occupied Ukraine, where both died, his mother by a bullet to the head when

This is a condensed version of J. M. Coetzee's essay "Paul Celan and His Translators," published in *Inner Workings: Literary Essays 2000–2005* (London: Vintage Books, 2008), 114–32, and in *Inner Workings* (New York: Viking, 2007).  Reprinted here with the author's kind permission. [T.N.]

she became unfit for work. Antschel himself spent the war years doing forced labor in Axis Romania.

Liberated by the Russians in 1944, he worked for a while as an aide in a psychiatric hospital, then in Bucharest as an editor and translator, adopting the pen-name Celan, an anagram of Antschel in its Romanian spelling.[1] In 1947, before Stalin's iron curtain came down, he slipped away to Vienna and from there moved to Paris. In Paris he passed his examinations for the Licence ès Lettres and was appointed lecturer in German literature at the prestigious École Normale Supérieure, a position he held until his death. He married a Frenchwoman, a Catholic from an aristocratic background.

The success of this move from East to West was soon dampened. Among the writers Celan had been translating was the French poet Yvan Goll (1891–1950). Goll's widow Claire took issue with Celan over his versions, and went on to accuse him publicly of plagiarizing certain of Goll's German poems. Though the accusations were malicious and perhaps even crazy, Celan brooded over them to the point of convincing himself that Claire Goll was part of a conspiracy against him. "What must we Jews yet endure?" he wrote to his confidante Nelly Sachs, like him a Jew writing in German. "You have no idea how many should be counted among the base, no, Nelly Sachs, you have no idea! . . . Should I name names? You would stiffen with horror."[2]

His reaction cannot just be put down to paranoia. As postwar Germany began to feel more confident, anti-Semitic currents were again beginning to flow not only on the right but, more disturbingly, on the left. Celan suspected, not without reason, that he had become a convenient focus for the campaign for the Aryanization of German culture that had not given up in 1945, merely gone underground.

Claire Goll never relented in her campaign against Celan, pursuing him even beyond the grave; her persecutions poisoned his days and contributed heavily to his eventual breakdown.

Between 1938 and his death in 1970 Celan wrote some eight hundred poems in German; in addition there is a body of early work in Romanian.[3] Recognition of his gifts came soon, with the publication of *Mohn und Gedächtnis* (Poppy and Memory) in 1952. He consolidated his reputation as one of the more important young German-language poets with *Sprachgitter* (Speech Grille; 1959) and *Die Niemandsrose* (The No-One's Rose; 1963). Two more volumes appeared during his lifetime, and three posthumously. This later poetry, out of phase with the leftward swing of the German intelligentsia after 1968, was not quite so enthusiastically received.

By the standards of international modernism, Celan up to 1963 is quite accessible. The later poetry, however, becomes strikingly difficult, even obscure. Baffled by what they took to be arcane symbolism and private references, reviewers called the later Celan hermetic. It was a label he vehemently rejected. "Not in the least hermetic," he said. "Read! Just keep reading, understanding comes of itself."[4]

Typical of the "hermetic" Celan is the following posthumously published poem, untitled, which I quote in John Felstiner's translation.[5]

You lie amid a great listening,
enbushed, enflaked.

Go the Spree, to the Havel,
go to the meathooks,
the red apple stakes
from Sweden —

Here comes the gift table,
it turns around an Eden —

The man became a sieve, the Frau
had to swim, the sow,
for herself, for no one, for everyone —

The Landwehr Canal won't make a murmur.
Nothing
stops.

What, at the most elementary level, is this poem about? Hard to say, until one becomes privy to certain information, information supplied by Celan to the critic Peter Szondi. The man who became a sieve is Karl Liebknecht, "the Frau . . . the sow" swimming in the canal is Rosa Luxemburg. "Eden" is the name of an apartment block built on the site where the two activists were shot in 1919, while the meat-hooks are the hooks at Plötzensee on the Havel River on which the would-be assassins of Hitler in 1944 were hanged. In the light of this information, the poem emerges as a pessimistic comment on the continuity of right-wing murderousness in Germany, and the silence of Germans about it.

The Rosa Luxemburg poem became a minor *locus classicus* when the philosopher Hans-Georg Gadamer, defending Celan against charges of obscurity, gave a reading of it through which he argued that any receptive, open-minded reader with a German cultural background can understand what it is important to understand in Celan without assistance, that background information should take second place to "what the poem [itself] knows."[6]

Gadamer's argument is a brave but losing one. What he forgets is that we cannot be sure that the information that unlocks the poem—in this case, the identities of the dead man and woman—is of secondary importance until we know what it is. Yet the questions Gadamer raises are important ones. Does poetry offer a kind of knowledge different from that offered by history, and demand a different kind of receptivity? Is it possible to respond to poetry like Celan's, even to translate it, without fully understanding it?

Michael Hamburger, one of the most eminent of Celan's translators, seems to think so. Though scholars have certainly illumined Celan's poetry for him, Hamburger says, he is not sure he "understands," in the normal sense of the word, even those poems he has translated, or all of them.[7]

"[It] asks too much of the reader," is the verdict of Felstiner on the Rosa Luxemburg poem. On the other hand, he continues, "what is too much, given this history?" This, in a nutshell, is Felstiner's own response to accusations of hermeticism against Celan. Given the enormity of anti-Semitic persecutions in the twentieth century, given the all-too-human need of Germans, and of the Christian West in general, to escape from a monstrous historical incubus, what memory, what knowledge is it *too much* to demand? Even if Celan's poems were totally incomprehensible (this is not something that Felstiner says, but it is a valid extrapolation), they would nevertheless stand in our way like a tomb, a tomb built by a "Poet, Survivor, Jew" (the subtitle of Felstiner's study), insisting by its looming presence that we remember, even though the words inscribed on it may seem to belong to an undecipherable tongue.[8]

At stake is more than a simple confrontation between a Germany impatient to forget its past and a Jewish poet insisting on reminding Germany of that past. Celan was made famous by, and is still most widely known for, the poem "Todesfuge" ("Death Fugue"):

> Black milk of daybreak we drink you at night
> we drink you at noon death is a master from Germany
> we drink you at sundown and in the morning we drink
>     and we drink you
> death is a master from Germany his eyes are blue
> he strikes you with leaden bullets his aim is true

(I quote from Hamburger's translation, in *Poems of Paul Celan*, p. 63, because Felstiner's version of the passage, quite as riveting in its own way, is controversial out of context.) "Death Fugue" was Celan's first published poem: it was composed in 1944 or 1945 and first appeared, in Romanian translation, in 1947. It absorbs from the Surrealists everything that is worth absorbing. It is not entirely Celan's brainchild: here and there he takes over phrases, among them "Death is a master from Germany," from fellow poets of his Czernowitz days. Nevertheless, its impact has been immediate and universal. "Death Fugue" is one of the landmark poems of the twentieth century.

"Death Fugue" has been widely read in the German-speaking world, anthologized, studied in schools, as part of a program of what is called *Vergangenheitsbewältigung*, coming to terms with, or overcoming, the past. At the public readings Celan gave in Germany, "Death Fugue" was always in demand. It is the most direct of Celan's poems in naming and blaming: naming what went on in the death camps, blaming Germany. Some of Celan's defenders argue that he is labeled "difficult" only because readers find the encounter with him too emotionally bruising. It is an argument that needs to account for the reception of "Death Fugue," a reception with apparently open arms.

In fact, Celan himself never trusted the spirit in which he was welcomed and even fêted in West Germany. In the line that German critics took with "Death Fugue"—to quote one eminent critic, that it showed he had "[escaped] history's bloody chamber of horrors to rise into the ether of pure poetry"—he sensed that he was being misinterpreted, and in the deepest historical sense, willfully misinterpreted.[9] Nor was he pleased to hear that in the classroom German students were being directed to ignore the content of the poem and concentrate on its form, particularly its imitation of musical (fugal) structure.

When Celan writes of the "ashen hair" of Shulamith, he is invoking the hair of Jews that fell as ash on the Silesian countryside; when he writes of "the sow" bobbing in the waters of the Landswehr Canal, he is referring, in the voice of one of her murderers, to the body of a dead Jewish woman. Against pressure to recuperate him as a poet who had turned the Holocaust into something higher, namely poetry, against the critical orthodoxy of the 1950s and early 1960s, with its view of the ideal poem as a self-enclosed aesthetic object, Celan insists that he practices an art of the real, an art that "does not transfigure or render 'poetical'; it names, it posits, it tries to measure the area of the given and the possible."[10]

With its repetitive, hammering music, "Death Fugue" is as direct as verse can be in its approach to its subject. It also makes two huge implicit claims about what poetry in our time is, or should be, capable of. One is that language can measure up to any subject whatsoever: however unspeakable the Holocaust may be, there is a poetry that can speak it. The other is that the German language in particular, corrupted to the bone during the Nazi era by euphemism and a kind of leering doublespeak, is capable of telling the truth about Germany's immediate past.

The first claim was dramatically rejected in Theodor Adorno's pronouncement, issued in 1951 and reiterated in 1965, that "to write poetry after Auschwitz is barbaric."[11] Adorno might have added: doubly barbaric to write a poem in German. (Adorno took back his words, grudgingly, in 1966, perhaps as a concession to "Death Fugue.")

Celan avoids the word "Holocaust" in his writing, as he avoided all usages that might seem to imply that everyday language is in a position to name, and thereby limit and master, that toward which it gestures. Celan gave two major public addresses during his lifetime, both acceptance speeches for prizes, in which, with great scrupulousness of word choice, he responded to doubts about the future of poetry. In the first address, in 1958, he spoke of his halting faith that language, even the German language, had survived "that which happened" under the Nazis.

> There remained in the midst of the losses this one thing: language. It, the language, remained, not lost, yes in spite of everything. But it had to pass through its own answerlessness, pass through frightful muting, pass through the thousand darknesses of deathbringing speech. It passed through and gave back no words for that which happened; yet it passed through this happening. Passed through and could come to light again, "enriched" by all this.[12]

Coming from a Jew, such an expression of faith in German might seem odd. Yet Celan was by no means alone: even after 1945, numbers of Jews continued to claim the German language and intellectual tradition as their own. Among them was Martin Buber. Celan paid a visit to the aged Buber to ask Buber's counsel about continuing to write in German. Buber's response—that it was only natural to write in one's mother tongue, that one should take a forgiving stance toward the Germans—disappointed him. As Felstiner puts it, "Celan's vital need, to hear some echo of his plight, Buber could not or would not grasp."[13] His plight was that if German was "his" language, it was his only in a complex, contested, and painful way.

During his time in Bucharest after the war, Celan had improved his Russian and had translated Lermontov and Chekhov into Romanian. In Paris he continued to translate Russian poetry, finding in the Russian language a welcome, counter-Germanic home. In particular he read Osip Mandelstam (1891–1938) intensively. In Mandelstam he met not only a man whose life-story corresponded in what he felt were uncanny ways to his own, but a ghostly interlocutor who responded to his deepest needs, who offered, in Celan's words, "what is brotherly—in the most reverential sense I can give that word." Setting aside his own creative work, Celan spent most of 1958 and 1959 translating Mandelstam into German. His versions constitute an extraordinary act of inhabiting another poet, though Nadezhda Mandelstam, Mandelstam's widow, is right to call them "a very far cry from the original text."[14]

Mandelstam's notion of poem as dialogue did much to reshape Celan's own poetic theory. Celan's poems begin to address a Thou who may be more or less distant, more or less known. In the space between the speaking I and the Thou they find a new field of tension.

> (I know you, you're the one bent over low,
> and I, the one pierced through, am in your need.
> Where flames a word to witness for us both?
> You—wholly real. I—wholly mad.)

(This is Felstiner's translation. In the freer version by Heather McHugh and Nikolai Popov, the last line reads: "You're my reality. I'm your mirage."[15])

*I*f there is one theme that dominates John Felstiner's biography of Celan, it is that Celan developed from being a German poet whose fate it was to be a Jew to being a Jewish poet whose fate it was to write in German; that he outgrew kinship with Rilke and Heidegger to find in Kafka and Mandelstam his true spiritual forebears.

Though Celan continued during the 1960s to visit Germany to give readings, any hope that he might develop an emotional involvement with a re-arisen Germany faded, to the point that he would call it "a most tragic and indeed most childish error."[16] He began to read Gershom Scholem on the Jewish mystical tradition, Buber on Hasidism. Hebrew words—*Ziv*, the unearthly light of God's presence; *Yizkor*, memory—appeared in his poetry. The theme of testifying, witnessing, came to the fore, along with the bitter personal subtheme: "No one / bears witness for the / witness."[17] The "Thou" of his now insistently dialogical poetry became, intermittently but unmistakably, God; echoes emerged of the Kabbalistic teaching that the whole of creation is a text in the divine language.

The capture of Jerusalem by Israeli forces in the 1967 war filled Celan with joy. He wrote a celebratory poem that was widely read in Israel:

> Just think: your
> own hand
> has held
> this piece of
> habitable earth,
> again suffered
> up into life.[18]

In 1969 Celan visited Israel for the first time ("So many Jews, only Jews, and not in a ghetto," he marveled ironically).[19] He gave talks and readings, met Israeli writers, resumed a romantic relationship with a woman from his Czernowitz days.

As a child Celan had for three years attended a Hebrew school. Though he studied the language unwillingly (he associated it with his Zionist father rather than his beloved Germanophile mother), his command ran surprisingly deep. Aharon Appelfeld, by then an Israeli but by origin a Czernowitzer like Celan, found Celan's Hebrew "rather good."[20] When Yehuda Amichai read out his translations of Celan's poems, Celan was able to suggest improvements.

Back in Paris, Celan wondered whether, in staying behind in Europe, he had not made the wrong choice. He toyed with the idea of accepting a teaching position in Israel. Memories of Jerusalem gave rise to a brief burst of composition, poems that are at the same time spiritual, joyful, and erotic.

Celan had long been troubled by fits of depression. In 1965 he had entered a psychiatric clinic, and later underwent electroshock therapy. At home he was, as Felstiner puts it, "sometimes violent." He and his wife agreed to live apart. A friend visiting from Bucharest found him "profoundly altered, prematurely aged, taciturn, frowning."[21] "They're doing experiments on me," he said. To his Israeli lover he wrote, in 1970: "They've healed me to pieces." Two months later he drowned himself.[22]

To the historian Erich Kahler, with whom Celan had corresponded, Celan's suicide proved that to be "both a great German poet and a young Central European Jew growing up in the shadow of the concentration camps" was a burden too great for one man to bear.[23] In a profound sense this verdict on Celan's suicide is true. But we cannot discount more mundane causes like Claire Goll's prolonged, mad vendetta, or the nature of the psychiatric care he underwent. Felstiner does not comment directly on the treatment to which Celan's doctors subjected him, but from Celan's own bitter asides it is clear they have much to answer for.

Even during Celan's lifetime there had developed a busy scholarly trade, principally in Germany, based upon him. That trade has today grown to an industry. As Kafka is to German prose, so Celan has become to German poetry.

Despite the pioneering translations of Jerome Rothenberg, Michael Hamburger, and others, Celan did not really penetrate the English-speaking world until he had been taken up in France; and in France Celan was read as a Heideggerian poet, that is to say, as if his poetic career, culminating in suicide, exemplified the end of art in our times, an end in parallel to the end of philosophy as diagnosed by Heidegger.

Though Celan is not what one would call a philosophical poet, a poet of ideas, the link with Heidegger is not fanciful. Celan read Heidegger attentively, as Heidegger read Celan; Hölderlin was a formative influence on both. Celan approved of Heidegger's view of poetry's special claims to truth. His own explanation of why he wrote—"so as to speak, to orient myself, to find out where I was and where I was meant to go, to sketch out reality for myself"—is fully in tune with Heidegger.[24]

Despite Heidegger's National Socialist past and his silence on the subject of the death camps, Heidegger was important enough to Celan for Celan, in 1967, to call on him at his retreat in the Black Forest. Afterwards he wrote a poem ("Todtnauberg") about that meeting and the "word / in the heart" he hoped to hear from Heidegger, but failed to get.

What might have been the word Celan was expecting? "Pardon," suggests Philippe Lacoue-Labarthe in his book on Celan and Heidegger. But he soon revises his guess. "I was wrong to think . . . that it was enough to ask forgiveness. [The extermination] is absolutely *unforgivable.* That is what [Heidegger] should have said."[25]

To Lacoue-Labarthe, Celan's poetry is "in its entirety, a dialogue with Heidegger's thought."[26] It is this approach to Celan, dominant in Europe, that has done most to take him out of the orbit of the ordinary educated reader. But there is an opposing school, to which Felstiner clearly adheres, which reads Celan as a fundamentally Jewish poet whose achievement it has been to force back into German high culture (with its ambition to locate its ideal origins in classical Greece), and into the German language, the memory of a Judaic past that a line of German thinkers culminating in Heidegger had tried to obliterate. In this view Celan certainly *answers* Heidegger but, having answered him, leaves him behind.

Celan is the towering European poet of the middle decades of the twentieth century, one who, rather than transcending his times—he had no wish to transcend them—acted as a lightning rod for their most terrible discharges.

*Paul Celan*

# Argument

> On the blank of the page the blood
> that flows is that of the wound
> —PIERRE-JEAN JOUVE[1]

A few years ago, on November 22, 1979, to be precise, I was in the small but pleasant "Salle d'actualités" on the ground floor of the Pompidou Centre in Paris, where a literary evening had been scheduled in memory of the poet Paul Celan, who, long practically ignored in his adopted city, was finally starting to make a name there. The almost simultaneous publication of poetry collections by him, especially *Poèmes de Paul Celan* in André du Bouchet's translation (Clivages, 1978) and *La Rose de personne* in Martine Broda's version (Le Nouveau Commerce, 1979), as well as of a special issue of *PO&SIE* journal dedicated to Celan, assumed in Paris the proportions and significance of a late but welcome recognition, on which the poet's friends, not so numerous, could congratulate themselves.

Happy to find myself at this event, at which Celan's widow and his son were also present, I could not help reflecting on the belatedness of the poet's posthumous glory in this capital, which he had chosen as the place for his self-exile and as his point of departure for eternity. Listening carefully to the presentation by Jean-Pascal Léger (the young editor of the volume *La Rose de personne*), the paper read by translator Martine Broda, and the other talks, I felt that I was attending an academic ritual performed according to the rules of a genre that was very fashionable in Parisian intellectual circles at the time. The image I myself had of Celan did not find a correlative in the erudite and doubtless interesting presentations of the speakers: they talked mainly about the difficulties involved in translating poetry and about the eternal dilemma of choosing between a literal and a free translation. Jean Launay, who, with Michel Deguy, had translated some texts by Celan (published in *PO&SIE*), opted for a *mot-à-mot* translation, word-for-word, while Martine Broda, relying on her own experience and on observations by Walter Benjamin,[2] declared herself in favor of free interpretation, one capable of creating "a compliment bestowed upon language." To be fair, I must add that Martine Broda was the only one who laid stress on the importance of *context* for understanding Celan's extremely difficult texts. But the discussions were mostly oriented toward detached analysis, in which the poet's existential drama was lost in a pretentious and, ultimately, hollow *metalanguage.* They spoke about "the oxymoronic value" of the rose, "flower of the absurd," about the almond metaphor and other such things—a whole forest of symbols that was hiding the living tree of Celan's poetry. He might have repeated what he said in 1958 when he received the Bremen Prize: "Reachable, near and not lost, there remained in the midst of the losses this one thing: language. It, the language, remained, not lost—indeed, despite everything" (Erreichbar, nah und unverloren blieb inmitten der Verluste dies eine: die Sprache. Sie, die Sprache, blieb unverloren, ja, trotz allem).[3]

Of course, any great poet is condemned to being reduced to his own words by criticism, be it academic or not. This is the fate of any body of work—to become the subject of discussions, aseptic food produced on the conveyor belt of the manufacturers of literary canned produce. For some decades now, language has tended to displace the author as subject and as hero of literature and criticism. The Russian formalists, the New Critics from America and France, the structuralists and poststructuralists of all shades—all have striven to eliminate the poet from poetry in order to make it possible for the latter to be "dissected" and "deconstructed" through an analysis that aspires to scientific status. Let us remember Osip Brik's extreme position, when he did not hesitate to affirm that *Eugene Onegin* would have been written anyway, even if Pushkin had not existed. Or the statement formulated over six decades ago by T. S. Eliot: "The more perfect the artist, the more completely separate in him will be the man who suffers and the mind which creates."[4]

Writers themselves have contributed to this odd metamorphosis through their legitimate reaction against excesses in sociological and biographical criticism, too inclined, in its turn, to confer on them the status of alienation. Flaubert's ambition to lose himself in his own work ("The man is nothing, the work is everything" [l'homme n'est rien, l'oeuvre est tout][5]) has been shared by many authentic writers in his time and in the contemporary age. The battle Proust fought against Sainte-Beuve, however justified, paved the way for the triumph of a certain type of criticism, ready to put in brackets or even completely ignore any referential element—be it biographical, historical, etc.

The primordial role ascribed to language in modern poetry is also well known—poetry as it has been written since Rimbaud and especially since Mallarmé, and the best definition of which seems to be the one formulated by Valéry: "a language within language" (un langage dans le langage). "Modernity begins with the search for an impossible literature" (La modernité commence avec la recherche d'une littérature impossible), said Roland Barthes. He also spoke of the "hunger of the Word, common to the whole of modern Poetry" (cette faim du Mot, commune à toute la Poésie moderne), a hunger that makes poetic speech "terrible and inhuman" (une parole terrible et inhumaine).[6]

Listening to the discussions on Paul Celan, I felt that, on the contrary, it was not the poet who practiced "terrible and inhuman" speech, but his critics. This is not meant to be a sweeping condemnation of the so-called "New" Criticism and its advocates, of various theoretical orientations. This type of criticism has indisputable merits and has proven its value and usefulness in various ways. But, by declaring itself to be the supreme and unique method of investigation, it runs the risk of breaking off from the vital source of literature and of transforming literary works into dead and interchangeable objects. When we speak of a poet of Paul Celan's importance, we must take into account precisely his singularity, his *uniqueness*, which cannot be reduced to language, although he expresses himself in it and continues to exist through it. If it is true that the only thing that matters is the work, it is no less true that this work bears the indelible mark of its author. To affirm, as Jacques Derrida and so many others do, that the aim of reading must be the deconstruction of the *text*, with the aim of thus finding an internal logic that has no connection with the author, seems to be denying the specificity of literature for the sake of an abstract and ridiculous "literarity."

Even for those who never met him personally, Paul Celan is, without a doubt, a poet who lives in his work, because he invested his own life in it. It is true that, especially in the last period of his poetry, starting around *Sprachgitter*[7] (1959), he wrote in an elliptical, seemingly impersonal, style recalling Malarmé's, in which the drama of language seems to be the only thing that affirms itself. Yet what takes place in the poems included in that volume, as well as in those of the later volumes, is the drama of the poet—more precisely, the drama of the poet *within* and *through* language. Henri Meschonnic might be overstating it when he says that Celan wanted to kill the German language—the language of his parents' executioners—but Celan's drama is not foreign to this essential fact of his biography.[8] Many researchers have emphasized the importance of the poet's biography in an exegesis that grapples with the various problems raised by such a difficult and enigmatic body of work. Michael Hamburger, who published a massive collection of Celan's poetry in 1980 that Hamburger himself translated into English, confesses his perplexity at Celan's work, which seems so paradoxical and obscure, yet in which nothing is arbitrary. After sketching his biography, Hamburger observes: "These fundamental facts of Celan's life [no comprehensive biography had been published at the time, and no biographical document had yet been made public] might suggest, in part, the abnormal and extreme nature of his situation as a poet." "That is why," concludes Hamburger, "a thorough documentation of Celan's life is necessary in order to clarify many of his late poems, and that is also the reason why he was perfectly right to insist on the fact that he was not a hermetic poet."[9]

In a review of Celan's posthumous volume *Zeitgehöft*, George Steiner, in his turn, raised the question of an "adequate biography": "There are, in his poetry, too many crucial moments which depend on the knowledge of certain specific personal contexts. One day, Celan's complicated life and paths will have to be clarified through documents."[10]

Even Peter Szondi, one of the best critics of Celan's poetry (with whom he was friends, and whom he would "imitate" in the final gesture of suicide), did not hesitate to appeal to his biography in order to decipher some obscure poems—and this despite his confessed preferences for a critical approach of the type professed by Roman Jakobson or Jacques Derrida. In his foreword to Szondi's volume *Celan-Studien*, Jean Bollack quotes from a letter received shortly before his death. Szondi was informing him that he had decided to write "a little book on Paul" (un petit bouquin sur Paul), which would consist of five studies. In one of them, Szondi meant "to give all the details" regarding Rosa Luxemburg and Karl Liebknecht that could have contributed to a better understanding of the poem "Du liegst im großen Gelausche,"[11] "showing, at the same time, how necessary it is to know the details in order to understand the poems of his last years" (tout en montrant combien il faut connaître de détails pour comprendre les poèmes des dernières années). "An anti-reading, therefore, but a fully justified one" (Une anti-lecture donc, mais pour cause), added Szondi in his letter.[12]

The details offered by Szondi concern a scene Celan caught a glimpse of in Berlin, during a visit there in December 1967, in the western part of the city and evoked in the above-mentioned poem published in the posthumous collection *Zeitgehöft*. If an understanding of this poem actually depends on clarifying the personal and historical *context* in which it was written, I believe that the same thing can be said of Celan's *entire* poetical work, a remarkably *unitary* work, despite its diversity and evolution over time. Of course, the poems of the final period—a period that can be said to be governed by quasi aphasia—demand a much more careful anti-reading than that required by the poems of the earlier periods, which are relatively clearer. What is the point of refusing the light that biography and history could shed on a work of such complexity? Why should we exclude Celan the *man* from the poetry he signed with his own blood as a poet?

In his introduction to a book published a few years ago, Gaëtan Picon protested firmly against the tendencies of certain critics who, under the influence of structuralism, tried to separate the author from his own work:

> It is too easy to say that the work does not express biographical personalities, the anecdotes of a life. Proust gave a very good answer to Sainte-Beuve when he said that a book "is the product of a different 'I' from the one we reveal in our habits, in society, in our vices." But everyone knows that a man is, at the same time, and above all, the experiences he wished to live but did not, the things he wished to do but did not, the sum of his desires, projects, dreams . . . How could we escape our I? How could we transgress its space? Psychoanalysis teaches us that every reaction is significant: the deep, responsible personality is not a privileged compartment within a whole, in which the rest might be insignificant; it is a totality, from which nothing can be removed.[13]

"An authentic work," added Picon, "is a life, not an object. The movement which constitutes its creation, that perilous road into the unknown and which leads it toward an ever-mysterious beyond, is also the movement that makes it visible to our eyes. The impact it has on us is precisely within itself: not so much as detectable structures, but as expressions, which are sometimes dormant, other times vivid, bringing it to life."[14]

If I am taking so many precautions, resorting to so many quotations, it is not in order to open up a breach in the fortress of structuralism or of the New Criticism, but because what I have to say about Paul Celan falls under the more or less explicit interdictions formulated by the critics of these two orientations. My ambition is more modest than that of a literary theoretician or an advocate of "biographism." Still, I can only be happy about a phenomenon that has been present in European critical awareness for a while now, a phenomenon defined by Eugen Simion as "the return of the author" in a study published not long ago under the same title with Cartea Românească.[15] (Incidentally, Eugen Simion himself had been a confessed adversary of biographism à la Sainte-Beuve.) This change in perspective is propitious for my task—the one I decided on while listening to the "terrible and inhuman" speech employed in the discussions of Celan's poetry one November evening in 1979. I swore to myself then that I would reveal what I know about my friend and make public some of the texts he entrusted to me.

This resolution runs counter, I know, to the decision made by Celan's widow, that of *not allowing* the publication of certain biographical documents and literary texts written before the poet's "French period." Mrs. Celan has, of course, her own arguments, which I have known for a long time—ever since I was preparing, with Nina Cassian, a representative collection of Celan's poetry in Romanian translation. This collection was to be published with an introduction by Alexandru Philippide, one of the Romanian poets most esteemed by Celan and one of the most competent connoisseurs of German literature. I delivered the introduction, translated into French, to Mrs. Celan in Paris, but she categorically opposed its publication at the beginning of the collection, so that the latter appeared (in 1973) without Philippide's foreword. The reason invoked by Celan's widow was that Paul did not customarily publish his work accompanied by prefaces. As for the unpublished texts left by Celan in Bucharest, Mrs. Celan would have liked them to remain unpublished forever, on the grounds that the poet himself had not considered them worthy of being included in the corpus of his work.

I do believe that nobody has the right to forbid the publication of authentic texts by a poet of Celan's stature, whose critics deplore precisely the lack of information capable of contributing to a better understanding of his exceptional life and work. Celan is like Rilke's rose:[16] he belongs to nobody, which is to say that he belongs to everybody, to posterity itself, which has every right to know as much as possible about both his life and his work.

What would Kafka's image be today if his friend Max Brod had respected his testamentary wish to destroy all the manuscripts the former entrusted to him? I do not claim that the texts in my possession have the same importance as Kafka's writings, but nothing that bears Celan's signature can leave us indifferent. It is not right, or logical, to keep hidden documents concerning the life of a poet who, according to George Steiner, created "the profoundest, the most innovative lyric poetry in western literature in our time."[17]

This said, I now need to clarify the nature of the documents. They are, first of all, the poems and prose texts written by Celan in Romanian; though not many, they testify to the poet's mastery of a language he acquired in all its intimate nuances—the Romanian language. Celan spoke this language for several decades, to the point of even writing in it—both prose and poetry—not to mention the translations he made *into Romanian* from German and Russian literature. The seven poems and the fragment of an eighth are related, as far as atmosphere and theme are concerned (if not precisely through their *diction*), to the poetry Celan wrote during a major phase of his maturity. The eight prose-poems written by Celan in Romanian assume, I believe, even greater significance when we consider that, in the poet's entire German-language oeuvre, there is *only one* prose-poem, "Gespräch im Gebirg" (Conversation in the Mountains), which is in fact rather an apologue.

The Romanian prose-poems deserve special attention not only because their style was influenced by Surrealism but also because they harbor autobiographical overtones. "A doua zi urmând să înceapă deportările" (The deportations about to begin the following day)[18] and "Partizan al absolutismului erotic, megaloman reticent chiar şi între scafandri, mesager totodată al haloului, Paul Celan" (A partisan of erotic absolutism, reticent megalomaniac even among divers, at the same time messenger of the halo, Paul Celan)[19]—the two prose-poems that begin with these words are among the few explicit confessions, as it were, to be found in the poet's work, usually so discreet and indirect as it is.

In this book, I will also quote from one of the games of Surrealist inspiration practiced by Celan during his stay in Bucharest: Questions and Answers. This game demonstrates not only Celan's solid knowledge of the Romanian language but also a certain "cheerfulness of the spirit," remarkable in a poet usually so gloomy. Playing with Romanian words in the style of Urmuz[20] or of the Surrealists, Celan displayed his poetic skills in this manner as well. Of course, the importance of these games should not be exaggerated; they have, rather, the value and significance of exercises that are, nonetheless, oriented toward his profound vocation, which involved a playful element as well.

The verse, the poems in prose, and the word games written in Romanian bear, in a different linguistic register, the stamp of Celan's genius. If we think that, in those more than twenty years he lived in Paris, Celan never wrote poetry in French (a language he knew to perfection and was fond of), then these Romanian texts constitute a spiritual territory that cannot be ignored, since it occupies a unique place in the immediate vicinity of the lyrical space the poet created in the German language. Without being an advocate of bilingualism, he knew how to create subtle but long-lasting bridges over a few literatures. His Romanian spirituality is one of the secret dimensions, still not uncovered and deciphered properly, of the great poet from Bukovina who, living in Paris and fertilizing the soil of German poetry like no other in the postwar, post-Auschwitz era, honored *all* his countries of residence, thus deserving, in his turn, to be honored by each and every one of them.

Personally, I cannot understand, let alone accept, the point of view sometimes expressed in the West about Paul Celan. "In 1947, there appeared in Vienna a young man named Paul Celan. He was coming, literally, from nowhere," said Milo Dor, for example, in an essay published after the poet's death.[21] In a 1959 review, Horst Bienek made a comment that strikes me as equally superficial: "Celan's origin in Romania, that landscape where the Hasidic stories are present, translated for us into German by Martin Buber, has generated many speculations. It seems pointless to me to discuss the particular constellation by virtue of which such a talent was made possible. It is very fortunate for us that some of the most beautiful poems created during the second half of the century were written by Celan in German."[22]

Much more reasonable and closer to the truth would seem to be the point of view expressed by Beda Allemann, in his afterword to the volume *Ausgewählte Gedichte* (Selected Poems), where he speaks of Celan's transformative contributions to the various traditions he incorporated in his poetry. Referring to the poet's translations from Russian, English, and French poetry, Allemann says: "The encompassing character of a poetry that embraces the East and the West is manifest in them as well, a character which inescapably compels both the language and the person speaking it to transcend themselves. It is finally being acknowledged that there are dimensions which have been added to the German language poetry through this step ahead."[23]

Although he emphasizes, among the roots of Celan's poetry, Hasidism (in which he sees a much stronger influence than that exerted by Surrealism and even finds an explanation for certain apparently Surrealistic features of his poetry), Allemann intuits very well the diversity of the horizons the poet integrated into his own vision. Yet what is missing in this rich, complex picture of the poet's spiritual biography is the period he spent in Bucharest, a relatively brief period (two years and a few months), but not at all unimportant or lacking in major consequences for his development. Besides, that period is closely connected to the previous one, which Celan spent in his native Bukovina, a period highlighted fairly accurately by Israel Chalfen in his biographical essay, published in 1979 and reedited in 1984.[24] Unfortunately, the last part of the study, concerning the Bucharest period, contains some errors, which makes it even more necessary to reconstruct that period as precisely as possible.[25] The conference organized in Bucharest in the fall of 1981 by the Cultural Institute of the Federal Republic of Germany in collaboration with the Writers' Union of Romania represented an opportunity for a useful exchange of views among the participants; above all, it facilitated the consolidation of some solid landmarks in the path that leads back in time to Paul Celan's youth. Uwe Martin, then manager of the Cultural Institute of the Federal Republic of Germany and the main organizer of the conference, summarized thus the importance of the Bucharest period: "To the poet, the Romanian capital meant much more than a short transitional phase in his life."[26] The memories recounted by some of his friends from Bucharest have brought to light several aspects of his activity and human profile. Presentations of a more academic nature were also given, concerning Celan's early poetry (the topic of a paper by Bianca Rosenthal from California State University) or the problems encountered by the critical exegesis of Celan's work (the subject of the paper delivered by Beda Allemann of the University of Bonn).

To me, personally, the Celan conference represented a strong stimulus to put into practice the decision I made in the fall of 1979 in Paris—namely, to share Celan's unknown texts and my own memories of the past. The first stage of this endeavor consisted of a series of three articles published in the journal *Neue Literatur*, titled "Paul Celans Bukarester Aufenthalt."[27] In these articles, I quoted substantially from my correspondence with Paul Celan. I believe that these letters are of particular interest for two reasons: first, they project upon the Bucharest period the nostalgic light of the poet himself; second, they contain the confessions the poet made somewhat later, in a period of crisis.

Even greater interest may be aroused by the letters Paul sent to our mutual friend Margul-Sperber,[28] more or less during the same period. Apart from the bitter confessions made *in German* to his former mentor in Bucharest, these letters contain revealing details pertinent to Paul Celan's evolution in the West. At the same time, they testify to the enduring nature of a friendship that, beyond all the differences and distances, bound Celan to the Bukovinian poet, who had watched over his debut and had helped him claim his place on the orbit of universality.

To better understand the unpublished texts by Celan and his correspondence, I have tried to *situate* them in the original context in which they were written. But, above all, what I am trying to do is explain to myself the figure of Paul Celan, which in the meantime has become enigmatic, approaching it from all possible angles, including the biographical. Such an endeavor involves difficulties that go beyond the merely theoretical, and which are part of any effort at evocation (not least in view of the disdain that hovers over biographism). First of all, there is the difficulty inherent in any reconstruction made *post festum*—that is, after the passage of a considerable number of years. The period I wish to evoke is very distant in time; it is close to the phase that made Jules Supervielle (a poet Paul Celan was fond of) say that "memories are [made] of wind, they invent clouds" (les souvenirs sont du vent, ils inventent les nuages).[29] Yet what I am interested in is recovering a *real* past, not in inventing a fictitious time or in projecting on the real one the light and shade of other temporal layers. But how can one perfectly isolate, in one's memory, an older region, in such a way as to prevent it from communicating with later temporal layers? Since Bergson and Proust, we have known that duration, the time of lived experience, involves the mixture and simultaneity of different layers. How to recover what Proust called "the permanent and characteristic essence hidden in things" (l'essence permanente et habituellement cachée des choses), that profound truth that lies buried in memory and transcends the mere record of facts? Even without entertaining Proust's titanic ambition, a memorialist is confronted with problems similar to those the great French writer encountered, or those James Joyce had to tackle when he started to write *Ulysses*. In order to reconstruct one day—*a single day!*—lived by his hero in Dublin (June 16, 1904), Joyce, who was no realist, did not hesitate to use a series of dictionaries that could indicate to him the state of the language in that period, as well as a number of books, to determine, for example, the color of the clothes worn by the inhabitants of Dublin in 1904. Between this scholarly enterprise and Proust's more poetical one—his reliance on sounds, smell, and gustatory memory in order to recover "lost time" (and draw it out of chronological order)—an entire fan of possibilities opens up, accessible to those who try to reconstitute a fragment of the past.

Fortunately, I have preserved a number of fixed points from where I can descend with some certainty into that obscured region buried in my memory. They are the texts written by my friend in Romanian, some photos taken in Bucharest and elsewhere, as well as a little notebook in which I wrote, in 1947, some of Celan's witticisms. It is not much, I admit, but my memory has something solid to rely on. There are also the "witnesses," those friends who are still alive and whose memories I could confront with my own.

In order to recreate the atmosphere of the years 1945–47, I had to resort to the press of the time, a fascinating read from many points of view. Without mixing up the external events (political or cultural) with the inner life of a poet of Celan's stature, I believe that the "air" of a period marked by so many dramatic events should not be eliminated from such a picture; on the contrary, it should be evoked as a background—a background ample enough to suggest the richness and variety of impressions that must have had an impact on young Paul Celan in Bucharest during those long-gone years.

I say Bucharest, although I know all too well that the city as it was then was radically different from the present one; many things have changed in the meantime—the streets, the houses, the shop windows are not the same. A terrible earthquake and a series of urban planning modifications, imposed by a demented dictator, have drastically changed the face of the capital. How to reconstruct the everyday atmosphere of the city as it was then, shortly after a devastating war? How to reestablish Celan's itinerary, which he traveled for over eight hundred days on his way to the publishing house where he earned his living? How to revive the "presentness" of those days, their dense network of worries and joys? How to capture the fleeting shades of a constantly revised picture, ceaselessly invaded by successive waves of light and darkness? What slogans, what songs, what shows, what anecdotes, what terrestrial and spiritual food were topical back then?

Even if I did succeed, thanks to my memory and the press of the time, in reconstructing part of this puzzle, I would still not be able to evoke the vibrant and organic "presentness" as it was experienced by my friend and myself during those years. One cannot bathe in the same river twice; still, trying to do so might prove necessary and worthwhile, even in the knowledge that the second time will only afford an echo of the first. There is no doubt that, apart from the difficulties already mentioned, there is also the risk of idealization. When trying, with as much fidelity as possible, to isolate in time a long-classified period, we are fatally inclined to confer on it an ideal status, a quasi-mysterious, even mystical aura, derived from the prestige of temporal distance itself. I do not claim that I will be able to avoid this all-too-human temptation, but I will strive to keep it within reasonable limits and to balance it with the weight of verified and verifiable facts. Paul Celan needs not a hagiography but a better knowledge of *all* the elements that compose his spiritual biography, so complex and so closely intertwined as it is with his work.

It can never be stressed enough that Celan was a poet with multiple roots—a different way of saying that he had no particular roots. At least four cities—Czernowitz, Bucharest, Vienna, and Paris—have good reason to claim him, just as seven fortresses claimed Homer or, closer to our times, as Prague, Paris, and several other cities could have raised a claim to Rilke. The analogy with Rilke appears even more natural if we think of the affinities between the two German-language poets and of the fact that the author of the *Sonnets to Orpheus* wrote in French as well. Although he lived in Paris for more years than Rilke did, Celan did not write poetry in French, yet he did write poems in Romanian, his second language, from this point of view. If Rilke's critics and admirers can pay due attention to his poems in French, I see no reason why the texts left by Celan in Bucharest, just as valuable, should be ignored.

In the speech he made upon receiving the Bremen Prize, Celan tried to make "a topographical sketch" of the landscape he came from, a landscape unknown to most of his German listeners. His native Bukovina, he said, was "a land in which there lived people and books" (es war eine Gegend, in der Menschen und Bücher lebten). "People and books" lived in the Bucharest of 1945–47, too, years that represented a turning point in the poet's destiny. My ambition has been to evoke the people and books the poet lived among, as well as to reconstruct his circle of friends and the particular atmosphere of the Romanian capital during those long-distant years. In general, the other periods in the poet's life are much better known: the six months he spent in Vienna, for example, are no mystery anymore (apart from his precipitous departure from the city). Much is also known about the poet's last uprooting—the visit to Israel, six months before he died. This visit was full of significance for the profound and, I would add, hopeless Judaism embraced by Celan following in Kafka's footsteps (whose Zionism sprang from the same desperate need to anchor himself in an impossible certainty). All these geographical and spiritual dimensions of Celan's destiny are known and valued. What is missing from this picture, I repeat, and it is quite a lamentable situation, is the Romanian dimension. Celan himself emphasized the significance of this dimension in a letter he sent me from Paris on September 12, 1962:

> J'ai connu—et traduit—un certain nombre de grands poètes français. (Comme j'ai connu la "fine fleur" des poètes allemands). Certains m'ont témoigné, dans des envois et dédicaces, une amitié dont je ne dirai que ceci: elle s'est avérée être bien "littéraire." Mais j'ai eu, il y a longtemps, des amis poètes: c'était entre 45 et 47, à Bucarest. Je ne l'oublierai jamais.

> I've met—and translated—a certain number of great French poets. (Just as I've met "the cream" of German poets.) Some of them have shown me, in the books they sent me and in their dedications, a friendship of which I can only say this: that it has proved to be quite "literary." But I had, many years ago, some poet friends: it was in Bucharest, between '45 and '47. I'll never forget them.

Many years before, in his first letter to me (from Vienna), Celan had spoken nostalgically about "cette belle saison des calembours" (that beautiful season of wordplay), a season that we shared and whose brief duration he truly regretted. How can I forget something that Paul Celan himself perceived as "unforgettable"? How can I fail to respect his memory—in all the senses of the word?

But enough of arguments! They are numerous and solid, fully justifying this journey into the past that I have been postponing for so long, for all sorts of objective and subjective reasons. Focusing on the legendary figure of Paul Celan, my journey is not possible, of course, without his "poet friends," whom he mentioned with such affection. The present book is due to them, too: to Margul-Sperber, Philippide,[30] Nina Cassian,[31] Vladimir Colin,[32] Horia Deleanu,[33] and especially to Ovid S. Crohmălniceanu[34] (to whom I express my gratitude here as well, for his tireless efforts to convince me to write it and for the valuable suggestions he made in the process of my writing it).

The list of those whom I ought to thank is too long, but names that must be mentioned are those of Ruth Kraft[35] and Uwe Martin, former manager of the Cultural Institute of the Federal Republic of Germany in Bucharest, who took the initiative to organize the 1981 Celan conference.

I dedicate these memories to the magnificent "cloud" that Paul Celan has become, for me and for all of us.[36]

# 1

# Bucharest in the Time of Paul Celan

> My memories about cities are
> like love memories.
>
> —VALÉRY LARBAUD[1]

In 1946, Bucharest still resembled the city described eleven years earlier by Paul Morand, in his rather sentimental but well-documented book. The war had, of course, left deep marks: several districts had been disfigured by German and American bombs, and some monumental buildings—such as the National Theater on Calea Victoriei—no longer existed. But, on the whole, the capital continued to be the city of "the joy of living," where so many foreign visitors felt "at home," if not better. "I, a Westerner with the forehead wrinkled by worries, have learned there [in Bucharest] that happiness can sometimes smile at you. This is the lesson this people gives us, one of the peoples worst treated by their conquerors."[2] Thus Paul Morand summarized his impressions after a long stay in Bucharest, where he had come to undergo "a therapy of carefreeness" (une cure d'insouciance). "The lesson Bucharest teaches us is not an art lesson, but a lesson in life."[3]

Four years of war and foreign occupation had undoubtedly weakened the foundations of this *bien-être*, and Paul Morand himself, returning to Bucharest again toward the end of the war (as ambassador of the Vichy government!), had to acknowledge the unfortunate, negative changes caused by the hostilities of the time. Yet the city on the banks of the Dâmboviţa River still had enough of its former charm and was starting to heal its deep wounds, inflicted by the war. Bucharest was still a picturesque capital, full of painful or delightful contrasts (depending on the visitors' point of view), a city where all styles of living, architecture, art, and clothing met, a kaleidoscope of brightly colored fragments, endowed with great combinatory potential.

It is very difficult to reconstruct today, so many years later, the image of Bucharest as it was in 1946, but certain landmarks have remained intact, especially in the area most frequented by Celan, with Calea Victoriei as its central axis. At number 155, there was a building in the neo-Gothic style, designed by architect Cerkez, not far from the famous Casa Moruzi, in the old Romanian style, or from the old Casa Manu, built in the neoclassical style. In the same area, there was—and still is today—the Ateneul Român (Romanian Athenaeum), built in 1886 after the French architect Albert Galleron's designs. This building has a cloister with a six-columned arcade, which confers on it "the appearance of an ancient Greek temple."[4] On the walls of some buildings and on the pedestals of some statues, one can, even today, decipher the signature of many French architects and sculptors: Albert Galleron, Théophile Bradeau, Paul Gottereau, Louis Le Blanc, and others, as well as names of sculptors such as Ernest Dubois and Antonin Mercié, which are, I think, better known in Bucharest than in Paris. One of the broadest avenues in the Romanian capital—which in 1946 was still called Lascăr Catargiu Boulevard—had been designed in imitation of Henry Martin Boulevard in Paris.

"Bucharest, savannah of gardens," a French traveler, Bellanger, wrote in 1856, quoted by Paul Morand in his book. This definition of the city was still valid in 1946. There were no gardens à la française or à l'anglaise—although some of them, belonging to the grand noblemen of yore, could have been easily called so—but, rather, gardens that displayed no stylistic ambition, just an exuberance of green and of "these Romanian flowers, invincible, which are creeping everywhere and survive anything, the stifling dust as well as the burning sun."[5]

There was also another permanent feature of Bucharest: the constantly fresh spectacle of girls in bloom. In a period when the other charms of the city were not so evident, the everyday show offered by these young women in Bucharest, some of them elegant in a modest way, others dressed after the latest Parisian fashion, delighted the passersby, making them turn their heads. This aspect needs no literary reference to confirm it. It is one of the things that have not changed in this city, which has undergone so many transformations between 1946 and 1984, when I am writing these words. And it is infinitely easier for me to evoke it than to reconstruct, in a precise manner, or at least in outline, the framework of my friendship with Paul Celan. The girls in Bucharest are always in bloom, while the man admiring them is past sixty years of age, and his friend crossed into the land of shadows long ago. The streets themselves, if they still exist, have changed their names and appearance.

Constantin Bacalbaşa,[6] one of the most competent chroniclers of the history of the city, wrote:

> The Dâmboviţa Gorges have completely changed entire areas of the city. A lot of streets had different names from the ones they have today: Calea Victoriei was called Mogoşoaia Bridge, Rahova Avenue was Craiova Avenue. When I look back, I realize what significant transformations Bucharest has gone through. In other big European cities, you can see not only many new commercial companies, but also many old ones. In Bucharest, commercial companies appear and disappear as if in a kaleidoscope, hardly anything is stable, everything is replaced."[7]

These words had been written right after the First World War. In 1946, the capital of Romania was entering a similar phase of renaming the streets and the companies, activity all the more intense since it was part of radical social and political changes. Officially, Romania continued to be a kingdom, but the actual regime was quasi-republican, and rapidly evolving toward socialism. History was in great haste, but people did not seem to match its pace. Of course, the political battle was fierce, important events were being planned, and others had already taken place. But what I would like to evoke here is not so much the political and social history of the years 1946 and 1947—this can be easily elucidated by consulting historical documents—as the atmosphere, the moral and intellectual climate in which Paul Antschel, the young man who arrived in Bucharest in the spring of 1945, found himself living.

Coming from Czernowitz, a city traumatized by war, Celan arrived here tormented by painful memories, still very fresh at that time. This delicate and handsome young man of twenty-five brought with him to Bucharest a bitter smile, but also an ardent desire to feel alive at last. Israel Chalfen meticulously reconstituted, in the above mentioned study, the period Celan spent in Czernowitz—a period profoundly marked by his parents' deportation to the other side of the Bug River, and their murder in the fall of 1942. Having miraculously escaped the same fate,[8] their only son spent the years 1942–44 in a forced-labor camp near Buzău, from which he was allowed to go home to Czernowitz once a month. On March 28, 1943, he wrote to his friend Ruth, who had remained in Czernowitz: "They say spring is now coming . . . For about two years now I no longer feel the seasons and flowers, and nights, and transformations at all."[9]

Taciturn, reserved, he used to answer those who asked him what exactly he had been doing in the forced-labor camp near Buzău with a single word: "Digging" (Schaufeln). In the camp, he avoided taking part in his companions' conversations, preferring to withdraw to the solitude of a corner, where he could ruminate over his dark thoughts. He wrote poetry in secret and, on Sundays, when the prisoners were allowed to write letters, he would write a bitter epistle to his girlfriend in Czernowitz or to the relatives who were still alive. In the fall of 1942, in a letter from his mother, Celan received the news of the tragic death of his father, shot by the SS because he no longer had the strength to work in the quarry he had been sent to. His mother was killed for the same reason soon afterward.[10]

Franz Auerbach, the former manager of the State Jewish Theater in Bucharest, was in the same camp—Tăbăreşti, near Buzău—as Paul. He remembers that Paul was very quiet and never spoke about his parents' death. According to the same witness, the living conditions in that camp were more livable than in other places: especially at the beginning, the prisoners were treated relatively humanely, being accommodated in the mansion of Brătescu, a kind man and a landowner who knew well that it was in his interest to spare them, since they were building an access road to his land. But afterward, the prisoners lived in mud huts. Auerbach also remembers that, during that period, Paul was engrossed in Shakespeare, whose sonnets he had started to translate, and in Ruth, to whom he would write whenever he had the opportunity.

This, in short, had been young Paul Antschel's life before arriving in the Romanian capital in the spring of 1945. When I first met him—in the fall of the following year—his wounds seemed to have scarred over; he was remarkably discreet about his own sufferings, and I do not think he ever spoke to me in detail about his parents' death. The portrait I am trying to reconstruct also contains, of course, information I received from others much later. I, for one, saw him then as a bright, witty, even cheerful young man, with chestnut-brown hair and brown eyes, elegant in his movements, and of notable distinction. We soon became friends—right from the beginning of our acquaintance, I might say: from the moment I entered the office where he had for a while been working as editor for Cartea Rusă (Russian Book), where I myself would be working for a few years, and I felt his kind gaze and heard his warm, enveloping voice. I suppose Marcel Aderca,[11] writer Felix Aderca's son,[12] had told him a few things about me. Marcel, who had been working at the publishing house for a long time and whom I had met during the war, helped me get a job there shortly after my return to Romania.

At this point, I must open a parenthesis to explain certain circumstances that are essential for understanding my friendship with Paul Celan. The subject of this parenthesis is a rather bizarre young man, whose name I still bear, but of whom I can only speak in the third person, so distant he seems to me not only in time but in my inner space as well. It is not a question of judging the adolescent I was, or of condemning his errors (he, too, would have the right to judge mine!), but simply of reconstructing a character from which, due to the force of circumstances,[13] my present self is very different. Here are the facts.

In May 1944, this character, with whom I share my name and memories, left his family and his native Bucharest and went to what was then called Palestine, a territory that had been under British administration by virtue of a mandate since 1917. It was a painful decision dictated by several considerations, the most important of which being encompassed by the word *war*: at the age of twenty-one, the character concerned was tired of that war, which seemed to have no end and which threatened to destroy him as well. At that time, the Jews in Bucharest—spared till then by the Antonescu regime[14]—were in danger of being sent to the immediate proximity of the front, on the Focşani-Nămoloasa-Galaţi line, where Marshall Antonescu's troops had retreated.

Our character had no hope, patience, political maturity, and many other things; on top of everything, he was fascinated by Rimbaud: all he dreamed of was a "descent into hell," a journey whose destination was, if not Abyssinia, at least the Middle East. Before departing, he wrote a testament in thirteen points, which he gave as justification to his friends, the poets Nina Cassian and Jean Colin, who had witnessed his inner turmoil and with whom he had played many literary games for months on end, despite all the obstacles—the bombings and the endless miseries that befell them. The character in question wrote a letter right before leaving, on the first days of May 1944, to the novelist Ury Benador,[15] who had supported some literary events organized by Nina Cassian, Jean Colin, and other young poets, including himself. In it, he tried to explain, in a grave, emphatic tone, his decision to depart:

> I'm writing to you because I don't have time to say goodbye in person, and because, despite all my faults, it's very important to me to be honest in this momentous hour of my dislocation. I'm leaving for Palestine—now, when I've started to gain a bit of substantiality as a Romanian man of letters. By leaving, I give up not only my vocation, but also a series of values that are more humane and, in fact,

> more dear to me. But it's too late now to change my mind about this painful decision. I'm young and maybe even childish, underneath my armor of seriousness: I imagine not only the risk of reaching Palestine, but also that of not being able to do so. In any case, I'll have an experience that I need in order to define myself, strengthen up, get used to life. As with any man who is about to embark on a new experience, I'll do my best to return a different man, more mature perhaps, or maybe more humble and cured of this thirst for experiences. I'd be happy to see you again on the other side of the precipice of this separation, and I believe it will happen so.

Indeed, so it happened, but not as soon as I might have thought: "the Palestinian experience" lasted over two years, a long time, during which our character summoned all his spiritual and intellectual energies up to prepare for his return, refusing any temptation to put down roots in that place. During his stay there, he gained a lot of life experience, working as a stevedore in the port of Haifa, as a day laborer in an oil and soap factory, as a warehouse man for a construction company belonging to the British army—but this is not the place to recount that rather painful experience in detail, whose unhappy significance cannot be explained solely by external circumstances but must also include our character's personality and vocation. Finding himself in a foreign environment, the poet in him—a Romanian language poet—reacted vehemently in his attempt to save himself.

Apart from the language, the other lifebuoy was the image of a girl who had remained in Bucharest. Her name was Maria (Marița), and they had studied together at the Colegiul Onescu, a college for Jewish students founded during the war by a group of scholars, including Alexandru Graur,[16] Mihail Sebastian,[17] Felix Aderca, and others, who had been forbidden to teach in state universities or to publish in the press. Maria's image acquired the proportions—and the role—of a redeeming myth, which had no connection to reality or to the truth. Somehow, idealizing Maria was his favorite way of preparing for his return. Maria was supporting the communist ideals—she even militated for them surreptitiously. Under the influence of these two idealizations, our character became converted to communist ideals, which he had not embraced in Bucharest, despite the efforts made by his friends Nina Cassian and Jean Colin.

Meanwhile, in Bucharest, his friends Nina and Jean and the mother of this self-exiled poet were struggling to obtain the repatriation papers in response to the desperate and insistent cries for help they received from the shores of the Mediterranean Sea. While waiting for a favorable decision and for the marine traffic between Haifa and Constanţa to resume, our character kept up an intense correspondence with his friends. Their letters strengthened his decision to go back, because they offered him an attractive picture of the new realities in the country, a picture that contained the literary landscape as well. I allow myself to quote here, for their value as testimonies, some fragments from this correspondence; they shed light on the climate in which young Paul Celan was already living, as well as on the personalities of some intellectuals who would become his friends in Bucharest.

In November 1945, Jean Colin wrote to his friend from far away: "A lot of joy and much sadness upon receiving your long-awaited message. We'd been thinking of you so often, cursing the space separating us. Dear Petrică, if only you knew how much we want you here with us, amidst these fresh challenges, breathing the air of freedom. So many things have happened since you left! Still, we often wonder what you'd say about this or that." As for literary news, Jean Colin informed him that a journal in Bucharest, *Viaţa Socială C.F.R.*, had published a poem by Rimbaud ("Vénus Anadyomène") in our character's translation. Another encouraging piece of news: an article published by the novelist Ovidiu Constantinescu[18] on the literary circle maintained during the war by the great literary critic Eugen Lovinescu[19] (deceased in the meantime) contained, in the list of the participants, a reference to "young P. Solomon, who is living now, somewhere, his Ahasuerus destiny . . ."[20]

Jean Colin sent his friend some other news as well: "Saşa Pană[21] is bringing out the journal *Orizont*, where Surrealists are sworn at and where social poetry of the worst quality is published"; that

Tudor Arghezi[22] "received the national prize for poetry"; that George Călinescu[23] "is the manager of the best weekly, *Lumea 1945*"; and that he, Colin, had adopted the pseudonym "Vladimir" Colin, which he had used to sign the Romanian version of "October Poem" by Mayakovsky.

Nina Cassian, Colin's wife at the time, defined the evolution of many intellectuals belonging to the young generation thus: "Many things could be said about our psychological climate. The crisis existed and has consumed itself. All my amazing formulas, which your common sense—in reality, only fear and lack of guiding principles—judged quite harshly, and all the abstruseness are now lying in corners." And, after informing him that she had become "a great composer," she added with humor: "In general, my name was on posters and dogs peed on me on the walls of the Capital."

In a letter from February 1946, Colin described a spiritual state that was not only his:

> Our life is unfolding toward the only possible objective. We've had defeats, but we've known victory, too, and we hold the most solid certainties!—as Geo Dumitrescu[24] used to say. Today we have them, we wake up with them and we go to bed with them. A certain maturity, certain serious changes transpire from your letter. Have you reached the point we are at? Will you come back as one of us, capable of staying upright next to us? I must believe you will. We want you by our side with all our hearts, here, in the middle of all this frenzy and enthusiasm. Forget about the fact that you used to write a certain type of poems, and about swearing at a certain part of literature. *We* are struggling to make it alive, real, artistic.

It had been a long time since our character stopped writing "poems of a certain type": that is, decadent poems, and he had also stopped swearing at "a certain type of literature," especially committed literature. On the contrary, he was writing social poems or poems with political, anti-imperialist themes—even the poems dedicated to Maria had "progressive" accents and connotations.

In the meantime, in Bucharest, the real Maria had evolved in an entirely different direction from the ideal image the exiled poet made of her. This is what his friends had been trying to suggest, more and more clearly. Their frankness had the effect of a cold shower on our character; yet Maria's image remained almost intact, because myths have a long life.

Still thanks to the same friends, some of his manuscripts, which they had scrupulously kept, started to be published—first the translation of Rimbaud's sonnet "Vénus Anadyomène" in *Viața Socială C.F.R.*, and in March 1946 the Romanian version of another poem by Rimbaud—"Le bal des pendus" (Dance of the Hanged Men)—on the first page of George Călinescu's new and prestigious journal. How could he resist the temptation to feel proud of this presence in Bucharest's literary publications, and how could he not see in it a sign that it was time to put an end to the long absence from his country?

To close the parenthesis about our character, I will only add that, toward the end of August 1946, he returned to Romania after a one-month voyage aboard the vessel *Transylvania*, which brought him from Haifa to Constanța. One last detail: when he exited the Port of Constanța, our character—a swarthy, scrawny fellow with a little moustache, holding in his hand a cylindrical metal box crammed full with the black olives he had bought in Salonica—had the pleasant surprise of seeing Nina Cassian with a small group of friends, with whom she had spent her holiday at the Black Sea! Among them, there was a beautiful blonde girl named Lia Fingherhut, the future lover of Paul Celan, to whom we shall return presently, after this detour.

So, I first met Paul in the editorial office of Cartea Rusă, shortly after my return: that is, in the fall of 1946. He had been working there for a year; he was, so to speak, a kind of veteran, much appreciated for his competence and seriousness as reader and translator from the Russian. The press had its headquarters on 120 Calea Victoriei, in a building that still stands to this day—one of those neoclassical houses that, in the old times, belonged to the gentry and which was greatly admired by foreign visitors. The editorial office was in a wing at the back of the yard, on the first floor, and you could get there by climbing up the creaking wooden steps of the massive staircase, with a banister. I feel I can still hear the creaking of the wooden floorboards under Mihail Sadoveanu's heavy steps[25]—ever rarer, as the great novelist was climbing higher and higher in public life. To the street, the building had a somber façade, with large windows framed by a little frieze above a balcony with wrought-iron latticework. In this main part of the building there were the administration offices and the very bright and spacious office of the general manager, Traian Cerbu.[26] There was also a sumptuous reception room, lit by enormous chandeliers that were rarely turned on—only when the management organized a welcoming party for who knows what "esteemed guest." I do not recall ever stepping into that reception room. The editors seldom used the wing to the street: they did their job in the small rooms on the first floor of the back wing, where the editor-in-chief, Armand Popper, was still working at the time.

At the back of the yard, in the buildings that used to be the stables of the gentry mansion, there was a budget shop for the press, which, like all such shops of other companies and institutions, offered its employees some basic foodstuffs and even clothing items at low prices. There were also some tall poplars outside; the master of the entire area was Gheorghe Faghiura, the janitor, a jack-of-all-trades who had a good heart but enjoyed drinking a bit too much, as far as I can remember.

Armand Popper had been appointed editor-in-chief in April 1946, so Paul was already working there when he started. He realized very quickly that Celan was "an indispensable man" because of his vast knowledge of the Russian language and Russian literature, and he also appreciated his distinction and spiritual delicacy. Without being a man of letters—he had studied economics—Armand Popper[27] nourished a profound respect for writers and had substantial knowledge of literature, extending up to Surrealism (besides, he had been good friends with Dolfi Trost[28] and had, I think, met Paul Păun,[29] too). Celan's "sad eyes," which Popper referred to as a fundamental feature of his, recalling their unique expression to this day, must have seemed to the editor-in-chief very different from those of another employee of his, a certain Andrei Ivanovski.

This character, who gave the impression of having descended from a Dostoevsky novel, was Paul's bête noire. In his turn, Ivanovski detested Paul—as he detested all the editors, among whom he cut a singular figure due to his poor command of the Romanian language and to his appearance and behavior. He wore a rubashka tied with a leather belt, was always smoking a stinking pipe, and was already tipsy in the morning by the time he came to work. Silvian Iosifescu,[30] an assiduous collaborator of the press at the time, remembers that once, during one of Ilya Ehrenburg's visits to Bucharest, Ivanovski told his colleagues that the Soviet writer was "a liberal" and "a cosmopolitan," and that "tolerance" of such fellows was drawing to an end. Although he was undoubtedly more knowledgeable than the others, Ivanovski was not really taken seriously. His colleagues either made fun of him or avoided him, while Armand Popper would put him in his place whenever he had the chance.

Popper remembers that Paul often came to his office to make a phone call or simply to have a chat. Most of the time, Paul complained about Ivanovski's negligent attire and quarrelsome attitude, which drove him up the wall—he who was otherwise a calm and patient person by nature. A tactful man, Popper would try to calm him down, although he himself could not stand Ivanovski, whose coarseness contrasted so blatantly with Paul's delicate sensibility. I think that, despite this divergence and certain little conflicts it led to, Paul ended up by perceiving his fierce colleague as a character in a novel, too bookish to fear. After all, literature is one thing, life another altogether.

When I started working at the press, Paul was working in an office in which there was no room for Ivanovski. It was only later that the editorial office would move to a more spacious room (in the central wing). Until then, Paul and Ivanovski—separated by a few rooms—did not have many opportunities to "collide."[31] Strangely enough, it was Paul who sometimes went to his colleague to ask for some clarification, because Ivanovski was a walking encyclopedia and knew a great deal about many things.

Another colleague at the press, Marcel Marcus, who was not working in the editorial office but in the administrative one, remembers that Paul had a tiny desk, although he could have received a normal-sized one. Everything about Paul was modest, from the gray pullover with its collar turned down to the cheap cigarettes he smoked—he always had a lit one between his slender fingers.

The atmosphere in the editorial office was relaxed, the relationship between the few readers and translators and their hierarchical superior had nothing solemn or rigid about it. Although the texts they all toiled at sometimes left room for improvement, the press was also publishing good books from literatures that were little known here at the time—Russian and Soviet. It was also publishing many advertising brochures, which had their own particular usefulness.

All in all, Paul found his job in the editorial office quite satisfying. It kept him in touch with a field he was very much interested in—that of translations and of translators themselves, some of them very talented. I think that Cartea Rusă was one of the most serious and professional publishing houses of the time. The books translated there—even those that might not have deserved such attention—were subjected to thorough confrontation with the original and to stylistic adjustments. The external collaborators were carefully selected, often at the editors' recommendations, and approved by the editorial board, which met quite frequently—most of the time in the presence of Alexandru Philippide, the literary advisor of the press. Compared to other publishing houses, Cartea Rusă paid better for the translations, and their authors were treated with much deference and understanding. Those who worked there felt that they were part of a somewhat privileged group and, without asking themselves too many questions about it, they were pleased to have the opportunity to do a useful job, appreciated both by the board and by the press collaborators.

It is important to remember that the press was frequented by many important Romanian writers, from Mihail Sadoveanu to

Cezar Petrescu.[32] Its editorial board included such scholars as historian Andrei Oţetea,[33] Professor Alexandru Rosetti,[34] and, starting with the summer of 1947, Iorgu Iordan[35] as well. Among the translators who collaborated with the press were renowned writers who strove to translate important works from classical and modern literature into Romanian, sometimes alone, at other times with the help of experts in the Russian language. *A Sportsman's Sketches*, translated by Sadoveanu and published during the time Paul worked at Cartea Rusă, was an important cultural event that marked Turgenev's recognition in our country. Another such event was the publication of Mikhail Sholokhov's epic novel *And Quiet Flows the Don*, translated by Cezar Petrescu and Ivanovski (whose competence was, I repeat, impressive, despite his personality). Among the active collaborators with the press during this period were Otilia Cazimir,[36] who translated Kuprin's *Sulamith* and other books; George Lesnea,[37] who translated Lermontov's *Demon*; and Ion Biberi,[38] who translated into Romanian *The Death of Ivan Ilyich* and other stories by Leo Tolstoy and dedicated an ample monograph to the Russian master, also published by Cartea Rusă. Tudor Arghezi, Radu Tudoran,[39] and many others would join the group of collaborators a little later.

The newspapers of the time provided elaborate commentaries on the most important publications, which were filling a void in Romanian culture. Writers such as Alexandru Philippide, Ion Biberi, Felix Aderca, Ion Călugăru,[40] Octav Şuluţiu,[41] Eugen Schileru,[42] Silvian Iosifescu, and many others wrote highly competent reviews in newspapers of wide circulation and of various ideological orientations.

I mention all these things to evoke the intellectual climate and atmosphere of the time, one in which Paul had no reason to feel uncomfortable or "exiled" in a job that was foreign to his vocation. If he had not felt well there, he could have found another job quite easily. Not only did he not do that, but he kept pleasant memories about the more than two years he spent in the editorial office, as attested by the words he used when talking about Armand Popper and other colleagues in the first letter he sent to me from Vienna.[43]

Paul knew the Russian language well and, although Horia Deleanu said that he spoke it with some mistakes, these disappeared in writing; at any rate, they did not prevent him from reading massively in this language, which he had acquired relatively recently. Knowing Romanian even better, he had no difficulties making some translations by himself, or confronting the Romanian versions of others with the original text. As Israel Chalfen shows, Paul Celan had learned Romanian at the Orthodox High School for Boys in Czernowitz and later on at Marele Voevod Mihai High School, where Aurel Vasiliu, a distinguished teacher and poet from Czernowitz, had been his teacher.[44]

At any rate, with his philological talent and sharp intelligence, the editor Paul Ancel—that was how he spelled his name at the time—did not encounter serious problems, nothing that could not be solved with the help of dictionaries. His translations from Chekhov (*Peasants*), Lermontov (*A Hero of Our Time*), or Konstantin Simonov (*The Russian Question*), signed Paul Ancel or A. Pavel, testify to a good command of semantic and stylistic nuances in both languages and a remarkable professional seriousness.

However transitory Paul's activity as a translator into Romanian had been, it did not pass unnoticed in Bucharest. His version of Lermontov's story *A Hero of Our Time* received particular attention, being considered by the press of the time as an important contribution to a better knowledge of the great Russian writer. Yet the fact that the Romanian version had a foreword by Alexandru Philippide must have made Paul happier than the praise it brought to him as translator.

As regards Paul's exceptional philological talent, I am inserting here some of Horia Deleanu's memories.[45] He had been Paul's colleague at the editorial office of the local newspaper *Bucovina Sovietică* in Czernowitz, where Deleanu in particular acquired the skills to be a journalist, a job which he would have in Bucharest (as editor-in-chief of *Veac Nou*) before dedicating himself to his vocation as theater historian and critic. When he returned to Czernowitz in the fall of 1944 after a long period of flight through the Volga region,

Deleanu found Paul as one of the editors of that newspaper. That same fall, both of them enrolled in the Department of Romance Languages of the University of Czernowitz, which had recently reopened under a new management.

In April 1945, Deleanu left Czernowitz for Bucharest, where his ex-colleague, Paul, would arrive soon afterward. Among the latter's first places of residence in the Romanian capital was Deleanu's home—a room on 8 Duiliu Zamfirescu. Deleanu's wife was in Iaşi working on her PhD in medicine, so Paul was able to live in that modest room for a while. In the spring of 1947, or maybe even shortly before, Deleanu asked Paul to read his thesis for the University of Bucharest—"Psychological Studies in Molière's Plays: *Tartuffe*, *Don Juan* and *The Misanthrope*"—and give him his critical opinion of it. The thesis was written in French, a language Paul mastered to perfection, and had to be presented before the very demanding professor Frédéric Dard. Paul read it very carefully, making a series of corrections and suggestions and, when he finished, returned the manuscript to Deleanu significantly improved stylistically (as was evident on the pages that were minutely annotated by Paul and which are still in Deleanu's possession). But he took it back with a bit of a delay, for the reason he himself confessed in a note, also kept by his friend:

> I didn't come this morning because, on my way to you, I realized the first sheet was missing. I looked for it everywhere, even at the office, but couldn't find it. Still, the misfortune—for which I apologize a thousand times—is not that big: the first two sheets have been mostly transcribed by me and can be replaced. Forgive me, please, I'll be at your place tomorrow morning.

Deleanu found this note under the entrance door of his place; soon afterward, Paul handed him the whole manuscript, including the sheets he had lost and which he had rewritten, partly with the help of his prodigious memory. Two of the sheets Paul transcribed refer to Dostoevsky, the Russian writer who, together with Esenin, most fascinated Celan. An interesting detail—the three sheets have the following heading:

> FRANZ V. M.
> successor Wenzel M
> Scientific Bookshop and Teaching Materials
> Stationery and Office Supplies
> Established 1884
> Czernowitz, 13 Piața Unirii

Paul often bought paper from that bookshop. It reminded him of his native city and of his past, forever lost now, but frequently invoked in the company of Horia Deleanu or other friends from Czernowitz.

Now I would like to describe the personality of a man who played a significant role in Celan's life in Bucharest. I am referring to Alexandru Philippide, the literary advisor and, at the same time, tutelary genius of our publishing house. The author of *Stânci fulgerate* (Blazing Rocks) was not only a great poet but also a perfect democrat, with a very open mind and highly distinguished behavior. Lacking any vanity or pompousness, feeling a strong passion for culture, and endowed with much wisdom, Philippide strove to orient the press in an aesthetic direction. The editorial meetings, held about once a week—on Wednesdays or Thursdays—were real intellectual feasts, and some of the decisions made during them, under the poet's influence and encouragement, materialized in the plans of the press, especially in the field of classical Russian literature.

Paul Ancel felt profound esteem for Philippide, whom he would call, for a long time, "the master" (a word with discredited connotations in our country, but with rich resonances for a German-language intellectual: Celan himself would be characterized as "Meister der Dunkelheit," master of darkness, a characterization which, to a certain extent, fits Philippide as well). The Romanian poet, who already had a substantial oeuvre and was highly appreciated by literary critics, treated young Paul Ancel as his equal, intuiting in him a poet of great merit (he was familiar with some of Paul's poems from

Margul-Sperber, their mutual friend). The fact that Philippide had studied in Berlin in his youth (though not literature, but philosophy and political economy) and that he mastered the German language perfectly made conversation with the young editor from Czernowitz easier. Another favorable element for the communication between the two was that, in his youth, Philippide had been friends with Benjamin Fundoianu,[46] a poet whose tragic destiny obsessed Celan. Philippide had also been closely acquainted with Ilarie Voronca,[47] whose unexpected suicide in the spring of 1946, soon after his return to Paris after a short stay in Bucharest, affected Celan deeply.

But who did not Philippide know? During the years he spent abroad—in Berlin and Paris—he had frequented Brâncuşi's studio, the cafés where the "vanguardists" of the time met and discussed noisily, and many other such places, yet he remained an unapologetically solitary figure, amused by but not attracted to gregarious manifestations in art and literature.

The words Philippide wrote about Celan's poetry shortly after the latter's death are revelatory of the way he perceived his ex-colleague's lyricism:

> The poetic thought of this poet, who was born in 1920 in Bukovina and died a month ago in Paris, hovers between the tyranny of memory and the need to forget. A life spent between these coordinates and which included the war years had to produce, in Celan's Aeolian harp–like nature, a terrible need for expression. But, along with this need, a new one, equally strong, was emerging within him—that of finding a new form of expression.[48]

This "Aeolian harp–like nature"[49] revealed itself to Philippide as early as 1946–47, when he knew little about Paul's poetry, which was, in fact, in full process of transformation. The attraction was mutual and was based on profound affinities, both literary and existential.

Like Philippide, Paul Ancel was, at that time, a man of the night—a *Nachtmensch*—in the sense that he liked spending the nights, till the break of dawn, writing poetry (the word *night* appears very often in his poetry and is thus related to that of so many German Romantic poets or even of Eminescu[50] and Philippide), strolling with some girlfriend, or having a drink and chatting with friends. He did not quite know how to drink, a little alcohol was enough to make him tipsy—but I will have more to say about our parties later. For now, let us go back to Cartea Rusă. For Paul, as for me, the job at the press was a convenient *gagne-pain*, in times when bread was hard to earn. The press employees had access to a journalists' canteen on Batişte Street—another important landmark in the geography of the city the poet lived in. One could eat relatively well and cheaply in that canteen, although at one point, because of the terrible drought in 1946 (which would strike again the following year), the menu was reduced to watery soup and boiled corncob.

From the editorial office, Paul and I would walk together on Calea Victoriei to the canteen, talking animatedly. A mutual friend, the poet Alfred Kittner[51] from Czernowitz, remembers that one day Paul went to the canteen with a book by Paracelsus under his arm, and "he was sitting at the same table with Petre Solomon, his colleague at the press . . . with whom he used to have endless conversations."[52]

A photo I have kept from those days restores the image of something that must have happened innumerable times. [This image appears on the cover of this English-language edition.] The snapshot captured us during one of our walks along Brătianu Boulevard, in front of the present National Theater, where at the time there was a long building with trelliswork sheltering a small restaurant and a few shops. It was an early spring day and we had probably just emerged from the canteen. Paul—bareheaded, but wearing a winter coat—was holding an open book in his hands, and I was walking by his side, also wearing a winter coat and a huge hat. We were both thin—especially I, with my famished figure and painful smile—and we seemed absorbed in our conversation. What was the book that Paul was holding in his hands? Anyway, it was the book that seemed to preoccupy us, not the ration card. We were young and knew how to endure material hardships, we had long been used to them. We were young and patient, like the protagonists in Joseph Conrad's story *Youth* (about some sailors on a ship to the Far East who encounter all sorts of calamities during their voyage, culminating with the sinking of their burning ship).

Both Paul and I liked to stroll the streets of Bucharest, which I had recently rediscovered and Paul had discovered not so long before. Our eyes were still fresh and eager for sights, though they had seen a lot already.[53] Walking and talking on the streets of the city situated on the banks of the river Dâmbovița, as he would do later on the streets of Paris, Paul felt at ease, in his element, as a city poet.

One of his constant pleasures was to linger in bookshops, in the hope of finding a rare book. Most often he would stop at the Studio 42 bookshop, owned by a certain Mr. Marcu, on Calea Victoriei, not far from Cartea Rusă. Miss Bertha, an ageing shop assistant from the old Hasefer bookshop, known even before the war by the intellectuals of Bucharest in search of foreign books, worked at Studio 42, which had taken over the distinguished customers of Hasefer. Ruth, Paul's girlfriend from Czernowitz, worked there as well. Although "nothing happened" between them—which made Ruth marry a young doctor from Bucharest shortly afterward—Paul remained friends with this woman, whom he had never dared to touch, preferring to idealize her. I think Ruth reminded him too much of the sufferings endured in Czernowitz, so it was difficult for him to regard her, in Bucharest, as a real person. The passionate poems Paul dedicated to Ruth during the war had placed her on a pedestal from which he found it hard to take her down. It was much easier for him, psychologically speaking, to fall in love with women who did not stir in him the complex feelings generated by a long platonic relationship. When still in Czernowitz, shortly after Ruth had left for Bucharest in the spring of 1945, Paul had a love affair with Roza Leibovici, a former fellow student from Iaşi. Meeting her again in Bucharest in the fall of 1945, he resumed the relationship with her, a happy, albeit brief one.

So was the relationship—happy and brief—between Paul and Viorica Schlesinger, a young poet returned like me from the Near East, and I was a witness to it in a sense, but I will speak more about my friend's love affairs later. I would only like to add here that a sort of literary circle used to gather in Viorica's house on Berzei Street.

Ovid S. Crohmălniceanu vaguely recalls a literature soirée during which Paul read some poems in German in the presence of Margareta Dorian, Nina Cassian, Colin, and me.

At that time, there were many literary circles in Bucharest, as short-lived as Paul's love affairs. *Revista Literară* of May 18, 1947, for example, announced that "since Saturday, April 26, the literary meetings held in Mrs. Postelnicu's house have been resumed"[54] (many writers participated in these meetings, such as Eusebiu Camilar[55] and Alfred Margul-Sperber, as well as a young novelist, unknown at the time, named Eugen Barbu[56]). Another literature circle was frequented by the algebra teacher Dan Barbilian, who, under the pseudonym "Ion Barbu,"[57] had reshaped the Romanian poetry by publishing the volume *Joc Secund* (Second Game) in 1930; in the two essays presented in French to the distinguished audience of that circle, he returned now, in 1947, to his poetic preoccupations, speaking about Rimbaud and Jean Moréas from an entirely original perspective.

The proliferation of literary circles was viewed by the journal *Revista literară* (May 25, 1947) as a symptom of "the stagnation in editorial activities and of the absence of a substantial number of publications." Yet many publishing houses and literary journals were active in the capital at the time—for shorter or longer periods of time, of course. An article in *Lumea* (27[31], March 1946) was titled precisely "The Inflation of Publishing Houses," in an analogy to the much more serious phenomenon in the financial sector; the author of the article deplored the fact that many presses proved to be, "with very few exceptions . . . rather small shops selling discolored bric-a-brac and cheap, false jewelry."

But what both Paul and I noticed was the rich variety of literary and artistic aspects and manifestations in Bucharest. That was because our points of reference were infinitely more modest: compared to Czernowitz (where Paul came from) and to the cities in the Near East (where I had spent the previous years), the Romanian capital seemed a real metropolis to us. Besides, even in Paris, the postwar period was not exactly one of great cultural prosperity; apart from Camus and Sartre, discovered by Parisian readers right after liberation—although they had made their débuts before the war—the "great names" remained the familiar ones of André Gide, Paul Valéry, François Mauriac, and André Malraux, along with the equally famous names of the former Surrealists Éluard and Aragon, who had in the meantime become committed writers. The fact that many talented writers such as Montherlant, Céline, Drieu La Rochelle, Giono, and others had compromised themselves by collaborating, to a greater or a lesser degree, with the Germans during the occupation or with the Vichy puppet government made the literary situation in France even worse, at the same time justifying a necessary, if dramatic, process of purging.

Counting the victims (Max Jacob, Robert Desnos, Benjamin Fondane, and so many others), punishing the guilty (Lucien Rebatet, Abel Hermant, and many others), reorienting intellectual energies in the midst of political chaos—all these phenomena delayed the emergence of a new, favorable literary climate. Many French writers, forced into exile during the war, had recently come back to Paris, enriching its diversity but also adding to the general confusion. Returned to the French capital in 1946 after an absence of five years, André Breton was trying, without much success, to resuscitate Surrealism, in a substantially different version with emphasis on esotericism and the fabulous universes of the imagination. Meanwhile, many of his former colleagues, from Aragon to Tzara, had evolved in the opposite direction, to that of political commitment to Communism—a direction abandoned by Breton soon after the second *Manifesto* (1929), in which he himself had legitimized such involvement.

Somewhat similar changes and phenomena were taking place in Bucharest, too, not only because the two historical situations were alike (the end of the war, the attack against Hitler's occupation, and so on), but also because the two countries shared a cultural tradition that was, up to a point, common to them both. Romania's liberation from the Fascist yoke meant, for the time being—and it is this "for the time being" that is relevant here—a corresponding freedom in the field of literature. It implied, among other things, the possibility of putting an end to the surreptitiousness of certain critical and artistic movements that had been kept hidden for a long time. One such movement was Surrealism, very active in the years Celan lived in Bucharest. Though occupying a marginal position compared to the main tendencies developing in the Romanian culture, Surrealism was active with a force inversely proportionate to its numerical weight. The small Surrealist group in Bucharest organized exhibitions, published manifestos and books in Romanian and French, and even indulged in the luxury of having internal, apparently suicidal, opposing factions.

In those years, Bucharest was visited by many first-rank personalities from various domains. In the field of literature, I would mention Elsa Triolet and Louis Aragon, who arrived in the capital at the end of July 1947, a few months after Tristan Tzara, the Romanian father of Dadaism, had become, like them, a "committed" writer. Celan did not feel any particular admiration for Aragon or Tzara: among the poets belonging to the Surrealist movement, the closest to his heart was Paul Éluard, who had remained faithful to his poetic vocation even during the periods of maximum political engagement.

I think Paul met Ilya Ehrenburg, who had been a guest of the Romanian capital several times since the fall of 1945. In Bucharest, the Russian writer addressed his audience in French, a language Romanian intellectuals spoke fluently. After one of his visits, the writer Ion Biberi, a collaborator of Cartea Rusă and highly esteemed by Celan, described Ehrenburg (in *Veac Nou*, October 19, 1946) thus: "Ilya Ehrenburg's appearance, as I perceived it during his brief stay among us, reveals a grieved man and an inner drama. The writer was a sad man, of an overwhelming sadness. In his lost look, in the features of his tired face and inner-directed expression, in his gestures, we all felt the echo of an immense sorrow."

Celan used similar terms to describe Ilya Ehrenburg, in whose melancholy he recognized his own. But he was not very thrilled about certain views the Russian writer had adopted, such as the latter's opinion of Kafka, expressed in the context of an investigation held by the French weekly *Action* under the alarming title "Faut-il brûler Kafka?" (Should Kafka Be Burnt?).[58]

Ehrenburg's response to this investigation was published in the journal *Veac Nou* (October 12, 1945) and focused on two questions: (1) "Whether society has the right to take defensive measures against a writer, if his activity appears to be jeopardizing the essential interests of the people"; and (2) "Whether Kafka's work describes, in a contagious manner, a certain condition of social decomposition and whether, by manifestly expressing morbid states of consciousness, it poses the risk of awakening or confirming similar processes in the reader." Although he gave a rather nuanced answer ("I understand the symbol hidden behind your question very well, but beware: the pessimists or the optimists might end up wearing a blue, green, or yellow star after this, as a distinctive mark"), Ehrenburg insisted on dissociating himself from Kafka: "If you want my personal opinion, I can tell you that I do not like Kafka very much, although I admire certain things in him. He is too egocentric, his universe does not have enough corresponding elements in the universe of the readers, of the masses . . ."

Celan, who admired the author of *The Metamorphosis* unreservedly and considered him one of his spiritual brothers, was unable to share this view. Fascinated by Kafka's poetic prose, suffused with existential symbols, he firmly rejected any attempt at reductionist or repressive interpretations of it—so little known then not only here but in the West as well. *His*, Paul Celan's, answer to the question "Faut-il brûler Kafka?" was to translate *into Romanian* four short stories by the great German-language writer: "Excursion into the Mountains," "Passers-by," "An Imperial Message," and "Before the Law."

Returning to the literary-artistic atmosphere in Bucharest at that time, I would also like to mention the intense and varied musical events that took place here. Apart from George Enescu and Constantin Silvestri, other soloists gave concerts and recitals—David Oistrakh, Lev Oborin, and Daniel Şafran, among others; in 1947, Yehudi Menuhin's magical violin, too, resounded in Bucharest. People could also attend the conferences held in the various halls by many intellectuals, Romanian or from abroad. Tudor Vianu,[59] Ion Marin Sadoveanu,[60] Eugen Schileru, and others filled the halls just like Tristan Tzara or Aragon. I remember Paul in the spacious lobby of the Dalles Hall, talking intensely with the German-language writer Oskar Walter Cisek[61] while waiting for I do not know what conference to start, one that he wanted to attend—a snapshot whose contours have blurred almost completely, save for my friend's elegant silhouette, engaged in conversation with another silhouette. Theater activities were also protean and interesting. In the Sfântul Sava Hall of the National Theater, the masque staged by the director Ion Sava after *Macbeth* was no longer performed—the show Colin had spoken about enthusiastically in one of his letters to me, in the spring of 1946—but was still the subject of intense commentaries, as if the event of performing it again was a constant possibility. In 1947, the Comedia Theater hosted Jean Cocteau's play *The Typewriter*, and at the Odeon one could see a show adapted from *Anna Karenina*, while a dramatization of *Les Misérables* attracted many spectators at Teatrul Mic (Small Theater). At the Victoria Theater, the Leny Caler-George Vraca Company presented (also in 1947) *The Latest News*, a comedy by Édouard Bourdet, with Ion Iancovescu in the leading role. I should also mention the great variety of films shown at cinemas—such as *Casablanca*, by Michael Curtiz, with Ingrid Bergman and Humphrey Bogart, which was on the screens of the Aro and Gioconda cinemas for months in the fall of 1947, or the superb English film *Brief Encounter* at the Orfu. However, both the theater and the cinema repertory also contained a substantial element of bad taste and "boulevard spirit."

Why do I mention all this? My intention is to evoke the great variety of spiritual nourishment at Paul Ancel's disposal in this city, which was not at all the "nothingness" from which Milo Dor claimed the poet emerged when he arrived in Vienna.

The nourishment was varied and accessible, indeed, but that does not mean that Paul consumed it every day. Books, for example, were very expensive—a novel cost twenty or even thirty thousand lei, *Revista Literară* was sold for seven thousand lei, and *Contemporanul* for ten thousand lei. After the drought in 1946, hunger was a serious threat in the country; on January 13, 1947, the newspaper

*Naţiunea*, whose manager was George Călinescu, published the following commentary on a law that had been drawn up by the Ministry of National Economy shortly before: "From the information we have, no restaurant will be able to offer snacks in the future. It is quite likely that until lunchtime and in the afternoon between three and seven these places will be closed."

Modest by nature and, at the time, a bachelor like me, Paul did not pay much attention to financial matters. He was content with the bare minimum, be it food or accommodation. Of course, awareness of the temporary nature of the situation made it easier for him to bear deprivations, but he continued to lead a frugal life even later, when he could have afforded to live in better conditions. In Paris, where I would see him again twenty years later, he lived modestly, in a small apartment on the fifth floor of a building without a lift. In Bucharest, he changed addresses quite often; but I remember only one of them, a furnished room in the semi-basement of a small block of apartments on Bitolia Street, close to Piaţa Confederaţiei, from which he would walk to the editorial office despite the fact that the distance was more than two kilometers. This habit of frugality made him receptive to the joys of the spirit and insensitive to lamentations generated by purely material deprivation. Unlike others, he did not consider it a tragedy when the law prohibited caviar to be sold by private traders (in February 1947). Besides, even if the salary he received from the press had become insufficient, the canteen and the budget shop provided him with the minimum for a decent life.

Unexpected gestures of help, lightheartedly accepted, did not miss the mark, either. For example, one day, the writer Ury Benador paid us a visit at the office—a generous man, full of initiative, who loved helping his colleagues. He invited us to the store across the street to try on some new clothes. The store belonged to a friend of his, a certain Cristian, who, apart from being a philanthropist, genuinely worshipped writers. Cristian came from Iaşi, where he had owned a large lingerie company and had known the Yiddish-language poet Iţic Manger,[62] whose father used to sew shirts. The poet himself had been an apprentice tailor at Cristian's company before embarking on his apprenticeship to glory in Czernowitz. And now there was another star from Czernowitz, lighting up Mr. Cristian's shop on Calea Victoriei.

I believe that even such small occurrences contributed to the consolidation of the friendship between Paul and me. Sharing the same bitter bread for hundreds of days, wearing our clothes away on the same desks loaded with dictionaries and other more or less literary texts, walking for hours on the same streets, sunny or immersed in darkness, we became a sort of musical duet, defined by Paul as "solo de Petronom, cu acompaniament de Paoloncel" (solo by Petronom, with accompaniment by Paoloncel).

# 2

# The Poet's Friends and Lovers

> . . . Mais j'ai eu, il y a longtemps,
> des amis poètes: c'etait, entre '45 et '47,
> à Bucarest. Je ne l'oublierai jamais.
>
> —Paul Celan[1]

Paul had what the French call "the gift of friendship"—an inborn gift, as was his poetic talent, but a gift that required certain propitious conditions in order to develop. The conditions were met in Bucharest during the period he lived there. The list of friends he managed to make in the Romanian capital, in the course of two years and a few months, is much longer than the list of friends he had in the more than twenty years of his sojourn in Paris. All I am doing is repeating what he himself declared in several letters and what I myself noticed, with astonishment, when we met again in the French capital. I am not looking for explanations of this *fact*—they are multifarious and complex, and have to do not only with the environment but also with my friend's psychological problems.

In Bucharest, Paul was still young, his nerves were still robust, and the traumas he had suffered in his native Bukovina did not seem to outrun his spiritual strength; on the contrary, the suffering he had endured required compensatory treatment—a "therapy of carefreeness."[2] The atmosphere in Bucharest agreed with him, that was obvious, and one of the symptoms of his recovery was his exuberant sociability. I shall not enumerate all his friends here—besides, I did not know all of them. Paul frequented certain groups—for example, his old acquaintances from Czernowitz—and, at a certain point, he even made friends with the tight circle of Surrealist poets. Yet, despite his sociability, he remained, like all of us, a man of secrets, of multiple potentialities, especially in his emotional life.

I will make a selection, frankly subjective at that, dealing here only with those of his friends whom I myself knew. I will begin with Nina Cassian, the dominant female personality of our group. As I try to evoke her physical and intellectual features as they were *back then*, I find it hard to keep them separate from the later ones, in order to avoid the mixture that derives from long association with a friend, whoever that may be. Although she had not yet published her poems in a collection, her presence in various journals of the time began to compel recognition of her distinct lyric voice—a strong, acute voice, which cultivated dissonances in subtle harmony with her entire iconoclastic generation. She possessed great intelligence, as well as an inimitable gift for expressing herself in a trenchant and striking way. Equally gifted in poetry, music, and even painting (she had taken lessons with George Löwendal and Hermann Maxy), Nina had, moreover, an extraordinary talent for acting, which she demonstrated both in public—at our literary meetings—and within the circle of her close friends, who were always numerous. Nina's presence in an otherwise heterogeneous group acted as a unifying force, as a social "binder" of instant efficaciousness. It was enough for her to show up in the midst of such a group for it to brighten, liven up, discovering its elective affinities. Whether improvising at the piano or playing pieces by Debussy, Bartók, or Constantin Silvestri, Nina found herself at the center of attention, which she stimulated in other ways as well, not least by her sparkling conversation. Self-conscious about her Dantesque profile, she insisted on proving her intellectual superiority in an often aggressive manner, meant to disarm those who might otherwise have faulted her for her "ugliness," which was, anyway, a figment of her imagination.

Hence, a certain element of maliciousness, a permanent disposition toward sarcastic rebelliousness, arousing hostile reactions in some people too superficial or too lazy to confront her barbs. I am not saying that Nina was easy to put up with—her pride (pride, not arrogance) could sometimes be quite disagreeable, as could her selfishness, which sometimes made her strike the attitudes of a spoiled child. But her *humane* qualities, not to mention her literary ones, far outweighed those defects—let us call them deficiencies of character or education—which nobody lacks. Paul was fascinated with Nina's personality, and along with that fascination went a considerable dose of fear. "She is straight but derilious,"[3] he would say of her, acerbically, with that extravagant wordplay typical of his humorous spirit. "Clever, but sterile"—his definition did not harbor any moral reservation, but simply conveyed a view, actually widely shared by others, of Nina's abundance of aggressive intelligence. There were also profound differences between the two poets springing from their biographies, as well as from their respective temperaments; yet these did not prevent them from communicating with and understanding each other, thanks to a spiritual affinity that was as profound as the differences mentioned above.

I often went with Paul to the apartment Nina and her husband, Colin, shared with her parents, on the first floor of a high block on 6 Poenaru Bordea Street. The door of the flat was always open to the numerous friends of the family, of whom I had been one for quite a while. Paul enjoyed himself very much in that comfortable apartment, whose walls were covered in paintings and whose living room was dominated by a massive Bechstein piano. Nina presided over some musical-literary evenings, in no way inferior to the meetings of certain then-famous literary circles in Bucharest. On such evenings, Surrealist games were often played, such as Questions and Answers, or Ioachim, a local version of the famous Cadavre exquis (Exquisite Corpse), perfected by Breton and his friends in the years following the First World War. The apartment resounded with songs, too—all sorts of songs, some innocent, others naughty, such as "Le père Dupanloup," whose refrain, "Zut. Merde. Pine et Boxon / Le père Dupanloup est un cochon," returned obsessively to our sinful lips. Paul himself contributed to these musical evenings, singing in his grave and resonant voice, either in chorus or solo. His rich and varied repertoire contained revolutionary songs about the Spanish Civil War, but also some medieval German songs of bizarre beauty.

In his presentation at the 1981 Celan conference in Bucharest, Ovid S. Crohmălniceanu described the original way in which the poet interpreted a German folk song, in which Death, riding a horse, traversed the settlements of medieval Flanders, ravaged by the plague: "Paul would sing *Flandern im Not* . . . which evoked a time when the plague devastated the Netherlands. At the end of each stanza, he would kick the floor with his foot and sing, in an increasingly grave voice, the refrain: *Ge-Stor-Ben* . . ."[4]

As regards the friendship between Nina and Paul, I would like to add that it grew stronger not only because they enjoyed sharing the same leisure activities but also thanks to the respect each felt for the other's poetic gift. Nina's solid knowledge of the German language and its literature made her a sagacious and competent interlocutor in a field where Paul felt most at ease. Her translations from Erich Kästner and Christian Morgenstern were examples of notable poetic equivalences. As far as poetry was concerned, their preferences were almost the same: Apollinaire, Desnos, Éluard, Esenin, Rilke, Arghezi, Ion Barbu.

In Nina Cassian's presence, Paul became very voluble; the pull was instantaneous, without any time wasted on etiquette, although behind his loquacity certain complexes or fears might have been lurking. Between them, there was also a certain coquetry—an expression of their mutual attraction as well as of the distance between them, which they inevitably noticed. To illustrate this coquetry, I will quote from the letter Paul addressed to Nina in the summer of 1947, when she was on holiday at the seaside, and I had taken the initiative of sending her a letter co-written with Paul:

> Ingrato!
>
> Nobilă şi arborescentă ca întotdeauna, când mă gândesc la tine, mâna mea arborescentă se grăbeşte să-ţi ofere ţie, adormitului meu covor pe care l-am întins mareelor, această oglindă din funingine albă şi tuş ritmizat—pentru ca să te poţi recunoaşte în ea ca Ibis (ceea ce-ţi dă posibilitatea să te vezi, în sfârşit, simultan realizată în dubla ta ipostază de pasăre adorată şi toc rezervor) şi

> pentru ca răuvoitoarele guri ale posterității să nu poată spune că nu ne-am iubit.
>
> Să vină marea peste noi şi să ne înghită rechinii-frați!
>
> Paul (mai african ca oricând).

> Ungrateful, you!
>
> Noble and arborescent as always, when I think of you, my arborescent hand rushes to offer you, sleeping carpet of mine that I have spread for the tides, this mirror made of white soot and rhythmicized Indian ink—so that you, like Ibis, can recognize yourself in it (which gives you the opportunity of finally seeing yourself simultaneously materialized in your double stance as adored bird and fountain pen) and so that the foul mouths of posterity will not be able to say that we did not love each other.
>
> Let the sea come over us and the brother-sharks swallow us!
>
> Paul (more African than ever).

Among those who often visited the flat on Poenaru Bordea Street was Ovid S. Crohmălniceanu, then a young engineer, a recent graduate (specializing in civil engineering) of the Polytechnic University in Bucharest. His real name was Moise Cahn, but his friends called him, for short, "Mony." Born in Galați, he had started a correspondence with Nina Cassian and Colin during the war; I myself had been included in this correspondence before I left the country.

Prior to Mony's arrival in Bucharest (in October 1944), Nina had found a quite bizarre pseudonym for him—"Ovid S. Crohmălniceanu"—because the polytechnic student harbored literary ambitions, which were justified by a talent exercised, at the time, mostly on parodies and critical interpretations of certain favorite authors. Passionate about detective fiction (Chesterton had been his idol in Galați) but also about modern poetry (while still in Galați, he discovered Rimbaud, Mallarmé, Jules Laforgue, Max Jacob, and Apollinaire, whose poetic works he copied almost in their entirety, in order to memorize them), Mony was a walking literary encyclopedia. In a portrait of him included in a recent survey of contemporary

Romanian literature, Eugen Simion (using information provided by Crohmălniceanu himself) mentions that he immensely enjoyed books as "aesthetic objects" as well: "His grandfather had been a book peddler, while his father, who often traveled to Bucharest, brought him books by Sadoveanu, Constantin Stere,[5] Gib Mihăescu,[6] Mircea Eliade, Cezar Petrescu, as well as detective novels, which he read with great passion."[7]

As the same literary historian says, in his debut articles (in *Ecoul*, ca. 1944), the young Crohmălniceanu evinced "a talent for pastiche"; his portraits of poets such as Vachel Lindsay, Erich Kästner, and Jehan Rictus contained, "beside precise and erudite information, a fictitious element: the young essayist invents texts in the author's style and imagines fabulous biographies."[8] Moreover, Mony was one of the few Romanian intellectuals of the time familiar with the literature of Surrealism, having up-to-date information about it plus powers of critical discernment that the fanatics of the genre lacked. Paul, who was attracted to Surrealism, found in Mony a lucid and competent critic, and it was no accident that, before leaving the country, Paul gave him one of Breton's fundamental books, *Arcane 17*.

In the letters she sent me between 1945 and 1946, Nina spoke about Mony in a way that accurately portrays the man as he was back then, and as Celan, too, must have known him. In one of them, after praising his erudition ("Mony has acquainted me with the German Expressionist literature"), Nina made the following confession: "It is formidable how much this boy has helped me see things clearly. He has been the cause of the entire revision of my aesthetic views; he has highlighted aesthetic principles for me and has even guided my own work with great intelligence." And she added, with affectionate irritation: "He, the idiot, doesn't even realize how much I owe him. I'd rather not show him my enthusiasm; he might get too full of himself. As it is, he's still under the impression that I'm very intelligent and that I'm helping him clarify his ideas. You should know that, although he'll be a construction engineer next year, the guy is perfectly capable of doing his share of the poems we three write—as before, still with jokes—as before—and which all remind us of 'the old days.'" Or, in another letter: "Mony's our Great Friend, next to whom Petrică[9] will rule as before. They share the same silly passion for the written word, the same all-absorbent sensitivity (remember?), the same self-congratulatory display on the high wire of their own personality. And I like you all, silly as you are." I have kept, from the time I finally met Mony, the following "certificate," which he wrote after losing I don't remember what bet to Nina:

> I hereby declare, in full possession of my mental and spiritual faculties, that Mrs. Nina Colin [Cassian] is the most intelligent, the most beautiful, and the most talented person, as well as the exemplar of the female gender, whom the undersigned has ever met or will ever meet in another life. We also confirm that she is gifted with a special talent which makes her, at the same time, the most agreeable woman ever. Whereupon the present certificate has been issued, to be used by her whenever necessary. [Signed:] Mony Cahn. Student-engineer at the Polytechnic School of Bucharest, Faculty of Constructions, fourth year, specialization Ferroconcrete and Civil Construction.

Crohmălniceanu would soon give up his career as an engineer, opting instead for that of literary critic, something that was noted from the very beginning by George Călinescu, in whose weekly *Lumea* he often published. In a note published on October 20, 1947, in his newspaper *Națiunea*, Călinescu typically extolled the reviews signed by Crohmălniceanu in the journal *Contemporanul*: "For a while now, the literary news section has been covered by Ovid S. Crohmălniceanu, a young man, I suppose. I shall not deal with the question of accuracy at this juncture. What is essential in criticism is the range of perception, the subtle verb, the rich cerebral associations. It is very likely that Mr. Crohmălniceanu will have a 'career as a literary critic.' His approach is Marxist, of course, but it is practiced with subtlety and without superstition." My friendship with Mony and especially the esteem he felt for our mutual friend Paul Celan led to the publication in *Contemporanul* (on May 2, 1947) of the first poem ever to be signed with the pseudonym "Celan," quite fresh back then and maybe as unusual as "Crohmălniceanu," though with a much more melodious sonority. I worked on the Romanian version of the poem with Paul himself, who helped me understand its profound nuances and connotations.

At the time, the poem bore the title "Todestango," which I retained in my own translation, made in close collaboration with Paul; although he had full confidence in my abilities as a translator (he knew some of my translations from Shakespeare, Rimbaud, and other poets), it was I who felt the need to consult him, mainly because I did not have sufficient command of the German language to be able to decipher all the nuances of such a poem. Both he and I wanted the Romanian version to be as close to the original as possible: he because, despite certain doubts regarding its chances for publication, he wished to present his poem in an equivalent form as a testing-board for prospective first readers, and I because, after reading it, I felt it was a masterpiece.

When Paul brought "Tango of Death" to me for the first time—at the beginning of 1947—I felt a real shock, triggered by the poem's verbal machinery, which seemed simple enough but was in fact quite ingenious. The shock derived, of course, also from the temporal closeness to the tragic events this incantatory poem made reference to, a poem devoid of any prosaic or journalistic element, yet so realistic in its substance. I perceived "Tango of Death" as a condensed but defining and definitive expression of an entire epoch that had just ended but which was still of great contemporary relevance. Since then, I have read numerous critical interpretations—some judicious, others extravagant—of this poem, which has become emblematic in the meantime, and which, as Siegbert Prawer emphasized, has as crucial a place in Paul Celan's oeuvre as *Guernica* in Picasso's work.[10] I am trying to ignore the immense bibliography generated by the "Todesfuge" in order to recover my original impressions of its rendering as "Todestango," and, of course, I can only partially succeed after so many years! I could not say, for example, when exactly the poem was born, but I would not swear that it was written in

1944–45 in Czernowitz, as Professor John Felstiner from Stanford University in California does in his otherwise extremely serious and well-documented study.[11] What I do know is that Paul continued to work on the poem even in 1947—a fact indicated by the title itself, still hesitant. Could it be that Paul decided to change it definitively into "Todesfuge" after its publication in Romanian as "Tango of Death"? It is a possibility one cannot rule out.

Professor Felstiner touches upon another thorny problem: that of the "sources" of Celan's poem, an issue that has created plenty of excessive—indeed, an enormity of—interpretations, as once maintained by Heinrich Stiehler in an essay published in the journal *Akzente*. In his view, Paul must have written the "Todesfuge" under the influence of a poem, similar in subject matter and structure, written in 1944 in Czernowitz by Immanuel Weissglas, a former colleague and friend of his. Even a moderately careful reading of the two poems—the one by Weissglas bears the title "Er" (He) and was published much later than "Tango of Death"!—will lead to a single conclusion: between them there is only a thematic resemblance, generated by the real situation on which both are based. Also, even if in "Er," too, there is a character—Death—who "ist ein deutscher Meister" (is a German master) and who "spielt im Haus mit Schlangen, dräut und dichtet" (plays with serpents inside the house, threatens and writes bad poems) while prisoners are forced to sing and dance, Weissglas's lines (supposing they were written before Paul's, which has not in the least been clearly established) remain very modest compared to the macabre symphony orchestrated in the "Todesfuge."[12]

In another article, Professor Felstiner shows that Paul could have started from a real event—one of the many horrors recounted by survivors returned to Czernowitz from the Nazi camp in 1944. In Janowska camp near Lemberg (Lvov) in Galicia, the Jews "selected" for extermination were forced by its commander to listen to a "tango of death" (Todestango) played by a violinist, after the music composed by the Argentinian Eduardo Bianco. Bianco's orchestra—says Felstiner—emerged in Paris in a period when Paul was studying in

France and, a year later, in 1939, performed in Berlin, in the presence of Hitler and Goebbels.[13]

Felstiner mentions yet another possible source for the poem: a little book by K. Simonov, published in 1944 under the title *The Extermination Camp in Lublin* (i.e., Majdanek), in which the Russian writer evokes a march of the prisoners toward the camp crematorium. "Tens of loudspeakers began to emit the deafening chords of some foxtrots and tangos," wrote Simonov. If we also remember that Paul would translate, in Bucharest, Simonov's play *The Russian Question*, the hypothesis becomes even more plausible.

At the time, Paul was intent on conveying a "message" through his poem, even if its form could have been perceived as unclear or ambiguous. That is why I believe Paul did not dislike the introductory note, placed by Crohmălniceanu above the poem: "The poem whose translation we are publishing here is based on the evocation of a real event. In Lublin, as in many other 'Nazi death camps,' some of the condemned were forced to sing melancholy music,[14] while the rest had to dig the graves."[15]

I wonder whether this note was drawn up on the basis of information provided by Paul himself, because, at that time, the full scope of the tragedies that had taken place in "the Nazi death camps" was not known. As John Felstiner observes, even the notion of "Holocaust," applied to the sinister sufferings inflicted by the Nazis during the war, would impose itself upon the European consciousness only around 1960 (in 1958, Elie Wiesel published his devastating report on Auschwitz-Birkenau, titled *Night*[16]). The note in *Contemporanul* had been, of course, a little tactical maneuver as well, adopted by Crohmălniceanu to convince Al. Buican,[17] the editor-in-chief of the journal (and himself a former prisoner in Auschwitz), to publish a poem that was, after all, difficult, written as it was in a very modern style that had already begun to be repudiated (for example, in the same number in which Celan's poem appeared, another poem, entitled "Tractorul" (The Tractor), was published as well).

Although at the time he was going through a phase of maximum closeness to Surrealism, it was very important to Paul that the "message" of his poem should be clearly understood. The publication of the Romanian version in *Contemporanul* gave him the opportunity to verify, for the first time, the impact the poem might have on its readers' consciousness. It was like a general rehearsal before a première that, of course, Celan had anticipated for a European audience, German in particular, because the "Todesfuge" was a poem written in German, meant to awaken and unsettle the conscience of the German people, who were guilty of the crimes evoked by him. The première was to take place only in 1952, when the poem, published in the volume *Mohn und Gedächtnis* (Poppy and Memory), would begin its journey to its main addressees. A very difficult journey, if we consider the reaction of the West German critics, most of whom, although praising the poem, kept silent about its profound meaning, which mattered to Celan at least as much as its lyrical form. To confine myself to only a few examples, here is what Heinz Piontek wrote in a review of *Mohn und Gedächtnis* in 1953, in which he did not even mention the "Todesfuge," the central poem of the volume: "His poetry is *poésie pure* . . . It has a French glow and a Balkan luster, the suggestiveness of a *chanson* and the modulations of melancholy. His poems are based exclusively on metaphor." Another reviewer, Helmut de Haas, emphasized—also in 1953—the qualities of the "Todesfuge" that seemed fundamental to him: "The elimination of any objective element, the ravenous rhythm, the romanticizing metaphor, the lyrical alchemy," plus an "integral element": namely, "the Zen Buddhist Satori experience" (das zenbuddistische Saturi-Erlebnis)! It is no surprise, therefore, that Paul Celan ended up distancing himself from his own poem, which had become the subject of such arbitrary interpretations and of such "beside the point" admiration. In 1958, annoyed by all these exegeses, which bled his poem of its meaning, Celan wrote to a critic: "To me, what matters is the truth, not euphony."[18]

The publication of the poem in Romanian translation had a certain impact in the literary press in Bucharest, without, however, generating a wave of critical interpretations. Its reception focused mainly on the question of "truth," to the detriment of "euphony," which was also perhaps due to the fact that the Romanian version was fatally diminished in the latter respect. A note published in *Revista Literară* on May 11, 1947, and signed "V. P." made reference, for example, to the "rich contribution" made by Nina Cassian and Sanda Movilă[19] through their poems, which had appeared in *Contemporanul* (32) saying also that "the poem 'Tango of Death,' by the German poet Paul Celan and translated by Petre Solomon, is remarkable for its structure and moving in its evocation." And further on:

> In the pages of the same publication, we recall having read another new poem a while ago, "Groapa comună" [The Common Grave], by the Croatian poet Ivan Goran Kovačić. The resemblance is valid, of course, only as regards the source of inspiration; more condensed and more restricted in its incursion into a landscape contorted by pain and helplessness, Mr. Celan's poem is testimony to a genuine sensibility, from which we expect other surprises in the future.

To this day I wonder who was hiding behind the initials V. P. Could it have been Veronica Porumbacu[20] or Virgil Prodan? I tend to believe it was Veronica Porumbacu, a poet who later, in her autobiographical novel *Voice and Wave*, would cite Celan's lament again—and whom the latter knew quite well. But it could also have been Virgil Prodan, a picturesque character, very active in the literary and nonliterary press at the time. His real name was Lucian Alfandary, but his friends nicknamed him "Dulă," which Paul himself used. Incredibly ugly, but with lively and intelligent eyes that twinkled under his bushy eyebrows, Dulă had a unique way of behaving and speaking. The son of very poor and distressed parents who lived in the notorious Crucea de piatră (The Stone Cross) district in Bucharest, he was very proud of his humble origins. The poetry he wrote was full of abuse and interjections directed at the bourgeois world. Some of his poems were published in *Lumea* and in other journals, under the above-mentioned pseudonym, which was not the only one Dulă used, because he sometimes signed himself as "Alf Prodan." In

*Lumea* of March 17, 1946, for instance, he published a poem titled "Nu suntem singuri" (We Are Not Alone):

> Mi-au venit în cale
> muncitorii ieşiţi istoviţi de la lucru,
> oamenii muncii, oamenii vieţii.
> Răsturnaţi-mă în cuptoarele voastre,
> loviţi-mă sub ciocane,
> sunt numai carne şi sânge, metal, energie.
>
> On my way, I met
> the tired workers, after the day's toil,
> work people, life people.
> Throw me into your ovens,
> hit me with your hammers,
> I am nothing but flesh and blood, metal, energy.

Such poems were still considered revolutionary and proletarian at the time. But their author did not claim to possess the unique and infallible "key" to lyrical knowledge; all he did was transpose his natural, hilarious way of speaking into a different register. For example, he was in the habit of calling some friends, saying: "Me!" or asking them, without any introduction: "Hen-house?!" (that is, a room) because he was always in search of a nest for his love affairs. During my absence from the country, he kept asking Nina and Colin: "Petrică?" which meant to convey, "Isn't he back yet?!"

Monosyllabic on principle and perhaps also from intellectual laziness, he considered that the times were propitious not so much for poetry as for real life—a life of pleasure and joy, which he had not experienced in his youth of poverty and anguish. That is why he chased girls (accumulating disappointments!), wore extravagant clothing, puffed away at his pipe, and got tipsy on strong drinks.

I am calling up Dulă here because he, too, was part of Paul Celan's circle of friends, a broad circle that included other such eccentric characters. In the long letter he sent me from Vienna, Paul described, in cryptic language, the adventures of the "Cap-Man," whom he had met in Budapest and who had been forced—not by him!—to go back to Bucharest, where the personage would linger for a few and increasingly difficult years before disappearing into a mysterious void, a mystery that, to this day, has not been solved by his old friends. . . .

It is only fitting that I should mention here Margareta Dorian as well, a discreet but important presence in the context, forever lost, of the years 1946–47. I had met her during the war at the University for Jewish students, which I have already spoken about; at the first opportunity, I introduced her to Paul, who would meet her again in Paris and who would continue to write to her for a while. In her first novel, published in the United States in 1967 under the title *A Ride on the Milky Way*, I rediscover the atmosphere in which Margareta lived in Bucharest, a life devoid of external drama but full of lyrical intensity. I can see the old house again, with its four high windows looking onto the street and its bay window suspended above the front door. I entered through that doorway so many times in order to talk to Margareta and her father, physician Emil Dorian, the author of some graceful poems (about his two daughters, Lelia and Margareta) and of some thesis-driven novels, meant to suggest the usefulness of fraternity among people and the absurdity of wars and of racial hatred.

In her novel, Margareta Dorian evokes her father's "monumental inkwell," his eyes, "dilated by his spectacles," his ironical and benevolent smile. The novelist also restores for me the atmosphere of our meetings: the garden of the suburban house, a huge garden, in which the numerous family friends often gathered in the summer around a table always adorned with a kettle or a coffee pot. The wooden fence that separated the doctor-poet's house from Cuza-Vodă Street was flooded, in May, by bushes of lilac in bloom; the garden also sheltered two poplars, an apple tree, and a plum tree—an entire flora that absorbed the guests' conversation, conferring on it a special resonance. "Es war Sommer und die Bäume flogen zu ihren Vögeln" (It was summer and the trees were flying toward their birds)—this line from Celan, placed as an epigraph to the second part of the novel, most poignantly evokes the atmosphere of that garden. Sometimes poems were read in it; I don't remember for sure whether Paul ever read any of his there, but he definitely listened to Margareta Dorian's. The latter had published, in the autumn of 1945, a booklet titled *Herbarium*, one of the five or six poetry chapbooks published by Forum Press, with a view to encouraging the young generation of poets. Margareta's poetry suggested a temperate spiritual climate, a sort of well-organized *hortus conclusus*, but not devoid of certain wild plants. She continued to write such poetry, which even appeared in journals—for example, *Studentul Român* of March 20, 1947, published her poem "Anotimpul Andersen" (The Andersen Season):

Nu putem să ne mai ascundem decât în gutui
şi să iernăm pe dulap cu genunchii la gură,
lângă jacheta mamei, mare, cafenie, pusă-n cui.
Oglinzile vorbesc sau nu de noi? . . .
Spune, dacă vrei să ne ascundem în gutui,
trebuie să le spui la revedere, să faci cu mâna frumos.
. . . Şi pe urmă, tavanul ăsta pustiu, tavanul ăsta lins . . .
Haide, astă-seară—ultima dată—să luăm masa jos.

There are only the quince trees left for us to hide in,
and we can only winter on the wardrobe, with our knees to our
 mouths,
by mother's large brown jacket, hanging on the nail.
Are the mirrors talking about us or not? . . .
If you want us to hide in the quince trees, say so,
you must say goodbye to them, wave beautifully.
. . . And then, this deserted ceiling, this smoothed ceiling . . .
Come, tonight—for the last time—let us dine below.

All sorts of gardens were being cultivated in the literary landscape of the time: intimist poetry coexisted with social poetry, and Margareta Dorian shook hands with Virgil Prodan on journal pages, as well as in the street or in the welcoming houses of mutual friends. The notion of "topicality" was quite broad, as George Călinescu himself defined it in an editorial published in *Lumea* on November 11, 1945:

> By "topicality," some people understand the present and suggest that it involves reportage—that is, reporting on everything that is happening in an objective manner, at the moment it is occurring. Of course, we will be doing this as well. But the theory of reportage ignores the fact that the notion of "topicality" in culture is broader, encompassing the subjective realm as well. Culturally speaking, the soul has its inner chronology, which does not correspond to objective chronology. In this sense, for many, what is out-of-date is actually topical. . . . Mature people in particular live retrospectively, self-actualizing in the past. For them, an old writer is present, while a new one is absent.

This description of the intellectual atmosphere of the period is necessary if we want to understand the times and, within those times, the personality of Paul Celan. Of course, Paul did not choose his friends on purely aesthetic or exclusively cultural grounds, and his liking for Margareta Dorian, for example, did not necessarily involve adherence to *her* type of poetry.

In fact, nothing could be further from the truth than a portrait of Celan as a man of letters to the core, concerned exclusively with the written or published word, consumed by that "frantic passion for art" which Baudelaire said could lead to the cancellation of art itself.[21] For him, being a poet—and few contemporary poets are more deserving of this designation—did not mean avoiding everything that was not directly linked to poetry. Although in the end what mattered, above all else, was "the alchemy of the verb," the windows of his alchemist's laboratory were open to the street. The raw material itself that was processed in this laboratory, passing through the poet's fine filters and transformed until it attained its purest essence, was nothing but the dull lead of real life or the blood-stained iron of history.

Celan was the opposite of an ivory-tower dweller. He liked being among people, whose grievances he listened to with an attentive ear.

His thirst for life, denied for so long, took the shape, in Bucharest, of intense amorous experiences. I do not claim to be an accurate chronicler of all the love affairs he had in the more than two years he lived here, but I can say that they were quite numerous, one giving way to the next at a vertiginous pace. After the long period of "fasting" in Czernowitz, in Bucharest Paul was living a belated, frantic adolescence. Whether influenced by the Surrealists or not (they, too, were in search of the "ideal woman," in all her terrestrial incarnations[22]), he passed quickly from one young woman to another, allowing himself, though, the time to actually fall in love with each of them. According to one of the women he courted, Paul was an affectionate man, of great charm, but perfectly capable of playing the spoiled child as well—capable, for example, of adding to his poetical compliments some very prosaic request: "Would you mind sewing on some buttons for me?" From the long list of "willing victims," I met only three—I am committing no indiscretion by naming them: Viorica, Lia, and Ciuci. The last two appear in Celan's letters as well, being insistently invoked by him over a long period of time.

I do not have very much to say about the first; nor did he: she was a fine girl, by all accounts, with an attractive body and a keen intelligence, inclined toward cynicism—maybe due to a rather unfortunate life (she had spent the war years far from her family and her country). The love between her and Paul did not last long, exhausting itself quickly without leaving any mark.

With Lia, it was totally different: a passionate love, which lasted relatively long (a few months). The daughter of a urologist from Bucharest, this "blonde Lia," the namesake of the one once celebrated by Tristan Tzara, was a person of irresistible vitality. Paul called her, affectionately, "Lala." In the spring of 1947, I had the opportunity to take a trip to the mountains with Paul and Lia, and with other colleagues from Cartea Rusă. I myself was accompanied by my future wife, the painter Yvonne Hasan, a friend of Lia's. We left for Sinaia by train on April 12, 1947; with our rucksacks on our backs and enthusiasm in our souls, we climbed up to the Voevozi chalet, from which we set off for Peştera and then onward toward Tătarului Gorges and Zănoagei Gorges, returning to Bucharest after a few days of happiness and thus free of the shackles of history. Nevertheless, in one of the last letters I received from Paul, he reminded me of a telling detail:

> I'm thinking of our trip to the Carpathians, over twenty years ago. Lia, Lia, Lia, drowned, drowned, drowned. Vanity of the written word. Do you remember the revolutionary songs I sang to you all on our way back, on the train—I have no other repertoire.

The poet's last "great love" in Bucharest was Corina, nicknamed "Ciuci," the daughter of a then-famous director, she herself a theater actress with an unfulfilled vocation. Refined, beautiful (in a different way from Lia—of a more statuesque kind), to Paul she looked like a goddess. According to Crohmălniceanu, Paul met Ciuci in the house of my future wife one night when we celebrated New Year's Eve there. Many people were present—around thirty—and the program for the evening was unusually diverse, including, among other things, a silly play, presented under the title *Pumnalul din cutia cu matzăs* (The Dagger in the Matzo Box[23]) by a trio made up of Marcel Aderca and his friends Max Haimsohn and George Rafael. Neither Marcel Aderca nor I or the much-regretted director George Rafael,[24] nicknamed "Rafi," would remember the subject of that Dada play later, in which Rafi played the part of Sherlock Holmes. There was also a "lady," and the plot was built around a crime of passion, committed with a dagger, hidden afterward in a box containing ritual matzos. Another number presented by the three was titled "The Female Trapeze Artist"—they looked radiant and came out in front of the audience after almost collapsing with exhaustion from the gymnastic exercises they had performed. George Rafael seems to remember that Celan, too, presented a number, performing a bizarre dance during which he took off his clothes, garment by garment, in a kind of striptease. Crohmălniceanu says that the dance must have been improvised specially for Ciuci, with whom Paul had fallen in love at first sight and to whom he whispered, at the end of the dance, some tender words, including "queen" and "princess."

"Anachronisms, catachronisms," as Paul would have said. Personally, I do not remember that night the way it imprinted itself on Crohmălniceanu's memory or George Rafael's. I cannot vouch for whether Paul met Ciuci in the house of my future wife, Yvonne. But that he fell in love with her, of that I am sure, and it matters little where or when exactly. After so many years, our memory must have mixed up the details of several memorable nights, ending by melting them into the recollection of an almost mythic New Year's Eve.

As for the real New Year's Eve party, the one I went to with Paul, I am a little more certain of my memories: it was my first New Year's Eve since my return to my country and, at the same time, the last I spent in Mariţa's company. I vividly remember that night as a landmark in my life, although I have forgotten many details. That particular New Year's Eve party took place in the apartment of an Italian-language teacher called Despina Mladoveanu, on Boteanu Street, in the center of the capital. Of the many guests, I remember only a few: Rafi and "Pitz" (Marcel Aderca), my friend Mihail "Milo" Petroveanu[25] (Veronica Porumbacu's future husband), and especially Mircea Ungureanu, a young man from a wealthy family (he was the son of an important manufacturer), for whom Mariţa would leave me that same memorable night.

Many years later—in 1984—Mariţa would recall the incidents of that night thus:

> You're asking me to tell you how I "lived" that New Year's Eve at Despina in 1946–7: it's been so many years since then, and my memory fails me. What do I remember? It was a sparkling moment in my life as a young woman, maybe the only such moment after the years of poverty and suffering in Iaşi and before the years of moral squalor in Paris. Rafi and Pitz were playing the undertakers in a funeral "act," singing through their noses; I pretended to be dead, and to this day I don't understand why that made

> me laugh uncontrollably. Maybe the fact that I felt loved by you, by Mircea, and by Milo gave me wings—I was floating—I was completely oblivious to the suffering I could cause, everything was a game, it did last, after all, only one night. Petrică, my dear friend, I know you'll be very disappointed: I only remember Paul Celan as a shadow, and that night, which was painful to you, was happiness for me. . . . I remember that Mircea and Milo fought, in a way, because of me, maybe also because everybody had had too much to drink, I remember that you came to pick me up and you gave me a box of chocolates, that you were young, delicate, pale, infinitely poetical and endearing, honest and fragile, I liked you, with that scarf of yours, that you often wore and which emphasized the impression of fragility you gave, I felt flattered by the interest you showed in me, you, who were a celebrity at the Onescu College and whom many girls desired—or dreamed of. But these are not the memories you are after; you would like to recover memories about Paul and I've forgotten everything about him, except his voice.

Paul's voice, that enveloping, slightly nasal voice, persists in my mind, too, but *in a different way*. That night and the following days, divining my suffering, Paul sought to soothe me with overflowing friendship and spiritual warmth. Himself fragile, having been hurt emotionally many times, my good friend insisted on helping me overcome this obstacle that could have easily turned into a precipice. At any rate, if I had not felt him close to me, it would have been more difficult for me to heal myself of the hurt I endured that memorable night, evoked by Celan in a poem written in Romanian and titled "New Year's Eve":

> În noaptea Anului Nou, anotimp fără ore,
> ai trimis catafalcul cel tânăr să-ți cheme iubita. . . .

> On the night of the New Year's Eve, a season without hours,
> you sent the young catafalque to bring you the woman you
> loved. . . .

Sensitive to other people's suffering, because he himself was all too familiar with suffering in all its protean forms, Paul thereby helped me to survive that painful New Year's Eve. Our friendship deepened even more afterward, acquiring the solidity that can come only from the cement of human solidarity. Other factors, of course, contributed to this friendship—certain spiritual and intellectual affinities or the cultivation of the same values: Shakespeare, Rimbaud, Arghezi, Kafka (the latter's writings being introduced to me by Paul). Trying to understand, so many years later, the somewhat privileged, special friendship Celan offered me—both during his stay in Bucharest and later—I cannot ignore other decisive factors as well. One of them seems to be the experience of being uprooted, which we both had: knowing my biography, Paul—the deracinated Paul Celan—perceived my case with understanding and sympathy, a case of uprooting that had been, of course, much less serious than his own. He knew only too well what it meant for a poet to be separated from his mother tongue, and he could understand better than others my decision to return to my native land. This understanding was also based on a personal experience: as described in Chalfen's monograph, Celan spent his childhood in a family atmosphere that was imbued with Judaism, but the increasingly acute conflict between him and his authoritarian father made him reject the "old man's" rather rudimentary Zionism from an early age. The Hebrew language, which he had studied for three years at a Jewish school in Czernowitz, would be repudiated by Paul as a *Vatersprache*, the patriarch's tongue.

The same desire to assert his separation from paternal authority made Paul reject his father's obsessive idea of sending him to Palestine, too. Naturally, the latter's tragic death, as well as his own experience during the war, would radically alter the way Paul perceived "the Jewish question," the Jewish element becoming more prominent in his consciousness, while the others remained unchanged. For him, being Jewish meant acknowledging evidence of a physical, rather than metaphysical, order, although later, after the bitter experience accumulated in the West, a certain metaphysical, even mystical dimension would become manifest in his attitude toward Judaism.

Between 1945 and 1947, Paul was determined to remain a German-language poet and to follow, in a way, the same path as Walter Benjamin—that of exile, which implied great existential risks, of course, but which suited his own vocation.

Unlike his good friend Gershom Scholem, who had emigrated to Palestine as early as 1923, Benjamin preferred to remain in Germany until Hitler's ascent to power and to go into exile to France afterward. The relationship between Scholem and Benjamin was further complicated by the latter's orientation toward Marxism, disavowed by Scholem, who was becoming increasingly immersed in the Kabbalah (being also a professor of Jewish mysticism at the University of Jerusalem). The fact that Scholem would continue to live, while his friend would commit suicide in the fall of 1940 in an unsuccessful attempt to cross the French border to get to Spain and, from there, to the United States, should not be viewed simplistically as a sign of the former's clear-sightedness and the latter's blindness. Benjamin was not the only German scholar to take his own life while in exile; the list of suicides is long, including such personalities as Ernst Toller, Kurt Tucholsky, Stefan Zweig, Ernst Weiss, and others—a group that Paul Celan himself would join many years later. Particularly for a writer, exile is a rupture with unpredictable consequences for one's vocation. There are no universally valid solutions for regaining spiritual and intellectual equilibrium after the trauma caused by exile. Some manage to survive and even have greater achievements (as is the case with Thomas Mann or Brecht), while others cannot adapt and succumb.

Returning to Walter Benjamin, I would like to point out—apart from the resemblance between his destiny and Celan's—an obsession common to both: that of language. In each of them, Judaism manifests itself preeminently in an obsessive investment in the *word* as the matrix of existence and repository of collective memory. From this point of view, they are very close to the biblical spirit and, at the same time, they prolong the multimillenary tradition of Jewish scholars, absorbed in the sacred texts, into modern times. To consider them as less *Jewish* and, particularly, as less effectual regarding their contribution to the spiritual treasure-house of humankind seems to me to be an attitude that is as unjust as it is narrow, even if endorsed by a distinguished scholar such as Gershom Scholem. Celan would become an admirer of Scholem, I know, but not an advocate of the solution the latter proposed. At any rate, in the period I refer to here, Paul was not in the least an advocate of Zionism.

As regards my episode in Palestine, I think that, for Paul, the essential fact was that I had been through a painful experience, right after the one endured during the war: the community work, the moral and financial squalor, the frustrations and humiliations, which he had himself suffered in Czernowitz and in the camp near Buzău. We both knew what it meant to shovel snow off the streets, or to dig ditches, obeying the commands of brutal and sadistic guards. Paul saw me as a victim of war, even as someone maimed by war, which he was himself in his turn—to a much greater degree, of course.

Besides, one should bear in mind the fact that Paul was also a leftist with a Marxist education, something that was still quite fresh at the time. Despite certain disappointments suffered during the war because of the harsh reality of his native Bukovina, he had not abandoned the ideals of his youth, to which he would remain faithful even later, judging by his correspondence with me and with other friends in the 1960s, in which he speaks about "mon vieux coeur de communiste" (my old heart of a communist), about his repertoire of revolutionary songs, and so on.

On the other hand, it must be stressed that his Marxist education did not preclude his adherence, emotional rather than theoretical, to some of Kropotkin's or Bakunin's ideas. Celan was an aggrieved Marxist—aggrieved by the transgressions committed in the name of Marxism during a certain period—and an aggrieved Jew, with a tragic awareness of Judaism. To him, nothing could be simple; everything was painfully complicated, as, after all, was history itself.

Yet during the time he spent in Bucharest, Paul was less concerned with politics, his spiritual and intellectual energies being focused on his vocation as a poet. He was not indifferent, though, to what was happening around him; on the contrary, he was highly sensitive to the struggles occurring in social and political life. As a confirmed anti-Fascist and victim of Nazism, he could only welcome efforts being made to ensure that the horrors that took place during the war would never be repeated. Loathing the legionnaires,[26] still quite active at that time, he approved of the measures taken against the propagation of their ideas and practices. Even the fact that he was working for Cartea Rusă—as he had worked, for a while, for *Scânteia* (as a translator of political texts, an activity that he had occasionally practiced for *Veac Nou* as well)—is relevant to his leftist orientation. But he could not ignore certain distortions, either, visible in the social, political, and cultural life of the country.

My friend's keen sensibility registered all sorts of details, amplifying them, and this tendency kept him in a perpetual state of alarm. His exactingness was absolute with regard to certain matters, such as anti-Semitism, and he refused to accept any kind of extenuating circumstances. It would persist and even deepen in the West, thus complicating his life there, of course, and increasing his solitude. The question of anti-Semitism often recurs in his correspondence with Margul-Sperber and me, assuming obsessional dimensions. While still in Vienna, long before becoming the victim of a slandering campaign whose plot included anti-Semitic undertones, Celan encountered certain adversities stemming from his Jewish origins. The supreme praise he could find for a distinguished Viennese artist—the painter Edgar Jené—was that he "is definitely without prejudices."[27]

Some time later, when in Paris, on August 2, 1948, Celan wrote the following sentence to a relative in Israel, which sums up his attitude toward the Jewish question: "Maybe I am one of the last people who must live the destiny of their Jewish spirituality in Europe to the end."[28]

Thanks to Paul and to the diffuse influence of his personality, I was saved, I think, from certain excesses and deformations, so common and widespread in those years. Also thanks to him I was able to recover my sense of humor, at least in part. The word games we played together and the conversations we had on literary and political matters prevented me from falling prey not only to a Zeitgeist that was beginning to be increasingly active in its manifestations, but also to certain personal inclinations favored by this phenomenon. To the tendency to simplify things in the cultural register and to reduce them to a frame of reference narrowed down to the immediate context, he opposed a complex and nuanced vision based on respect for true values.[29] Of course, my friends Nina Cassian and Vladimir Colin also contributed to this process of saving my soul, they who had remained true to their vocation, convinced that literature could serve the Revolution without disavowing itself. Alexandru Philippide made a contribution, in this sense, by the example he gave in protecting his poetic gift from contextual compromises and expressing his political opinions only in print or at cultural conferences, an otherwise honest and profound stance dictated by his old and steadfast democratic convictions. Yet, as I was with Paul almost every day, his influence on me was stronger and more direct, but this did not prevent me, unfortunately, from falling into the trap of compromises with my own vocation and from paying the due price. Without Paul, that price would have been much higher and more damaging. But enough about me!

I cannot end this chapter about friendship, in which I have included myself, insisting on my own image maybe a little too much (not from a lack of modesty but to highlight Paul's character), without evoking the personality of Alfred Margul-Sperber, who played a pivotal role in Paul Celan's poetic career. The latter's arrival in Bucharest in the spring of 1946 had been preceded by the revelation of his poetic genius to Margul-Sperber, to whom Ruth, Paul's friend from Czernowitz, had shortly before given a notebook containing a hundred poems. At that time, Margul-Sperber was a man of forty-seven with an already well-established reputation as a poet and scholar. During the war, I, too, had met this generous poet, of an imposing two-meter stature and an even higher moral standing. Together with some other friends, among them Nina and Colin, we had visited him in the book-crammed apartment he occupied on the top floor of an aristocratic house, later demolished, on a street near Piața Victoriei. The flat had a splendid terrace, which was flooded in the summer by a waterfall of ivy that ran down to the foundations of the house. Born in Storozhynets, Margul-Sperber settled in Bucharest in 1940, after a very agitated life: uprooted several times—first, during the First World War, as a soldier in the Austro-Hungarian army, then, in peacetime, as a student in Paris and as a journalist in New York—he had returned to his native Bukovina suffering from tuberculosis as well as from nostalgia. After a long period of journalistic activity in the leftist press in Storozhynets and Czernowitz—where he was responsible for the literary section of the newspaper *Czernowitzer Morgenblatt*—events forced him to move to Bucharest. But he would not be free from history's hostility there, either. Arrested at his home at the beginning of the war in order to be deported, he was saved at the last moment by an intervention from Ion Pillat,[30] a poet who was his friend and who had many connections in the higher spheres of the ruling powers. His prodigious activity as a translator from Romanian poetry—literary as well as folk poetry—had brought Margul-Sperber a degree of fame at least equal to that which he enjoyed as an original poet writing in German. In fact, as an original poet, he was known mostly in Bukovina and abroad and less so in Bucharest. Besides, he seldom published original poems, his generosity manifesting itself also in his relative neglect of his own poetic production in favor of other people's work.

In the preface to his first volume of poetry, *Gleichnisse der Landschaft* (Parables of the Landscape), published in 1934, Margul-Sperber had also made the mistake of openly declaring his aesthetic convictions, which ran counter to the prevailing modernisms of the time: "The author sincerely confesses that, as regards the form, choice, and style of his themes, he prefers everything that is old-fashioned and traditional and also declares that he does not wish to be considered one of the modern poets at all." Despite this polemical position, rooted in a conviction that was justified by a context saturated with "isms," the poet from Bukovina was not at all refractory toward authentic values in modern poetry. In his youth in Vienna, he had frequented Expressionist circles and had retained from their aesthetic and practices the pacifistic, antibourgeois vision—much more than their propensity to formal innovation. Philippide, who was a good friend of his and had in-depth knowledge of German literature, rightly observed that "Margul-Sperber's poetry is often a poetry of ideas, yet he never expresses these ideas in an abstract manner" but "converts them into images,"[31] an aspect that distinguishes him from the Expressionist poets spiritually related to him. Besides, Margul-Sperber had been friends with some of them—for example, Yvan Goll—and these friendships, based on mutual esteem, would be advantageous to Celan as well. Margul-Sperber had been in correspondence with many prominent literary personalities—among them T. S. Eliot—and had even had the privilege of meeting Kafka!

In his volume of memoirs, Saşa Pană recounts how, in 1942, in the yard of Caritas Hospital, he was "accosted by a huge poet (two meters tall), with an incredibly piercing yet gentle gaze [who] had met Kafka and wanted to set right a statement in one of my old articles: Kafka had not been a clerk in the water supply department but a general inspector at the Worker's Accident Insurance Institute."[32] A writer who had met Kafka, Yvan Goll, and so many other masters of modern literature could not be narrow-minded, even if, on the personal level, his evolution was taking a rather traditionalist and classicist direction. The spectrum of his tastes was always broad, and his generous character was only waiting for the right opportunity to prove itself.

Paul's arrival in Bucharest offered him such an opportunity. The friendship between the mature, forty-seven-year-old poet and the twenty-five-year-old one, then unknown, developed quickly, on the basis of a *coup de foudre* triggered by the reading of Celan's poetry. After Celan arrived in Bucharest, one of his first visits was to Margul-Sperber; he even lived in Margul-Sperber's apartment for a while until he could find accommodation of his own. One of the most important outcomes of Paul's visits to Margul-Sperber (which continued until the day before he left the country, even after Margul-Sperber moved to 31 Maria Rossetti, where the generous poet from Bukovina used to receive his poet friends every Sunday morning) was choosing a pseudonym, now fixed in stone for all time but devoid of any recognition then. "Plotting" with Margul-Sperber his future poetic trajectory, Paul thought that his family name, Antschel—quite a common name in Bukovina—did not have enough magical weight. The discussions on this topic, probably heated, were settled by Margul-Sperber's wife, Yetty, who suggested the pseudonym Celan, obtained by anagramming his family name (phonetically spelled Ancel and already used by Paul to sign some of his translations from Russian literature[33]). In the above-mentioned monograph, Israel Chalfen states that the pseudonym Celan had been suggested to Paul in Czernowitz by a certain Jakob Silberman, but I know for sure, both from Paul and from the Margul-Sperbers, that the "midwife" of the pseudonym was Yetty Margul-Sperber. Chalfen also puts forward the hypothesis—not at all plausible—that Paul "might have remembered" Thomas of Celano, an Italian scholar of the thirteenth century and author of three hagiographies about Saint Francis of Assisi.[34]

Another important literary outcome of the friendship between Margul-Sperber and Paul was the publication of three of the latter's poems in the only issue of the journal *Agora*, which appeared in May 1947, a few weeks after *Contemporanul* had published "Tango of Death," thus making the name Celan known for the first time. The three poems—"Das Gastmahl" (The Banquet), "Das Geheimnis der Farne" (The Secret of the Ferns), and "Ein wasserfarbenes Wild" (A Watercolored Deer)—were taken by Margul-Sperber himself to the poet Ion Caraion,[35] the manager of the ephemeral journal, who published them in its sole issue in a print run of one thousand copies, plus twenty-six "deluxe" copies. The journal had, on its front page, a new version of Ion Barbu's poem "După melci" (Looking for Snails), and the pages that followed contained a new poem in Italian, by Eugenio Montale, a version of "Miorița"[36] collected by Margul-Sperber, and two sonnets by Eminescu translated into German by Lucian Blaga,[37] ending—on pages 69, 70, and 71—with the three poems by Paul Celan.

The three poems, published in *Agora* on Margul-Sperber's personal recommendation, were part of the volume *Der Sand aus den Urnen* (The Sand from the Urns) and would be republished by the poet in the volume *Mohn und Gedächtnis*—the last of the three with a different title: "Die letzte Fahne" (The Last Flag) (instead of "Ein wasserfarbenes Wild"). It can therefore be said that the absolute debut of Celan's poems occurred in Bucharest in May 1947, first in *Contemporanul* with "Tango of Death," and, shortly thereafter, in *Agora* with the three poems in German.

In order to offer an accurate characterization of the friendship between Margul-Sperber and Celan, it must be mentioned that the latter dedicated a poem to the man who had become his mentor, a poem from the cycle titled *Der Pfeil der Artemis* (Artemis's Arrow). Even though the poem was not included by Paul in his debut volume (his *real* debut volume, *Mohn und Gedächtnis*, published in 1952, since the booklet published in Vienna in 1948 was withdrawn from circulation by Celan himself because of its typographical errors), the fact that it bore such a dedication is important in itself, given the scarcity of poems with a dedication in Celan's oeuvre. In a letter he sent in December 1947 to Max Rychner, the chief editor of the newspaper *Die Tat* in Zurich, with whom he had started a correspondence facilitated by Margul-Sperber, Paul pressed him to include both "Der Pfeil der Artemis" and "Schlaflied" (Lullaby), dedicated to Ruth, in the group of poems scheduled to appear in that journal. Inexplicably, Rychner—though a good friend of Margul-Sperber's—left out precisely the poem dedicated to Margul-Sperber, instead including "Schlaflied" among the seven poems published in the issue of the journal for February 6, 1948, but without the dedication. The grouping was accompanied by a quite erroneous biographical note: "Paul Celan is a young man from Romania who, being born in a village where people spoke Romanian, has learned the German language with remarkable ardor and has thus made his debut in our literature."[38]

Misrepresentations, confusions, typographical errors, and a host of setbacks marked Celan's entrée into the West, postponed, in fact, until around 1952. But the decisive impulse was given him in Bucharest, under the favorable circumstances of that time and, above all, through the providential meeting between Celan and Alfred Margul-Sperber, the generous man who, believing from the start in his talent, influenced, in a way, his whole trajectory.

# 3

# The Beautiful Season of Wordplay

> Language has been given to man
> in order to use it in a Surrealist fashion.
> —ANDRÉ BRETON[1]

Perhaps nothing characterizes better Celan's emotional state during the years he spent in Bucharest than the expression he himself used when trying to evoke that period nostalgically, soon after he left Romania: "cette belle saison des calembours." Although wordplay might not enjoy a very good reputation (Victor Hugo defined it as "la fiente de l'esprit qui vole" [the dung of the mind which soars], which did not prevent him from practicing it assiduously!), it has its usefulness and importance, being able sometimes to hide a by no means negligible potential for poetry or even philosophy. Not all languages lend themselves to wordplay; German, for example, does not really have a vocation for the pun, unlike French and Romanian, which possess it in abundance. A German-language poet, Celan could not play with its words—very few German poets were able to indulge in this luxury (I am thinking here of Christian Morgenstern in particular). Celan dislocated German syntax, created unwonted collocations, but he did not play with the words of this language. He played, instead, with Romanian words, the only language to which he entrusted the ludic dimension of his poetic genius. Why did Celan not play with the words of another language, one even better equipped from this point of view, such as French? This question is worth looking into.

Modern linguistics pays much attention to wordplay, seeing in it certain fundamental mechanisms of language and even of poetry.

"Phonemic similarity is sensed as semantic relationship," Roman Jakobson observed. "The pun, or to use a more erudite, and perhaps more precise term—paronomasia, reigns over poetic art."[2] Since the essence of wordplay is phonemic or semantic ambiguity, it is not surprising that literature—especially poetry—has always practiced it in order to enrich its expressiveness. This method was quite common in the modern age, owing precisely to the evolution of poetry toward a better knowledge of its own potential. The field of wordplay is vast, and the pun is only one of its many and diverse forms. A serious and competent linguist such as Pierre Guiraud even tried to classify these forms. In an ample study dedicated to wordplay,[3] he distinguishes two main types: those obtained through *substitution*, the pun belonging to this category, and those obtained through *concatenation* (*enchaînement*), based on verbal automatism, like the word games cultivated by Surrealists or by the advocates of so-called potential literature. Guiraud also identifies a third type: the inclusion in speech of certain sounds or meanings belonging to other contexts (such is the case of the anagram, or what the French call *contrepèterie*).

Puns, in their turn, can be of various types: the best are based on lexical polysemy, thus aligning themselves very closely with poetic images. One of the most amusing forms of polysemous punning, Guiraud writes, consists in ignoring the figurative meaning by *ad litteram* interpretation of an expression: for example, in a sentence like "Il embrassa cette profession à pleine bouche." Ambiguity can also derive from the homonymy of certain words, a phenomenon that is very widespread in French and has been exploited by many important writers, not only by professional quippers. Even Mallarmé practiced homophony—another source of puns—by rhyming, for example (in *Prose pour Des Esseintes*), "désir, idées" with "des iridées."

The Surrealists rehabilitated the anagram and the pun, intensely cultivated prior to classicism—by Rabelais, for instance, who did not hesitate to publish his masterpiece *Gargantua and Pantagruel* under the pseudonym "Alcofrybas Nasier," obtained through the anagram of his name. Rabelaisian verse reemerges, in different historical circumstances, among self-declared Surrealist poets or among those who were influenced only by André Breton's ideas—Boris Vian, Raymond Queneau, Jacques Prévert, and Henri Michaux. Automatic writing is one of the most efficient modern techniques of "systematic dislocation of language," meant "to create new and original semantic—and sometimes syntactic—relationships between words."[4]

The most recurrent, if not the most important, function of wordplay is its "ludic" function, the French linguist shows.

> He who plays with words is an actor who plays the role of the fool or the naïf; it takes a certain measure of art and intelligence in order to do this in an effective and convincing way. On the other hand, the ludic defunctionalizing of language may have yet another origin, more natural and more spontaneous, to the extent that play is also a form of freeing oneself from social constraints.

Hence the sometimes subversive character of wordplay, of absurd language; this practice flourished, for instance during the so-called Belle Époque, in which "the Artist, despising the bourgeoisie (who, in their turn, despised the Artist), acquires this reputation (see Alphonse Allais, Alfred Jarry, et al.)." The real function of wordplay, Guiraud concludes, "is the fight against taboos."[5]

The French linguist's analysis is based on various examples offered by the literature of his country, but the British domain of puns is also rich, including in it important writers such as Lewis Carroll and James Joyce—the latter being perhaps the best creator of puns of all time (see *Ulysses* and, especially, *Finnegans Wake*, a unique performance in this regard).

At the time Celan was living in Bucharest, the practice of wordplay was very popular. The literary press of the time offers ample proof of this, but the street itself seemed to be living under the sign of the pun and of involuntary humor. For example, Oscar Lemnaru,[6] a master of intelligent and deliberate puns, in an article in *Lumea* (December 9, 1945) speaks of a very elegant butcher's shop on the Calea Dorobanţi, on whose huge sign "there were painted two ox heads," below each of which one could read the name of the merchant: Savu Pavel. Celan, who used to walk on the Calea Dorobanţi every day on his way to the publishing house and back home, must have noticed this sign with amused delight, as he might have noticed another shop sign Oscar Lemnaru mentioned: "On Romană Street, corner of Elena Pherechide Street, there was, and I think there still is to this day, a candy store, yoghurt store, and tavern—all in one place—on whose enormous sign there is an image of a ruler on his throne, horses, and the court—all in supernatural sizes and having the following words below it: 'Upon the raising of Romania to the rank of a kingdom.'" The "serious" literature—in fact, the most "serious" at the time—did not despise wordplay at all; on the contrary, it cultivated it ostentatiously. The still-young generation of poets who had been traumatized by the war and were weary of the horrors and privations they had been forced to endure for so long was also displaying its anticonformism and spirit of rebellion by deliberately prosifying poetic diction. Considered today the leading representative of this generation, Geo Dumitrescu published his volume *Libertatea de a trage cu puşca* (The Freedom to Shoot a Gun) (1946), which was full of intentionally banal poetry (written during the war as a reaction to the jingoistic and chauvinistic exaltations of some official bards).[7]

Detecting beyond these lyrical lines a bolshevist and defeatist attitude, Antonescu's censors had forbidden their publication, but, in a bitter irony of history, they would be received, upon their publication in 1946, with a blatantly premonitory coldness. Yet the fact that a book of poems like *Libertatea de a trage cu puşca* could be published, albeit in a small print run, and could be awarded the Young Writers' Prize (offered by the Foundation for Literature and Art), was in itself a propitious sign. It was not the only one, since in the same period many other books of prose and poetry were being published without hindrance, some of them even more incendiary than Dumitrescu's chapbook—for example, those written by Surrealist poets. In the latter's texts, black humor was given free rein, linguistic clichés were dislocated, and wordplay was practiced unremittingly, since their objectives were not, of course, purely aesthetic. Thus, the pun was experiencing a brief but indisputable age of glory, raised as it was to ontological status. In an article published on the front page of the journal *Studentul Român* (December 25, 1946), Robert Klein—a brilliant essayist who would later become a great specialist in Renaissance art—broadened the sphere of the notion of "pun" considerably to make it capable of encompassing Picasso's art, Le Corbusier's architecture, or Husserl's philosophy. "Pun knowledge," observed Robert Klein, using a term from Blaga, "is not, therefore, merely the result of a decaying intelligence . . . but also the effect of a certain metaphysics of the object."[8]

In the same issue of the journal, Ovid S. Crohmălniceanu, in a long essay on Robert Desnos, endorsed the poet as "a prodigy of French avant-garde poetry":

> Breton invented the Surrealist *dicté* when Desnos had already surpassed it, managing to fall into a hypnotic sleep voluntarily and to speak in the same manner in which he wrote his poems and to be delirious in a deliberately automatic way, putting words together one after another—just as Duchamp "created" his curious machines-inventions-objects. It was from him that he took the name ROSE SELAVY, which he syllabified in his sleep. His phrases rolled like the wheels and skeletons of Duchamp's objects; the pun and the wordplay obeyed the same mechanism.

In the same issue of the above-mentioned journal, Nina Cassian mocked the inventiveness of Isidore Isou,[9] which resembled, in its own way, the punning—the so-called Lettrism—that was causing a stir in Paris at the time:

> It seems that it is ours, the Romanians', destiny to make a literary revolution in Paris. After Tristan Tzara, another fellow countryman, Isidore Isou ("nom d'oiseau," as the French say) is making what is vulgarly called "noise" and, in more pretentious terms, a "literary school." An advocate of pure sound, to the detriment of words, he offers us a few samples of indisputable art, for example: "Batouca zefir cafoufou pentaloun." Isidore Isou used to walk on

> the banks of the Dâmbovița, about which a Frenchwoman said, "la Seine pue aussi, mais quand même" (the Seine stinks, too, but still). He used to go to improvised literary circles and support his cause: "motism." After that, in a journal which "passed away" after only two issues, he promoted "verbism" and then, finally, in Paris, "lettrism." Isou was an uneducated man back then (is he still?). We believe he preferred the pure sound because he could hardly, if at all, regard it as a possible constitutive part of a word. He wanted, at whatever cost, to go to France. And he did. And there he is. Tzara told us that nobody was taking him seriously. Foul mouths even claim that he is being laughed at. But, regardless, the thing is: has he become "somebody"? He has. Has Paris swallowed what Bucharest refused even to consider? It has.

After confessing to feel a touch of envy, Nina Cassian dedicated "to the father of Lettrism" a poem "to his taste," titled "Areu" (*Bocet*—lament) and written in the "Spargese language":[10]

> Areu, areu
> Lortul mai mild, mai setău
> Alna mai velnică-n labe,
> Veltul mai lind în mirabe.

Nina Cassian's Lettrist poem, reprinted in a slightly modified version in the volume *Loto Poeme* in 1972 (Albatros Press), looked in 1946 like a paradoxical replica of Isou's productions but was, in fact, anterior to them. The difference between Nina and Isidore Isou was that she did not take herself seriously: when she invented the Spargese language, Cassian *was playing*, just as Virgil Teodorescu had been playing when he invented, in 1940, "the Leopard language." (Virgil Teodorescu's poem in the Leopard language was "bilingual" and began with the line: "Sobroe algoa dooy toe founod," translated into Romanian thus: "Peste câteva zile-ți vei găsi umbra" [In a few days you'll find your shadow]).

Puns or even wordplay represented a practice that great names engaged in, such as Queneau, Michaux, or Prévert. In Romanian literature, as exemplified above, it was not a rare occurrence at all: since Urmuz, the pun (in its broader sense) had gained the right of citizenship in the republic of Romanian letters, where Tristan Tzara,[11] too, was born. Tudor Arghezi, the second national Romanian poet after Mihai Eminescu, titled his debut volume *Cuvinte Potrivite* (Fitting Words), a telling title in this regard. Arghezi's journal itself was called *Bilete de papagal* (Parrot Notes), referring, through its name, to the Dadaist formula of random word selection.

After all, Isidore Isou's innovations, too, belong to the category of the pun, as defined by Robert Klein. Only that, in this case, the pun—"the discrepancy between an expression and what it intends to express, by producing a shock effect" (according to Klein's article)—was based on the transfer of some Romanian words and sonorities into a language saturated with its own clarity and willing to receive such exotic inputs.

Celan did not have the opportunity to meet Isou: when the latter was setting off for Paris, Celan was heading for Bucharest. Isou had in his suitcase a strategic plan, which was designed to conquer the French capital; Celan had only a bunch of poems in German and had no plans for going to Paris—at the furthest, to Vienna. When he arrived in Bucharest in the spring of 1945, Celan found himself in an atmosphere that was propitious to his poetic genius. In the meantime, after discovering he also had a vocation as a poet in Romanian, a language with vast expressive possibilities, which he had known since childhood, he started to use these potentialities in their playful, as well as their solemn, registers.

I had rarely had the chance to witness such a brilliant and constant verbal eruption as in my friend. I myself, recently returned to Romania after a long exile in a foreign language, was trying to keep up with him, rediscovering, in my turn, the ludic virtues of my mother tongue. That was how the orchestra Celan spoke of was born, modestly claiming for himself the role of accompanist, when in fact it was I who was the accompanist. Often, I was not even the accompanist, merely the witness and, at times, the faithful chronicler. Being with Paul in the editorial office as well as outside of it, I felt the need, at a certain point, to write down bits of his brilliant conversations. Unfortunately, I did this only intermittently, and only during the year 1947. An agenda of that year, which had a calendar full of Orthodox saints, contains in its now brittle pages some laconic notes, grouped under the title *Carticica de seară a lui Paul Celan* (Paul Celan's Little Evening Book)—a title that makes reference to Tudor Arghezi, one of our shared literary passions.

The first note, next to which Paul Celan himself wrote the date—11.III.47—reads as follows: "Paul confirmă că va face amor propriu cu Ciuci" (Paul confirms that he will make self-love to Ciuci). On March 15, this dialogue: "Mi-e somn.—Somn sau nisetru?" (I feel sleepy.—Sleepy or sleeper shark?[12]). On March 20, another terse dialogue: "Bună dimineața.—Nu trebuia" (Good morning.—You shouldn't have). On March 22, one of Paul's statements: "În primăvara asta, vom face nişte excursii care vor rămâne în istoria munților" (This spring, we'll take some trips which will remain in the history of the mountains), a statement that would be followed, very soon, by a trip to the Carpathian mountains, a truly memorable one—at least for me and my friend. On March 24, a note on Margareta Dorian, whom Paul addressed thus: "Spune-mi ceva în altă dezordine de idei, Margareta" (Margareta, tell me something in another disorder of things). Again on March 24: "Chiar aş mânca o bucată de Viorica" (I really feel like eating a piece of Viorica) (Viorica being the young poet I mentioned earlier).[13] The same day, a dedication in a book of poems: "Ai fost sicriul din care am coborât ca să scriu aceasta" (You were the coffin out of which I descended to write this). And a quotation from Ernst Jünger: "Când unul tace din gură, cuvintele sale devin proverbe" (When somebody is silent, his words become proverbs). On the same day, one of the poet's self-definitions: "Paul Celan: persona gratata."

On an undated page, an allusion to Tzara's visit to Romania, where Saşa Pană had been his host: "Saşa Pană e . . . umbra care şi-a găsit în sfârşit omul" (Saşa Pană is . . . the shadow which has finally found its man). Another dialogue, again without a date: "La ce te gândeşti?—La tabla înmulțirii" (What are you thinking of?—Of the multiplication table). Then, "Un gând pentru Margareta: E bine să simţi vântul, dar să te simtă şi el" (A thought for Margareta: It's good to feel the wind, but it should feel you as well). On the next page: "În poezie nu se aşteaptă tonul când se telefonează" (In poetry, you don't wait for the tone when you dial). Then Paul's opinion of Aragon (who would be soon arriving in Bucharest, with Elsa Triolet): "Aragon: un mare poet. Éluard: un mare poet mare" (Aragon: a grand poet. Éluard: a great grand poet). In April, when the date of our long-awaited trip to the mountains was drawing near, this dialogue between a "She" and a "He": "În ce calitate să vin în munţi?—În calitate de soră de caritate. Sau în caritate de soră de calitate" (In what capacity should I come to the mountains?—In your capacity as a nurse for charity. Or in your charity as a nurse for capacity).

The puns abound in these little pages and, however simple and unpretentious they may seem, they testify to a great joy of the spirit, which might appear surprising in a poet generally considered solemn and tragic. Paul liked, above all, to play with proper names, deforming them in all sorts of ways. Thus, Margareta became Gargareta, Colin—Mayacolin (because he had translated Mayakovsky), and, from wordplay to wordplay, he changed his own name from Ancel into Celan through an anagram.

Here are some more examples from *Paul Celan's Little Evening Book*: "Dl Alafon la Telederca" (Marcel Aderca, asked on the phone in the editorial office): "echifest de manivoc" (probably derived from a cliché in the press of the time: manifestly equivocal); "subinginer de suflete" (instead of the famous Stalinist formula "engineer of the human soul," applied to writers); "cărăm o angajuţă" (instead of "angajăm o căruţă"); "nici în declin, nici în demânecă" (instead of "nici în clin, nici în mânecă"); and another short dialogue: "Ce funcţie are ăsta?—Sinus" (What function does this guy have?—Sine). Finally, the pun I quoted earlier, but not in its entirety: "Muzică de anticameră. Solo de Petronom cu acompaniament de Paoloncel" (Antechamber music. Solo by Petronom, with accompaniment by Paoloncel). There is also the note written for Hölderlin's commemoration at the literary circle "Lovinescu's friends":

"Hölderlin şi Lovinescu se vor întâlni în eter pentru a cânta un imn etilic" (Hölderlin and Lovinescu will meet in ether in order to sing an ethylic hymn).

This string of pearls ends with a few parodies of some of Benjamin Fundoianu's lines (from the cycle *Cântece simple* [Simple Melodies]): "Şi va veni o seară când voi pleca de-aici" (And there will come an evening when I leave this place) became "Şi va veni un plec când vom zili de-aici" (And there will come a leaving when we survive the day); "Şi va veni o vreme când vom muri de foame" (And a time will come when we die of hunger) became "Şi va veni o foame când vom muri de vreme" (And a hunger will come when we die of time). These are dated May 1, 1947, when Paul was already preoccupied with his departure for Vienna. On the same date (which was written by Paul in my little notebook) I find his note: "Petre Solomon, stagnând în str. Batişte. O şoaptă de amor: Avansaţi în batistă!" (Petre Solomon stagnating in Batiste Street. A whisper of love: Advance in the handkerchief!). A note written in mid-November: "O telegramă din Budapesta anunţă că Paul a plecat la Ploieşti" (A telegram from Budapest informs that Paul left for Ploieşti).

It is far from my intention to see in Celan's wordplay some masterpieces of the genre, although some of them could easily stand beside gems by Queneau (or by Oscar Lemnaru). Apart from their ludic function, such wordplay also served, for Celan, to provide access to the intimate mechanisms of a language that he was using in a grave register as well. By playing, childishly, with Romanian words and "fooling around" with more or less uncomplicated puns, he was discovering, delighted, the potentialities of this language, temporarily chosen as the linguistic medium most favorable for a poetic exercise that was necessary for his own evolution. Simplifying things, of course, one could say that in German Celan had become, at the time, the prisoner of prosodic and stylistic patterns that he felt the need to unsettle. Even a cursory look at the poems from the Czernowitz period reveals the tyrannical presence of certain leitmotifs and symbols derived from his reading, though charged with the poet's personal experience. Rilke, Trakl, and Hofmannsthal are present *in* and *between* the lines. Many of Celan's early poems have strict rhyme and rhythm, often containing a musicality that recalls a romantic ballad by Heine. It is only in the "Todesfuge" that the melodious flow breaks, under the burden of the unbearable meanings it communicates, but even here a certain atmosphere of romance persists, a certain musicality, impossible conceptually, but tenacious, insidious, and disturbing.

I think it was only in Bucharest that Celan found his specific rhythms—maybe he would have found them anywhere else, but the fact remains that he had found and experimented with them here, both in Romanian and in German. The explanation—not the only possible one, of course—seems to reside in the poet's direct and active contact with Surrealist practices. Without going into detail about the aesthetics of Surrealism—which wishes to be, above all, an ethics—I would like to mention here the by now classic definition of the poetic image given by Pierre Reverdy, a definition that André Breton took over wholesale:

> The image is a pure creation of the spirit.
>
> It cannot be created out of a comparison, but by bringing together two more or less distant realities.
>
> The further-off and more appropriate the connections between the two realities brought together, the more powerful the image, and the more intense the emotive force it contains and the poetic reality it creates.[14]

During his stay in Bucharest, Paul Celan—who had discovered Surrealism long before (maybe in 1938, when he was studying medicine in Tours)—was decisively exposed to the influence of this fundamental poetic principle that defines Surrealism. Back then, there was a very active group of Surrealist poets in Bucharest, called the "new wave" of a movement that had already been noticed during the interwar period but was less rigorous and committed. I will not go so far as to say, as Marin Mincu did in his introduction to a recent anthology of Romanian avant-garde literature, that this group, formed at a time "when Surrealism was already exhausted" (in France), might have resuscitated European Surrealism.[15] It is true that Breton himself would acknowledge and praise the merits of the Romanian group, especially for the slogan it launched: namely, "la connaissance par la méconnaissance."[16] But Marin Mincu forgets that the activity of the Romanian group had ceased by the end of 1947, unlike that of the French Surrealists, who, once again gathered around André Breton, would continue to be active throughout the following two decades.[17]

It is no less true that, during its brief period of glory, the Romanian Surrealist group was intensely active on various levels, something that was in fact remarked upon by their French colleagues, whose primacy the group did not even dream of contesting. Strictly on the literary level, the Surrealist poets in Bucharest—Gherasim Luca,[18] Gellu Naum,[19] Virgil Teodorescu,[20] Paul Păun, and Dolfi Trost—were very productive, not only in Romanian but also in French: another sign of their subordination to the Surrealist center in Paris.

Unlike their forerunners in the first wave, the representatives of this new wave published their writings not in journals but directly in brochures and chapbooks, in limited editions, admittedly, but on high-quality paper (Vidalon Moyen Âge, Papier Vergé-Chamois, etc.). They published them with their own publishing houses or collections, called *Les éditions de l'oubli*, *Surréalisme*, *Negation of Negation*, *Intra-Noir*, again with the obvious desire to attract a Western readership. Their books were illustrated with reproductions after their own cubomania or graphomania images, or with drawings by Victor Brauner, Jules Perahim, and other Surrealist painters. They had bizarre or even downright terrifying titles, such as *Teribilul interzis* (The Forbidden Terrible) (Gellu Naum), *Le vampire passif* (The Passive Vampire) (Gherasim Luca), *Au lobe du sel* (Salt of the Lobe) (Virgil Teodorescu), *La conspiration du silence* (The Conspiracy of Silence) (Paul Păun), or *Le profil navigable* (The Navigable Profile) (Dolfi Trost).

Concomitantly, there was intense activity in the field of Surrealist art, even more visibly under the sign of automatism. Apart from the above-mentioned illustrations, the Romanian Surrealists organized exhibitions where they presented their various techniques and innovations. At the first of these exhibitions, organized in January 1945 in a hall on Brezoianu Street, they presented "colored graphs, cubomania collages and objects," "explained" in brochures that had titles like *Oniriser la vie*, *Puissance du regard*, or *Initiation voluptueuse.* Although Celan missed this exhibition, he did not fail to visit (together with Ruth) the second great exhibition of the Romanian Surrealists, organized in Bucharest between September 29 and October 18, 1946, at Cretzulescu Galleries on the Calea Victoriei. Gherasim Luca, Paul Păun, and Dolfi Trost exhibited many unusual objects there—for example, a "seductive chair" (la chaise seductrice) or some "dumbbells of fear" (haltères de la peur), as well as smoked lamp glass. The catalogue—signed by the three exhibitors and by their colleagues Gellu Naum and Virgil Teodorescu—strove to offer, in French, a poetic equivalent of the objects exhibited: "La pensée exprimée dans les filaments durs *du silence et de la convulsion* précède la racine impossible, elle la précède et la poursuit à l'aide d'une machine à élever des tonnes de regards et tout *le fluide d'entre les plantes*."[21] The catalogue ended with a programmatic text, "Une question," which reiterated the fundamental credo of the movement: "La poésie, l'amour, la révolution ne font qu'un" (Poetry, love, revolution are merely one).

The title of the exhibition, placed on the front page of the catalogue, was even more original: *L'Infra-Noir: Préliminaires à une intervention sur-thaumaturgique dans la conquête du desirable* (Infra-Black: Prolegomenon to a Surthaumaturgical Intervention in the Conquest of the Desirable). Naturally, the exhibition prompted diverse reactions, some of them very hostile, others merely sarcastic. To limit myself to one example, I quote from an article published by Nina Cassian in *Studentul român* (December 20, 1946):

> The LATEST SURREALIST EXHIBITION represented a great step forward on the path to knowledge, through the display of the twenty-two blackened lamps marking the only—but how essential!—difference

> between this and the previous exhibition of the group. We have long pondered the deep and stubborn problem of the smoke that settles on lamp glass, considering it a real opportunity to positivize the theory of objectified hazard. Could it be that these twenty-two lamps (twenty-two or maybe fifty-five) prove that Surrealism is, as Pierre Mabille wrote, more like a *Weltanschauung* than merely an artistic school?

Immune to press banter and the hostility of their readers, the Surrealist poets continued their activity. What is more curious is that their group, so limited in number, afforded the luxury of some factional battles, having, at the same time, a common front before "the enemy." Gellu Naum, Virgil Teodorescu, and Paul Păun had not hesitated to attack, as early as 1945, in a manifesto called *Critica mizeriei* (Critique of Squalor), the views of their friend Gherasim Luca. They accused him of sliding into mysticism and other such deviations from the classic theoretical principles of Surrealism, reaffirmed by them with great determination, although Breton himself had abandoned them in the meantime. Gherasim Luca, Trost, and, at a certain point, Paul Păun as well multiplied their theoretical interventions, using a rhetoric that was, in fact, quite similar.

In a *Mesaj adresat mişcării suprarealiste internaţionale* (Message Addressed to the International Surrealist Movement) (1945), written in French, Gherasim Luca and Dolfi Trost defined the position of the Romanian group, united at that time, as follows: "Separated from our friends, since the beginning of the global imperialist war, we do not know anything about them. But we have always kept alive the secret hope that on this planet, on which our existence seems to be becoming more and more unbearable, the genuine functioning of reason has not ceased to guide the group, which holds in its hands the highest ideological freedom ever—the international Surrealist movement." Addressing themselves particularly to André Breton, the authors of this message communicated to him "some theoretical conclusions" they had reached during the war: "Being Surrealists, we continued to see the possibility of permanent confrontations between inner reality and outer reality within our adherence to dialectical materialism, within the historical destiny of the international proletariat, and within the sublime theoretical conquests of Surrealism." More Catholic than Breton, the Romanian Surrealists criticized "the artistic deviations" committed by some of their French colleagues: Gherasim Luca and Trost found the cause of these "deviations" in "the mimetic use of the techniques invented by the first Surrealists." The two poets vehemently condemned "this Surrealist mannerism, which risks turning Surrealism into an artistic movement, to make it accepted by our class enemies, to grant it a harmless historical past—in short, to force it to lose the spirit that has animated, through all the contradictions of the external world, those who saw in the revolution their own raison d'être." In order to keep Surrealism "in a constantly revolutionary state," the authors of the message proposed "a dialectical position of permanent *negation* and of *negation of negation*." Another standpoint consisted in "a limitless eroticization of the proletariat," regarded as a "revolutionary necessity": "The objective hazard makes us see in *love* the general revolutionary method characteristic of Surrealism . . . We proclaim love, freed from social or individual, psychological or theoretical, religious or sentimental constraints, as our main method for knowledge and action." Finally, the two authors of the message proposed "a revolution against nature," meant to counteract "the vexing influences of human biology or the abstract indifference of cosmology." This proposal, original in fact, translated into what Gherasim Luca called "a non-Oedipal standpoint": "Due to revolutionary movements, the father's *position* has been greatly undermined, both in its direct aspects and in its symbolic forms. But the castrating vestiges of natal traumatism persist nevertheless, supported, in fact, by the position, favorable to the brother, adopted by political movements."[22] This radicalism on the part of the Romanian Surrealists manifested itself in the realm of dreams: "We cannot accept regressive dreams, as we cannot accept religious folly, because our trust in these grandiose revolutionary instruments prevents us from hiding certain reactionary elements, seeking shelter in a resistance which only serves to keep on hold, through mechanical procrastination, the coming close of daytime and nighttime."[23] The dry, scientifically pretentious language used by the authors of the message translated quite faithfully a dogmatic way of thinking characteristic of the entire Surrealist movement whenever it attempted to become socially and politically active. The Romanian Surrealists were no exception, which explains the resemblance between their rhetoric and the political rhetoric of the time (minus, of course, "the eroticization of the proletariat" and "the revolution against nature"!), both of which have the same revolutionary pathos and the same desire to change the old order of things on the elected territory "at 44°5' latitude north and 26° longitude east," as the authors of the message specified.

However, it should be added that, at that time, the language used by the Bucharest Surrealist group had not yet been trivialized by repetition; on the contrary, it sounded quite fresh, distinguishing itself from the political rhetoric. The Romanian Surrealists—I repeat, only a handful of people—launched their slogans in an atmosphere loaded with the electricity of certain long-suppressed political passions and, skirting illegality, acted on the periphery of leftist parties, trying to influence them as Breton had tried to do during the interwar period.[24]

What could Paul Celan have in common with the Romanian Surrealists? *L'amour, la liberté, la poésie*—the permanent values extolled by Surrealists everywhere were the values he himself had always believed in. But he was not at all attracted to the fanaticism some doctrinaires of the movement displayed, or to their dogmatic exclusivism, exaggerated to the point of ostracizing some deviationists on absurd grounds (as was the case, for example, with Desnos, accused of "too much self-indulgence"). If he had been included in their group, Celan would have been excluded sooner or later, for one reason or another.

As regards his participation in the activities of the group, nothing certain can be said. Gellu Naum is unhesitatingly sure about it: Celan was never part of the group, "which not anybody could join." Besides, Naum does not remember ever having seen him. A little more conciliatory and less categorical, Virgil Teodorescu remembers that Paul was "a follower," quite close to the Bucharest group.

Paul Păun tends to agree with Virgil Teodorescu, in the sense that, without having participated directly in the activity of the group, young Celan was evolving in its immediate proximity. Like Teodorescu, Păun thinks that it was Ira Hager, the wife of a Czernowitz librarian, who introduced Celan to the Surrealist circle. But Păun does not remember having spoken much with the young poet, seen only at a few parties ("Altogether, I don't think I spent more than *an hour* talking to him").

In his monograph, Israel Chalfen says that Celan frequented the Surrealist circle of Gherasim Luca, Paul Păun, and Dolfi Trost, participating in "their amicable meetings, where beautiful women were also present," including the Frenchwoman Nadine.[25] Horia Deleanu remembers vaguely that one evening Celan took him to a party, somewhere on Nicolae Iorga Street, where poems were read, but which also included some less innocent entertainment. According to Edith Silberman, on that street lived Leonid Miller, a good friend of Paul's from Czernowitz. Leonid Miller's sister, Nata, was very fond of parties.

Beyond this (false) controversy, what is really important is whether Celan can be inscribed in the Surrealist movement, understood "not as a new artistic school, but as a means to knowledge, especially knowledge of some continents hitherto unexplored systematically: the unconscious, the miraculous, dreams, madness, hallucinatory states—in short, the opposite of the logical realm."[26]

To the extent that the Surrealists subscribed to the definition of the movement formulated by Maurice Nadeau, they could not have left Celan indifferent. But their activity as a group left him quite unimpressed; what interested him were the individual cases of some poets exposed to the black sun of Surrealism. I have already spoken of Celan's affectionate esteem for Paul Éluard and his relative dislike of Aragon; both feelings illustrated a sense of discrimination that Celan also exercised in his relations with the members of the Bucharest group. If we think of the friendship that would develop between Celan and Gherasim Luca in Paris, it might be inferred that its foundation had been set in Bucharest. Despite his prodigious activity as theoretician of the group (he and Trost undoubtedly made the greatest contributions regarding the position of the movement), Gherasim Luca was a genuine poet, with a very likeable personality. Beyond the ostentatious elements in his texts, Luca impressed with his overflowing imagination and engaging humor, which proved that the doctrinaire was not as sadistic as he pretended to be.

Celan was very attracted to the ludic dimension of Surrealism—an essential dimension, which belongs to his configuration, characteristic of the south rather than the north. Breton had defined the role of humor in Surrealism thus: "Humor, as the paradoxical triumph of the principle of pleasure over actual conditions at the moment in which the latter are regarded as highly unfavorable, is naturally called upon to assume a defensive value in the age we live in, burdened as it is with menace."[27] Obsessed with theories, the Surrealists exercised humor as a privileged way of introducing "the objective hazard," also elaborating, with this view, a set of techniques, all based on verbal automatism. Their purpose was to capture a message and not at all to achieve literary effects. As early as the *Manifeste du surréalisme*, Breton had formulated the rules of the individual game as follows:

> After you have settled yourself in a place as favorable as possible to the concentration of your mind upon itself, have writing materials brought to you. Put yourself in as passive, or receptive, a state of mind as you can. Forget about your genius, your talents, and the talents of everyone else. Keep reminding yourself that literature is one of the saddest roads that can lead to anything. Write quickly, without any preconceived subject, fast enough so that you will not remember what you're writing and be tempted to reread what you have written. The first sentence will come spontaneously.[28]

The recipe for games for two or more players was a little more complicated, but it was based on the same principle of free and spontaneous expression, without any trace of inner censorship or control. The prototype of these Surrealist games was the famous Cadavre exquis, called thus after the phrase "Le cadavre exquis boira le vin nouveau" (The exquisite corpse will drink the new wine), a phrase obtained by the participants in playing one of these collective games.[29]

As mentioned above, Celan's circle of friends played a version of this game called Ioachim. Both Paul and I looked forward to the evenings or afternoons when we played Ioachim, usually at Nina Cassian's place: seated before a blank sheet of paper, we would start writing words at random, according to the Surrealist instructions for Cadavre exquis. The moment of reading aloud the collective texts was wonderful, eagerly expected by each of the participants. After the intense concentration on the sheets of paper, relaxation finally came—peals of laughter accompanied the reading of the results of this verbal lottery to which everybody contributed ("Le surréalisme est à la portée de tous les inconscients" [Surrealism is the capacity of everything unconscious] announced a *papillon* at the launch of the first manifesto in 1924).

During the war, Nina Cassian, her husband, and I had often played a version of Ioachim in verse, on given rhymes, so I was prepared, in a way, but Paul was only now discovering the delights of this Surrealist game, for which he had, of course, a much more profound affinity than I did. Unfortunately, I have not kept any of the many Ioachim games we played then, but I can relive their spirit through a passage from Marin Preda's novel *Delirul* (Delirium). The young journalist Paul Ştefan, the protagonist of this unfinished novel, spends the night of New Year's Eve at a colleague's place, where a number of people have gathered. From the very first moment of his arrival, Ştefan, who is a serious man, and a bit self-conscious about his peasant origins, is surprised by the decorations in his colleague's apartment: "Next to a painting, he saw a little fragment of a thin bone hanging by an invisible string. 'Fragment from a Thracian parrot, discovered in Fleaşca de Jos village,' he read." At a certain point, a girl named Luchi sits down at the piano with another guest and they start playing advertisements—"he with his voice, she accompanying him on the keys."

Later, Luchi brings a pie containing insulting messages, such as "For two lei, you would be capable of trampling on your parents," or "How can you not feel embarrassed, since you have no character?" After the message, the game Questions and Answers follows: "Wait, does everybody know the game?" says Luchi. "Ştefan, you'll get it quickly, the questions are spontaneous and the answers must also be so. Nobody is allowed to think [of them]."

Finally, the guests begin to play Ioachim:

> Luchi was already giving each of them a sheet of paper and a pencil. The new game, she explained to Ştefan, consisted in allowing your imagination to roam free, on a given topic. But the topic was not familiar to him, he said, when he heard that it was about two women, called *the two orphans*. That's no problem, said Luchi, write whatever you feel like, it'll be even funnier that way. . . . Ştefan would have preferred not to participate, he did not understand what he was supposed to do, but he did not want to ask for an explanation a second time, either. Who were the two female orphans? It was stupid, they knew them, whereas he had no idea. . . . He did not write anything and in no time he found himself facing a sheet of paper that somebody had passed along to him: "The population of Bucharest had long been accustomed to seeing two majestic, unfortunate women on the boulevard, named Miss Carapancea and Miss Cămărăşescu. Nobody will ever forget the bizarre and dense charm of these two orphan women. Life had not treated them kindly. . . . At the young age of . . ."—and the story continued in the same manner, the same Urmuzian style of an abrupt ending, and Ştefan had to continue. But nothing came to his mind, so he passed the sheet on, without having written anything on it.[30]

Marin Preda was not very tolerant toward those who played these games, and he approaches the scene in a most caricatural manner, in order to cast into relief, by contrast, his protagonist's seriousness. As he himself had for a while attended Nina Cassian's literary group, he met Celan during one of the meetings held at her place—not necessarily on the New Year's Eve evoked in the novel. In fact, this New Year's Eve is a fictitious and composite reconstruction of many evenings, about which Marin Preda had heard much without directly participating in them. In order to be able to describe it, the novelist appealed to Nina and myself, and both of us gave him some texts and background information. The game Questions and Answers included by Preda in his novel is a faithful reproduction of one of those texts, unfortunately the only one I have kept and which I placed at Preda's disposal: "Ce este singurătatea poetului?—Un număr de circ neanunţat în program" (What is the poet's solitude?—A circus act unannounced in the program); "Ce este o lacrimă?—Un cântar în aşteptarea greutăţilor" (What is a tear?—A set of scales waiting for its weights); "Ce este beţia?—O filă albă între altele colorate" (What is drunkenness?—A blank sheet among colored others); "Ce este uitarea?—Un măr copt în care s-a înfipt o suliţă" (What is forgetfulness?—A ripe apple into which a spear has been thrust); "Ce este întoarcerea?—Aproape nimic, dar ar putea să fie un fulg de zăpadă" (What is a return?—Almost nothing, but it could be a snowflake); "Ce este ultima seară înainte de plecare?" (What is the last night before departure?). The answer, which Marin Preda omitted, was: "Plecarea de la o expoziţie de porţelanuri vechi" (Leaving an exhibition of old china). "Ce este un an nou?—O poveste de dragoste care se sfârşeşte" (What is a new year?—A love story reaching its end); "Ce este tristeţea?—Un drum care se împotmoleşte înainte de a ajunge la liman" (What is sadness?—A road that comes to a standstill before reaching its haven); "Ce este un revelion?—Un pahar de vin în care s-a turnat otravă" (What is a New Year's Eve?—A glass of wine into which poison has been poured); "Ce este femeia iubita?" (What is the beloved woman?).

The novelist omits the answer to this question, too—"Trezirea tristă după o noapte fără constelaţii" (The sad awakening after a night without constellations)—just as he omits the following questions and answers: "Ce este un duel?—Un somn adânc într-o pădure de fagi putreziţi" (What is a duel?—A deep sleep in a forest of rotten beech trees); "Ce este bâlciul culorilor?—Poezia nescrisă care ne va roade adânc vieţile" (What is a color fair?—The unwritten poem that will gnaw deeply at our lives); "Ce este un tren pe care-l pierzi?—O batistă care mai flutură încă" (What is a train you miss?—A handkerchief that is still fluttering).[31]

Being an essentially realist novelist, Marin Preda had a weaker taste for the Surrealist imagination and for black humor of the Urmuzian type, which did not mean that he had no ear for or appreciation of such games. Anyway, the questions and answers quoted above bear Celan's mark (he wrote almost all of them with his own hand), and some of them are of no poorer quality than those written by Breton and his friends during the glorious times of Surrealism (for example, "Qu'est-ce que le jour?—Une femme qui se baigne à la tombée de la nuit" (What is the day?—A woman bathing at nightfall), or "Qu'est-ce que la raison?—C'est un nuage mangé par la lune" (What is reason?—It's a cloud eaten by the moon)—Paul Éluard's response to a question asked by Breton).

There is, however, one question that is harder to answer than those posed in such games: is Celan a Surrealist poet or not? Without a doubt, his poetic orbit is not too far from that of the Surrealists. At the same time, as a poet, he distances himself from their group, even if he has certain connections and affinities with them. Eminently a poet (and not a "pohète," as Jacques Vaché said scornfully, or as Gellu Naum would reiterate, many decades later), Celan extracts from Surrealism only what suits and interests him: that is, the poetic part—the part that belongs to the realm of dreams, of nights, of the miraculous, as well as the part defined by playfulness, verbal humor, freedom of the imagination. In short, it was not the movement per se but the Surrealist frame of mind that attracted Celan, solitary sniper at the avant-garde, reluctant to be classified in any way.[32]

His sporadic contacts with some members of the Bucharest group, as well as the more constant ones with those friends who, without being Surrealists, played passionately the games perfected by Breton and his colleagues, facilitated the transition to a new phase in his evolution as a poet. Questions and Answers, Ioachim, and even the puns he created in Romanian can be regarded as exercises in intellectual elasticity, meant to strengthen his "poetic muscles," and not as mere entertainment, as activities of collective fun. "Surrealism," Michel Carrouges wrote, "is the most powerful mental explosive ever created. It can be said, without abusing the terms, that it tends to effect, within the field of language and images, and even of sensations, the most spectacular chain reaction."[33]

One of the chain reactions generated by the Surrealist games Paul Celan played in Bucharest was his poetic work itself, written in Romanian and closely connected to his creations in the German language.

# 4

# The Adolescence of a Farewell

> Just as, within a state, we enjoy certain goods which belong to everybody and to nobody—roads, gardens, markets, similarly, in the republic of language, there are well-worn paths which belong to everybody. But one's real wealth can be found in one's own home, and in its home the Romanian language is a good administrator and has plenty of everything.
>
> —Mihai Eminescu[1]

Paul Celan's Romanian texts could be compared to a meteorite fallen, not entirely unexpectedly, on the lyrical landscape of Romania; a meteorite detached from a poetic comet which was, at a certain point, on a trajectory visible only within the space between 44°5' latitude north and 26° longitude east, which coincides with the place from which the Romanian Surrealists sent their message to André Breton in 1945.

But the impression of singularity the reading of these texts generates comes from the fact that they do not actually resemble anything else, not even the Surrealist texts to which they seem, however, to be related. They also present vague similarities with some more traditional aspects of Romanian poetry—no poet can completely avoid the tradition sedimented in the words of the language he uses even temporarily. Yet it would be unavailing to try to detect in Celan's texts traces of, let us say, Blaga or Arghezi, even if it is possible to identify certain analogies and parallels. Celan will be Celan, even in Romanian. The interesting fact is that his Romanian texts do not much resemble his German texts, either, with which they have, of course, the most incontestable affinities. The prose poems in particular are singular, unique, like an astral body, without any correspondence in German, a language in which, as far as I know, Paul did not write such texts, except the apologue titled "Gespräch im Gebirg" (Conversation in the Mountains).[2]

As regards the poems he wrote in Romanian, they are somewhat easier to situate within the early period of Celan's lyric poetry which, in a sense, they extend. Nevertheless, the shift to a different linguistic medium leads, in the case of his Romanian poems as well, to certain metamorphoses. It is as if, in Romanian, Celan were able to evade the sort of intellectual burden that the German language forced him to carry, and to try out new tonalities, with a greater degree of freedom than his mother tongue allowed him. This aspect should not be very surprising: for a writer, writing in a different language is often a salutary exercise, with stylistic and self-revelatory benefits. For Samuel Beckett, for example, writing in French meant a real liberation of his creative energies. As Al Alvarez, one of the most penetrating critics of Beckett's work, observes, the French language allowed the great playwright to escape "from the whole weight of Irish rhetoric . . . with its insidious cadence and genius for baroque linguistic flourish." Beckett "needed a medium at once more neutral and more precise," such as the French language. "This was exactly what Beckett required as he completed his break with the traditional novel and shifted into those plotless, placeless monologues, delivered in a monotone in some no man's land of the spirit." Thus, "it was most likely easier to achieve this despairing degree of abstraction in a language other than English which, despite every experiment, remains stubbornly specific, thick with local associations and echoes of other voices. In comparison, French seems a model of clarity and logic."[3]

Of course, what Paul Celan found in the Romanian language was different from what Beckett found in the French language. Like English, Romanian is a language "full of voices," endowed with vast potential to express the concreteness and color of things but containing, at the same time, possibilities of ascending toward the high realm of philosophical abstractions. Whatever the explanation, Celan allowed himself to be tempted by the Romanian linguistic potentialities in order to express his thoughts and his emotional states, as well as to experiment with methods inspired by the Surrealists or occasioned by his contact with them.

As mentioned above, Celan entered the Romanian language through the most accessible gate, that of wordplay, but he did not stop there. Besides, he did not arrive entirely unprepared. Even in his early poems, Celan had shown a strong inclination to free association, metaphoric thinking of the paralogical type characteristic of Surrealist poetry, itself a descendant of German Romanticism. But, under the influence of Trakl and particularly Rilke, these free associations lost their power to shock, in favor of a different musicality, which did not disregard such effects: "Die Wäldern winken den Wolken" (the forests wave to the clouds), in a poem from 1942 titled "Mein Karren knarrt nicht mehr" (My Cart No Longer Creaks).

Many of Celan's early poems have strict rhyming and meter, recalling classical models or the German Expressionist poets rather than Rilke or Trakl. Even a poem full of the utmost emotional tension such as "Nähe der Gräber" (Nearness of the Graves, in *Der Pfeil der Artemis*) enters a prosodic matrix that is, in a way, incompatible with the gravity of the "message": "Kennt noch das Wasser des südlichen Bug, / Mutter, die Welle die Wunden dir schlug?" (Does the water of the southern bend, Mother, know the wave that struck wounds in you?). Admittedly, the final couplet proclaims the incompatibility in the interrogative form: "Und duldest du, Mutter, wie einst, ach, daheim, / den leisen, den deutschen, den schmerzlichem Reim?" (And can you bear, Mother, as long ago at home, the quiet, German, pain-laden rhyme?).

Certainly, some of the original connotations are lost in translation, but I think that the spirit of song remains visible and audible. Still, the poet would long endure "den leisen, den deutschen, den schmerzlichem Reim," beloved since childhood, thanks to his mother, who had initiated him into German poetry. The conflict expressed here persists, unresolved, until very late, leaving its imprint on many poems. This applies not only to prosody—with which he had taken certain liberties even in Czernowitz—but to a whole series of constitutive aspects of his early poetry. The imagery and the lexicon of the poems often seem to counterpoint the grave message of horror and revolt implicit in their lines. Instead of transmitting shock, they stifle it; the shock wave is dispersed in the melodious flux of "the German rhyme."

At a certain point in his evolution as a poet, Celan must have asked himself, in anguish, whether one could still write poetry after Auschwitz—a question to which Theodor Adorno gave a negative answer. An authentic poet cannot be resigned to silence, not even in an extreme situation such as the one that made the famous German philosopher answer in the negative. On the other hand, Celan felt the inadequacy of his poetic diction for the message he meant to transmit and which he could not suppress within himself. His dilemma was existential and poetic at the same time, and involved his way of relating to his mother tongue and to his own destiny.[4] Whoever does not understand this dilemma will understand next to nothing of Celan's poetry, which, in its entirety, is a desperate dialogue between the poet and his mother tongue. Later, the poet would subject the German language to a process of radical transformation, by breaking its syntactic patterns and by introducing foreign lexical elements (especially from Yiddish and Hebrew, the languages of the victims of the Nazi Holocaust). But, at the time I speak of, he only felt the need to shake off some clichés that were pulling him back in time, toward poetry before Auschwitz. The contact with Surrealist ideas and practices facilitated this endeavor. André Breton had said that "la beauté sera convulsive ou ne sera pas" (beauty will be convulsive, or will not be at all) and Celan embraced this fundamental principle, which was consonant with his own convictions as well as with the historical situation.

The respite he took from his mother tongue was one of his ways of "taking revenge"—I retain here the original sense of this word *răzbunare* (revenge), as revealed by Noica:

> *Răs-bunare* (re-venge). Initially, it meant restoring the good qualities of something. All at once, the word "revenge"—such an

> ominous, grim word—becomes a positive one and its dark connotations disperse, just as rain clouds disperse (vremea se răzbună): that is, it becomes good and clear again.[5]

In the Romanian language, Celan felt free to experiment, to apply the lessons learned from the Surrealist poets, so active at the time. The break he took in another language was, of course, temporary, like that of an astronaut outside his spaceship when he wants either to repair or merely observe it. The return to his mother tongue was implicit from the very beginning. In fact, it was not even a total break but a parallel evolution, in two different linguistic realms. Celan continued to write in Bucharest as he did in Czernowitz; it is impossible to draw a precise chronological line between the poems brought from Bukovina and those written in the Romanian capital, but careful analysis reveals certain significant changes. The Romanian poems are situated temporally in the immediate proximity of the German poems, belonging to his most mature cycle written in Bucharest, *Der Sand aus den Urnen* (The Sand from the Urns), a collection that also contains some poems written in Czernowitz but finalized here. As regards their themes and prosodic style, the Romanian and the German poems have many similarities. Let us consider, as an example, the poem in German titled "Marianne" and its equivalent in Romanian, "Poem pentru umbra Marianei" (Poem for Mariana's Shadow), the presence of the same name in both titles being a (relative) clue to contemporaneity. The prosodic matrix is approximately the same:

> Geliebte, auch du bist das Schilf und wir alle der Regen;
> ein Wein ohnegleichen dein Leib, und wir bechern zu zehnt;
> ein Kahn im Getreide dein Herz, wir rudern ihn nachtwärts;
> ein Krüglein Bläue, so hüpfest du leicht über uns, und wir schlafen.[6]

> You, too, my love, are the reed, and we are all rain
> a peerless wine is your body, and the ten of us drink it
> a boat in the wheatfield your heart, we row it toward the night;
> an ewer of blue, how lightly you leap over us, while we sleep.

The Romanian poem seems like an extension of the one in German:

> Izma iubirii-a crescut ca un deget de înger.
> Să crezi: din pământ mai răsare un braţ răsucit de tăceri,
> un umăr ars de dogoarea luminilor stinse,
> o faţă legată la ochi cu năframa neagr-a vederii,
> o aripă mare de plumb şi alta de frunze,
> un trup istovit în odihna scăldată de ape.

> The mint of love has grown like an angel's finger.
> Believe it: out of the earth another arm, twisted by silences, rises,
> a shoulder burnt by the blaze of the faded lights,
> a face, the eyes blindfolded with the black veil of sight,
> a large wing of lead and another one of leaves,
> a weary body in the water-bathed rest.

The Romanian poem differs from the German one insofar as it abounds in metaphors, obtained by putting together a concrete term and an abstract one. Such metaphors appear in the German poem as well, but they seem more artificial, maybe due to the connecting copula "like": "Von Auge zu Aug zieht die Wolke, wie Sodom nach Babel" (The cloud spreads from one eye to the other, like Sodom after Babel).

In "Poem pentru umbra Marianei," there is only one *ca* (like): "Izma iubirii-a crescut ca un deget de înger." Everything that comes after this line is written in a succession of metaphors that impose, without forcing it, the shift from the concrete to the abstract and vice versa: "din pământ mai răsare un braţ răsucit de tăceri" (out of the earth another arm, twisted by silences, rises), "o faţă legată la ochi cu năframa neagr-a vederii" (a face, the eyes blindfolded with the black veil of sight), "un trup istovit în odihna scăldată de ape" (a weary body in the water-bathed rest), and so on.

Both poems are governed by the same oneiric atmosphere, one in which something is happening, a love drama, something hard to understand, especially in the German poem, with its multitude of symbols. There is this phase in Celan's poetry, characterized by a sort of baroque imagery, which complicates understanding to the extreme. The poem written in Romanian is relatively clearer, despite the unwonted nature of the metaphors, which, taken separately, remain obscure.

The dialogic, or dialogued, structure typical of his early poems, and even of some later ones, is brought into sharper relief in "Poem pentru umbra Marianei" than in its German equivalent. In the Romanian poem, the dialogue with the lover unfolds in a much more dramatic fashion, leaving in suspension the question "Ne iubim sau nu ne iubim?" (Do we love each other or don't we love each other?), and the entire succession of images, cumulatively, is oriented toward that question. These observations are not value judgments on the two poems; they seek only to highlight certain differences in nuance between the one text and the other. A careful reading of Celan's other Romanian poems may lead to even more interesting observations.

In the poem titled "Azi-noapte" (Last Night), the atmosphere is, from the beginning, Surrealistic: "Din pomii sădiţi de amurg în odăile noastre incendiate / vom desprinde încet porumbeii de sticlă" (From the trees planted by the dusk in our burnt rooms / we shall slowly set the glass pigeons free).

Without using the word "like" at all, the poet associates seemingly incompatible terms in this poem, too—not in an isolated manner, but in an uninterrupted flux that transforms the entire poem into a metaphor. Apart from this continuous metaphorization, what contributes to the impression of singularity is the use of verbs in the future tense—"vom desprinde" (we shall set free), "ne vor creşte pe umeri şi braţe" (they will grow on our shoulders and arms), "vei vorbi în neştire cu mine" (you will talk to me endlessly).

This aspect is very important, because it is related to the ontological roots of Celan's poetry. In his admirable essay *After Babel*, George Steiner observes that "man alone has developed a grammar of futurity"[7] and cites Celan, who noted, in *Atemwende* (Breathturn), that only man "can cast nets 'in rivers north of the future.'"[8] Steiner also makes reference to one of Mandelstam's comments on Dante, in whose *Inferno*—the equivalent of a grammar without futures—"we literally hear how the verbs kill time."[9] The use of verbs in the future tense implies hope, which, of course, should not be generalized or interpreted as a sign of optimism; Celan's poems are mostly gloomy, even when they offer time a slightly open door. Still, some of his poems seem to suggest hope, despite the somber spiritual landscape it has to cross. For example, in "Regăsire" (Reunion) the use of verbs in the future tense effects a subtle metamorphosis:

> Pe dunele verzi de calcar va ploua astă-noapte.
> Vinul păstrat până azi într-o gură de mort
> trezi-va ținutul cu punți, strămutat într-un clopot.
> O limbă de om va suna într-un coif cutezanța. . . .
>
> It will rain tonight on the green calcareous dunes.
> The wine, kept to this day in the mouth of a corpse,
> will awaken the land of bridges, transmuted into a chime.
> A man's tongue will toll courage inside a helmet. . . .

The meditation on time—a constant theme in Celan's poetry—acquires, in a poem like "Orbiți de salturi uriașe" (Blinded by Huge Leaps), a direct, almost didactic expression:

> Orbiți de salturi uriașe, ne-am întâlnit, călători prin miragii,
> în singura sărutare-a renunțării.
> Ora e cea de ieri, dar o arată un al treilea ac, incandescent,
> pe care nu l-am văzut niciodată în grădinile timpului—
> celelalte două zac îmbrățișate în sudul cadranului.
> Când se vor despărți va fi prea târziu, vremea va fi alta,
> acul străin se va roti nebun până va aprinde orele toate cu un foc
> contagios
> și le va topi într-o singură cifră, care-n același timp
> va fi oră, anotimp și cei douăzecișipatru de pași ce-i voi face
> în clipa când voi muri,
> apoi va sări prin geamul plesnit în mijlocul odăii,
> invitându-mă să-l urmez ca să-i fiu tovarăș într-un nou orologiu
> care va măsura un timp mult mai mare.
> Eu, însă, prefer ca vremea să fie măsurată cu clepsidrele.

Blinded by huge leaps, we, travelers through mirages, met
in the unique kiss of renunciation.
The hour is that of yesterday, but a third hand, incandescent, indicates it,
one that I have never seen before in the gardens of time—
the other two lie embracing in the south of the quadrant.
When they separate, it will be too late, the time will be different,
the foreign hand will rotate wildly until it inflames all the hours
in a contagious fire
and will melt them into a single number which, simultaneously, will be
hour, season, and the twentyfour steps I will take the moment I die,
then it will jump through the shattered window into the middle of the room,
inviting me to follow it, to be its companion, inside a new clock which will measure a much vaster time.
But I prefer time to be measured with hourglasses.

The use of the future tense does not imply, in Celan, any kind of facile optimism, and this aspect is also demonstrated by his "Cântec de dragoste" (Love Song), which I quote in full for its bizarre beauty:

Când vor începe şi pentru tine nopţile dimineaţa,
ochii noştri fosforescenţi vor coborî din pereţi, nişte nuci sunătoare,
te vei juca cu ele şi se va revărsa un val prin fereastră,
unicul nostru naufragiu, podea străvezie prin care vom privi
camera goală de sub camera noastră.
o vei mobila cu nucile tale şi-ţi voi pune părul perdea la fereastră.
va veni cineva şi-n sfârşit va fi închiriată,
ne vom întoarce sus să ne-necăm acasă.

When for you, too, nights begin in the morning,
our phosphorescent eyes, resounding walnuts, will descend from the walls,
you will play with them and a wave will overflow through the window

our only shipwreck, a translucent floor through which we will
    watch
the empty room beneath our room.
You will furnish it with your walnuts and I will drape your hair
                    curtain for the window.
somebody will come and it will finally be let,
we will go up again, to drown at home.

Celan uses with equal subtlety a tense that appears mostly in his German texts—the past tense, much more appropriate than the future for conveying sadness. The poem titled "Reveion" (New Year's Eve) consists of a succession of sentences that recount painful events: "ai trimis catafalcul cel tânăr să-ţi cheme iubita" (you sent the young catafalque to bring you the woman you love), "inelul stins în pahar s-a suit pe fereastră" (the ring extinguished in the glass climbed up the window), "s-au dus despletitele mâini s-o aştepte la poartă" (there they went, the loose hands, to wait for her at the gate), "un zar a căzut între lespezi" (a die fell among the gravestones), "turla cetăţii de lemn a plecat cu o umbră" (the tower of the wooden citadel left with a shadow). The constant use of the same modal register in the "narrative" contributes to the dramatic character of the poem.

Finally, a poem like "Tristeţe" (Sadness)—the only one written in a somewhat classical manner, with strict rhyming and meter—reveals an older style of Celan's, one that has not been influenced by Surrealism and does not hesitate to allow a Romantic undertone, much like the poems he wrote in German in Czernowitz. On the other hand, the poem testifies to a confident mastery of the expressive resources of the Romanian language and a manifest desire to use them. The middle stanza is exemplary in this regard:

cerul cu zimţi, de nea, peste tâmple,
nor înflorit, pe o geană să-l duci,
tu, rătăcită-n veşminte mai simple,
râzi: oare mâine şi toamna din nuci?

> the snowy, saw-toothed sky, over the temples,
> cloud in bloom, on your eyelash to carry it,
> you, adrift in simpler garments,
> laugh: maybe tomorrow the autumn in the nuts, too?

The question at the end, "Cui îi dau roua?—Lacrima—cui?" (To whom should I give the dew? the tear—to whom?),[10] is also relevant for Celan's ability to employ the most refined means of the Romanian language. As Constantin Noica—one of the rare thinkers who knew how to listen to what words say, deriving from their profound meaning an entire philosophy—emphasizes, the possibilities in Romanian for using the interrogative form involve special skill. First of all, the interrogative *oare*, with which one can formulate any question, be it total or partial, is full of hidden meanings, retained throughout its long semantic evolution (derived from the Latin word *hora* [hour]). Just like the interrogative *au*, *oare* suggests a state of indeterminacy favorable to deep clarification: "The question 'fills' the world with possibilities. It can stir to life more than the answer can satisfy."[11]

The lexicon of Celan's Romanian poems is less rich than that of his German poems, but inside this limited and sometimes conventional perimeter the poet drills deep in order to discover and bring to light treasures of equal value. In both linguistic registers, he uses carefully selected words, among which the most recurrent are *urnă* (urn), *păr* (hair), *ochi* (eye/s), *vis* (dream), *rouă* (dew), *aur* (gold), *lacrimă* (tear), *nor* (cloud), *vânt* (wind), *ceață* (fog), *tăceri* (silences), *noapte* (night), *inimă* (heart), and so on. They might seem banal, but what confers on the poems in which they appear their unwonted character is the imaginative skill of associating these words with adjectives that qualify them in such a way as to ascribe meanings that transcend their everyday usage. Celan "dematerializes" the words, not by annulling their meaning but by multiplying their semantic connotations, thus opening frontiers in unexpected directions.

From this point of view, he belongs to the long tradition of modernity as defined by Hugo Friedrich: "Poetic diction took on the character of an experiment, bringing forth combinations which created, rather than grew from, the meaning. Familiar linguistic material appeared in unusual senses. Words from areas of remote specialization were given a poetic charge. . . . The oldest elements of poetry—simile and metaphor—were handled in a new fashion: the poet avoided the natural term of comparison, forcing an unreal union of logically and objectively incompatible elements."[12] However, the Surrealist techniques Celan appropriated during his Bucharest period produce a very personal style, since the creation of "unusual senses" is the result of strong pressures, not only of cultural mimeticism. The poet's evolution is characterized by something imperious, organic, that derives from his very existence. Focusing on this evolution in a study of remarkable analytical acuity, Harald Weinrich shows that, starting with his second volume—*Von Schwelle zu Schwelle* (1955)—Celan's poetry undergoes a process of contraction (the study is titled *Kontraktionen*). Celan's rhythms and metaphors shrink; the stone motif becomes increasingly important, thus indicating that his lyricism is solidifying.[13]

During the time he spent in Bucharest, and even in Vienna, Celan goes through a phase of dilation, of lyrical expansion, related, of course, to his youth, but not only. Heated iron dilates and becomes malleable, but in a cold environment it loses its malleability and contracts. Naturally, things are much more complicated in poetry, but I do not think I am mistaken in seeing a connection between the dilation I have been speaking about and the spiritual warmth Celan received in Bucharest and which he himself emanated. In any case, the poems written in the Romanian capital, like those written in Vienna, are characterized by an expansion that manifests itself at the most visible level in their length. The singularity of these poems does not derive from dislocation, as would be the case later, but from associations of radically opposed terms. At this juncture, the violence the poet had suffered had not yet turned against the German language, and even less against the Romanian language. To him, Surrealism meant not so much a break as a continuation, an expansion of the Romantic-Expressionist lyrical style practiced at the beginning. Besides, as many critics have pointed out, Celan does not surrender completely to the principle of automatic writing professed by the Surrealists; he is "a Surrealist who controls his spontaneity and abstains from automatic writing."[14]

The Romanian poems, few as they are, indicate quite clearly the limits within which Celan meant to keep the influence of Surrealism. The poems have an internal structure, a convergence of images, and even a sort of narrative sequence, untranslatable into everyday parlance, of course. "Something is happening in them," something very dramatic, in an impressive crescendo. What adds to their dramatic dimension is the dialogic form, the polarity "I–thou," which represents the structuring principle of almost all the poems written in that period, including those written in German.[15]

That the poet followed Breton's indications regarding verbal automatism only up to a point is proven also by the fact that he carefully revised his poems. For example, the poem "Azi-noapte" (Last Night) presents, in its initial version written in pencil, a number of lines over which Celan hesitated a lot before giving them their final form: the second line—"ci o baltă de umbre va fi" (but a pool of shadows it will be)—was initially "ci o mână de umbre va fi" (but a handful of shadows it will be); in the sixth line, "iar viața va fi acea barcă la mal părăsită de vâsle" (and life will be that boat on the shore deserted by oars), Celan wrote the word "rămâne" (remains) over the words "va fi acea" (will be that), which was meant to replace them; then he erased that as well.

The prose poems Celan wrote in Romanian are more difficult to categorize than the poems proper, and I do not think I am overstating too much when I compare them to a meteorite that has fallen into Romanian literature, yet it is still ignored. One can come close to such a meteorite only when equipped with fine measuring instruments, which I do not claim to possess. I will try, nonetheless, to provide a description, let us call it phenomenological, although it would be more precise to call it impressionist, leaving to other, more competent critics, the task of interpreting them with the attention they deserve, in all their aspects. I begin by revealing the autobiographical nature of some of these prose texts.

The one that begins with the words "Partizan al absolutismului erotic, megaloman reticent chiar şi între scafandri, mesager, totodată, al haloului, Paul Celan" (A partisan of erotic absolutism, reticent megalomaniac even among divers, at the same time messenger of the halo, Paul Celan) is the only one that is dated: "11.03.1947," a date that resonates with the other prose texts as well. To my knowledge, it is the first text signed with the pseudonym Paul Celan, written by himself, probably very soon after his final choice. The fact that the pseudonym appears among a constellation of images that are clearly Surrealist adds to the chronology the indication of spiritual affiliation, of intellectual adherence to part of the program of the Surrealists, "membri acefali ai Conspiraţiei Poetice Universale" (acephalous members of the Universal Poetic Conspiracy).

It is tempting to compare this text with Gherasim Luca's prose piece, similar up to a point, titled "Inventatorul iubirii" (Inventor of Love), dating from 1945. Celan's text is very short, unlike Luca's, yet it is not the length that counts here but the quality of the two texts. In "Inventor of Love," there are many compound sentences, such as the following:

> Port cu o eleganţă specială acest cap de sinucigaş pe umeri şi mut dintr-un loc într-altul un zâmbet infam, otrăvind pe o rază de mai mulţi kilometri respiraţia fiinţelor şi a lucrurilor. . . . Mă privesc în oglindă şi-mi văd faţa plină de ochi, de guri, de urechi, de cifre. Sub lună, corpul meu aruncă pe pământ o umbră, o penumbră, o groapă, un lac liniştit şi o ceapă.
>
> I carry with special elegance this suicidal head on my shoulders and I circulate an infamous smile from one place to another, poisoning the breaths of beings and of things over a range of several kilometers. . . . I look at myself in the mirror and I see my face full of eyes, mouths, ears, numbers. Under the moonlight, my body casts a shadow, a half-shadow, a pit, a quiet lake, and an onion.

Such sentences can be easily subsumed under the topic of the author's "non-Oedipal" position, thus sublimating his poetic effectiveness.

In Celan, theoretical statements are not permitted to stifle poetic vibrancy. The self-portrait remains a poem about himself, about "the halo, Paul Celan."

The concentrated (not dry, or deformedly sparse) form of this poem contrasts with the discursivity of the prose in "Inventor of Love" and in other Surrealist texts. Excessively preoccupied with theory, the Romanian Surrealists—consistent with the antiaesthetic principle of the movement—rarely leave room, in their prose, for elements that might suggest the slightest intention to literaturize. Their daring images float in a rhetorical magma, quite banal as a matter of fact, despite the radicality of the terms used. There are two types of discourses in this kind of prose, the poetic and the theoretical, each developing independently with no connection to the other. Even in Gellu Naum, perhaps the most consistent among the Romanian Surrealists, this parallelism between the two discourses is visible—for example, in *Castelul Orbilor* (The Castle of the Blind) (1946), where sententious prose of the type "poezia este un avans, un promiţător avans, o profeţie a gândirii noi şi reale" (poetry is an advance, a promising anticipation, a prophecy of new and real thinking) alternates with verbal delirium sprinkled with unusual images, such as "În camera de sticlă insectele devorau dirijabile" (In the glass room, the insects were devouring, compliantly).[16]

Like Gherasim Luca, Gellu Naum is very clear and, at times, terre à terre when he makes propaganda for the ideas so dear to the Surrealist group, but he becomes obscure and incoherent when he allows his inner demon to speak.

Celan's prose poems are undeniably touched by the wing of Surrealism, but at the same time they testify to a will to structure that distinguishes them from the prose of the above-mentioned poets and makes them comparable with the genre inaugurated by Baudelaire's *Spleen de Paris*. In his preface to a recent anthology of Romanian prose poems, Mihai Zamfir observes that this genre is defined by "a picturesque vocabulary, specially chosen," "a discontinuous, symmetrical and elliptical syntactic structure, drawn to rhythm and using metaphorizing language. The lexicon of a prose poem does not follow a visible order: that is, it does not organize around clearly delineated semantic fields. What defines it is a carefully studied semantic dispersion. Consequently, the reader's attention is fixed on each word in itself. . . . Such a poem does not demonstrate anything [and] does not propose any reality other than the text itself."[17] Celan's prose poems would have deserved a place in Mihai Zamfir's anthology, since they match the definition of the genre almost perfectly. Moreover, they have documentary value in proposing—apart from "the text itself"—the reality of a singular self-portrait, with no equivalent in the confessions Celan made in German.

From this point of view, the poem that begins with the words "A doua zi urmând să înceapă deportările" (The deportations about to begin the following day) is the most significant because it evokes the tragic events in the poet's Czernowitz biography—the separation from his parents, the deportation of Jews, and so on. The poem unfolds in a dramatic manner, recalling the famous "Todesfuge," based on the same realities and the same experience. The oneiric or, rather, nightmarish atmosphere enveloping Celan's prose does not cancel the horror of the events evoked; on the contrary, it brings it into sharp relief. The keynote of this text is despair: the character called Rafael (maybe an analogy to the biblical angel) is dressed "într-o vastă deznădejde din mătase neagră" (in a vast despair of black silk) and throws a similar robe across the narrator's shoulders. Rafael tries to save the people condemned to deportation with the help of a chandelier rising toward the sky—the symbol is quite clear. But their ascension proves to be unavailing and ridiculous, as the narrator wonders at the end: "Unde este cerul? Unde?" (Where is the sky? Where?).

Any attempt to paraphrase the poem risks turning it into something banal, of course, but it is no less true that, within the oneiric space created by Celan, something happens, in fact, that transcends the text, drawing it toward an essentialized, hence all the more horrifying, reality.

> A doua zi urmând să înceapă deportările, noaptea a venit Rafael, îmbrăcat într-o vastă deznădejde din mătase neagră, cu glugă,

privirile arzătoare i se încrucişară pe fruntea mea, şiroaie de vin începură să-mi curgă peste obraz, se răspândiră pe jos, oamenii le sorbiră în somn.—Vino, îmi spuse Rafael, punându-mi peste umerii mei prea strălucitori o deznădejde asemănătoare cu aceea pe care o purta el. Mă aplecai înspre mama, o sărutai incestuos, şi ieşii din casă. Un roi imens de mari fluturi negri, veniţi de la tropice, mă împiedica să înaintez. Rafael mă trase după el şi coborârăm înspre linia ferată. Sub picioare simţii şinele, auzii şuieratul unei locomotive, foarte aproape, inima mi se încleştă. Trenul trecu deasupra capetelor noastre.

Deschisei ochii. În faţa mea, pe o întindere imensă, era un uriaş candelabru cu mii de braţe.—E aur?! îi şoptii lui Rafael.—Aur. Te vei urca pe unul din braţe, ca, atunci când îl voi fi înălţat în văzduh, să-l poţi prinde de cer. Înainte de a se crăpa de ziuă, oamenii se vor putea salva, zburând într-acolo. Le voi arăta drumul, iar tu îi vei primi.

M-am urcat pe unul din braţe, Rafael trecu de la un braţ la altul, le atinse pe rând, candelabrul începu să se înalţe. O frunză mi se aşternu pe frunte, chiar în locul unde mă atinsese privirea prietenului, o frunză de arţar. Mă uit împrejur: nu acesta poate fi cerul. Trec ore şi n-am găsit nimic. Ştiu: jos s-au adunat oamenii, Rafael i-a atins cu degetele sale subţiri, s-au înălţat şi ei, şi eu tot nu m-am oprit.

Unde e cerul? Unde?[18]

The deportations about to begin the following day, Rafael came to me that night, dressed in a vast despair of black silk, with a hood, his scorching glances crossed on my forehead, streams of wine began pouring down my cheeks, they spread onto the ground, people sipped them in their sleep.—Come, said Rafael to me, placing on my too-shiny shoulders a despair akin to the one he was wearing. I bent down toward my mother, I kissed her incestuously, and went out of the house. An enormous swarm of big black butterflies, come from the tropics, hindered me from moving forward. Rafael pulled me after him and we descended towards the railway. I could feel the tracks under my feet, I could hear the whistle of a locomotive, very close, my heart clenched. The train rattled past over our heads.

> I opened my eyes. In front of me, on an immense expanse, there was a huge chandelier with thousands of arms.—Is it gold? I whispered to Rafael.—Gold. You will climb up one of its arms so that, once I have lifted it high up in the air, you can fasten it onto the sky. Before the break of dawn, people will be able to save themselves by flying there. I will show them the way, and you will receive them.
>
> I climbed up one of the arms, Rafael passed from one arm to another, touched them all in turn, the chandelier started to rise. A leaf settled on my forehead, right where my friend's gaze had touched me, a maple leaf. I look around: this can't be the sky.[19] Hours pass and I have found nothing. I know: down on the ground, people gathered, Rafael touched them with his slender fingers, they, too, rose towards the sky, but I still have not stopped.
>
> Where is the sky? Where?

A note from Kafka's *Diary* would have been appropriate as an epitaph to this poem: "Should I greatly yearn to be an athlete, it would be the same thing as my yearning to go to heaven and to be permitted to be as despairing there as I am here."[20]

Invoking Kafka when speaking about a text by Celan is one possible way of situating these enigmatic prose texts more precisely than their classification under a certain literary genre can achieve. This is so because, although they comply with the exigencies of the genre, they retain their singular character, thus justifying attempts to explain them by reference to models outside the definition cited above. Kafka is one of these models, even if, at first reading, nothing seems further from Celan's prose poems than Kafka's parables: stylistically speaking, there is no relation between them. Kafka is precisely at the opposite pole from Celan, because Kafka cultivated a factual style, full of minute descriptions and devoid of metaphors; the singular dimension of Kafka's texts is produced by the sudden movement form the banal to the fantastic. Still, a certain measure of affinity between the two writers can be detected at deeper levels than the stylistic one. Margul-Sperber was not mistaken in recommending

Celan as the author of a work that represents, for poetry, what Kafka's work represents in prose. Personally, I think that, through Kafka, Celan corrected his imagistic exuberance, of Surrealist inspiration, diverting it toward the parable. Without being apologues, the prose poems seem to aspire to allegories, although what is *visible* is the flux of metaphors. Beyond the words that "make love"—to use Breton's expression—the poems prompt reflection and evoke an existential reality discernible in the filigree of the images.

Some of Celan's prose poems translate a typically Kafkaesque situation into metaphorical language: the impossibility of reaching a goal. Such is the case of the poem that begins with the words "Din nou am suspendat marile umbrele albe în văzduhul nopţii" (Once more I have suspended the big white umbrellas in the night air):

> Sub picioarele mele desculţe nisipul se aprinde, mă ridic în vârful degetelor şi mă înalţ într-acolo. *Nu mă pot aştepta la ospitalitate . . . Nu sunt primit.* Un crainic necunoscut mie mă întâmpină în larg ca să mă anunţe că *mi se interzice orice escală.* Ofer mâinile mele pentru a veghea ca echilibrul acestei flore postume să fie păstrat în afară de orice pericol. *Din nou sunt refuzat.*

> Under my bare feet, the sand catches fire, I stand on tiptoe and rise in that direction. *I cannot expect hospitality . . . I am not accepted.* A herald I have never met approaches me on the open sea to inform me that *I am forbidden any halts.* I offer my hands to make sure that the equilibrium of this posthumous flora is kept out of any danger. *Again I am denied.*

The narrator would like to continue his voyage but, exhausted, closes his eyes "pentru a căuta un om cu o barcă" (in order to look for a man with a boat). We encounter here the poetic equivalent of the desperate efforts made by Kafka's heroes to get out of the labyrinth. The narrator in the poem about deportations rises toward the sky, but does not find it. The narrator of the poem that begins with the words "Fără balustradă" (Without a handrail) goes up and down the steps of the mysterious staircase, repeating "performanța cu o viteză din ce în ce mai mare" (the performance at an increasingly high speed).

Enigmatic in terms of the message they seem to transmit as well, Celan's prose poems are animated by metaphoric energy, which in its turn causes perplexity. Released from prosodic constraints, the poet allows himself greater freedom to associate opposite terms than in the poems, Romanian or German, written in the same period. Here, the imagery erects multiple bridges between the abstract and the concrete, which exist, as we have seen, in his poetry as well. The "dictatorial imagination" that Hugo Friedrich considered to be a distinctive trait of modern poetry[21] works fully here, without, however, inducing a sense of the arbitrariness of the absurd. In most cases, the associations possess poetic legitimacy, like the flashing images of Rimbaud in *Illuminations*—another possible way of approaching Celan's poems. "Steagul vaporos al întâlnirii cu tine însuți" (the ethereal flag of a meeting with yourself), "dantela neagră a plăcerii de a nu iubi pe nimeni" (the black lace of the pleasure of loving nobody) (a "black lace" is attached, in another poem, to "mânecile costumului de cenușă" [the sleeves of the ashen suit]), the mirrors that "se apleacă mereu ca să-ți culeagă umbra" (always bend down to pick up your shadow), people who "tatuează ora morții în pielea frunzoasă a frunților de dansatori spanioli" (tattoo the time of their death on the leafy skin of their Spanish dancers' foreheads), their tattoo being made "cu săgețile timide încă, dar nu mai puțin veninoase, ale adolescenței unui adio" (with the spears, still shy but poisonous nonetheless, of the adolescence of a farewell)—all these images, and many others, stud Celan's prose poems like stars, radiating a bizarre luminosity in which objects and beings assume fresh contours.

The richest prose poem in such unusual associations and images is the one that opens with "S-ar putea crede" (One might think). Here are some examples:

> Ai golit începuturile luminii din oglindă, te-ai desfătat cântând acrostihul neprihănitului călător întru miasme, mâhnit și clarvăzător ca floarea cepii.

(You have emptied the beginnings of light found in the mirror, you have delighted in singing the acrostic of the untainted traveler into miasmas, aggrieved and clear-sighted like an onion flower.)

Pustietatea în care te-ai aventurat cu sandala molipsită de poezia adolescenței tale de hârtie.
(The desert into which you ventured with your sandal contaminated by the poetry of your paper adolescence.)

curiozitatea dantelată a pieptului.
(the lacy curiosity of your chest.)

pasionat de extremitățile alogene ale plimbărilor.
(passionate about the allogenic extremities of walking.)

paşii tăi înaintau spre plictiselile de puf.
(your steps were advancing toward the velvety boredoms.)

vasta încăpere a posibilităților periclitate de ulii cu cercei.
(the vast room of the possibilities jeopardized by ear-ringed hawks.)

Even taken out of context, these bizarre collocations suggest an unusual associative power. Read in their context, they gain extra value, hard to define in conceptual terms but evident to anybody who expects from poetry something different, special, and not a message transmissible by other means.

An important element of Celan's prose is its rhythm, the cadence imposed on the unfolding of the sentences; their flow, phonetically natural, softens the arbitrariness of certain comparisons or makes it enter a realm of "normality": "Era un zvon în aer, un zvon de monete celibatare, venite să te vadă plecând" (There was an echo in the air, an echo of celibate coins, gathered to see you leaving); we read this fragment, from the same poem, and we are not surprised by the presence of "celibate coins," as we would be if it had not been part of that particular verbal ensemble. The alternation of long, complex sentences with short ones is created with exquisite musical sense.

The lexicon of Celan's prose poems deserves, in turn, careful analysis. Apart from the words that usually appear in his poems—hair, eyes, sand, urn, night, clouds, and so on—what we also encounter here is a series of more erudite terms, along with other more prosaic ones: "vegetaţie antropomorfă" (anthropomorphic vegetation); "reabilitarea solstiţiilor" (the rehabilitation of the solstices); "aşteptări infructuoase" (fruitless expectations); "capetele concrescute ale mulţimii" (the grown-together heads of the crowd); "ochii tufelor antropofage" (the eyes of the anthropophagous bushes); "eforturile precare ale cititorului în stele" (the precarious efforts of the star-gazer); "un act de curaj monosilab" (a monosyllabic act of courage/an act of monosyllabic courage); "mesager al absciselor" (messenger of the abscissa); "ondulaţiile inegale ale posterităţii" (the uneven undulations of posterity), and so on.

However, the prose poems present, on the whole, a lexical landscape dominated by words with lyrical connotations and resonance. From this point of view, they might seem less exuberant than the prose of the Surrealist poets, who do not hesitate to resort to linguistic violence in order to convey their apocalyptic visions. Celan keeps his writing within the limits of a kind of decency that perhaps derives from his cautious approach to words in the Romanian language.

The same reservations prevent him from dislocating the syntax of Romanian, which he keeps within its traditional patterns but into which he nonetheless pours incandescent lyrical matter. He is more adventurous with regard to his choice of words, which he leaves in their usual order.

In any field, including the linguistic, timidity begets clumsiness. Such occurrences are not entirely absent from Celan's Romanian texts either, and I have insisted on their qualities because these are much more significant and far outweigh the stylistic imperfections or deviations, very rare in fact, from grammar rules. One should not forget that Celan was a *German-language poet*, Romanian being for him a language he had learned at school and heard intermittently in a city with a tumultuous history. He was, of course, a polyglot, a natural polyglot, much as the ancient Greeks were polytheists.

Along with German and Romanian, he knew Russian, French, English, Latin, Hebrew, and Yiddish—eight languages he commanded at various levels of proficiency. Celan's case differs from that of Elias Canetti, who was born in Bulgaria and whose family moved to England and then to Vienna a few years later (and afterward to Zurich). Canetti learned German later—the language his parents spoke, as a sort of secret code for their love:

> To each other, my parents spoke German, which I was not allowed to understand. To us children and to all relatives and friends, they spoke Ladino. That was the true vernacular, albeit an ancient Spanish. . . . The peasant girls at home knew only Bulgarian, and I must have learned it with them. . . . All events of those first few years were in Ladino or Bulgarian. It wasn't until much later that most of them were rendered into German within me.[22]

For Celan, German was his mother tongue from the very beginning, and the languages he acquired later—gradually, without invalidating one another—doubtless contributed to the enrichment of his mother tongue and to a deepening of the keen linguistic awareness so characteristic of the poet.

His case is different from that of another famous polyglot, George Steiner, who confesses, in *After Babel*:

> I have no recollection whatever of a first language. So far as I am aware, I possess equal currency in English, French, and German. . . . I speak and I write them with indistinguishable ease. . . . I dream with equal verbal density and linguistic-symbolic provocation in all three. . . . This polyglot matrix was far more than a hazard of private condition. It organized, it imprinted on my grasp of personal identity, the formidably complex, resourceful cast of feeling of Central European and Judaic humanism. Speech was, tangibly, option, a choice between equally inherent yet alternate claims and pivots of self-consciousness.
>
> At the same time, the lack of a single native tongue entailed a certain apartness from other French schoolchildren, a certain

> extraterritoriality with regard to the surrounding social, historical community.[23]

Steiner formulates a series of questions that can be asked with reference to Celan as well, although his polyglotism developed upon the foundation of a single mother tongue: "Does a polyglot mentality operate differently from one that uses a single language or whose other languages have been acquired by subsequent learning? When a natively multilingual person speaks, do the languages not in momentary employ press upon the body of speech which he is actually articulating?"[24] It is hard to find a clear, precise answer to these questions, but it is beyond any doubt that multilingualism exerts a significant influence on one's expressive linguistic competence.

The more than two years Celan spent in Bucharest allowed him to expand his knowledge of the Romanian language to a level close to perfection. Romanian became a second mother tongue to him, through a series of factors, among which was his emotional and intellectual conflict with German, the language of those who had killed his parents. The respite he took in the Romanian language proved to have been long enough to allow him to experiment in this language with some things that German permitted only with a certain degree of difficulty, as it is the case with wordplay (practiced by philosophers more than by poets).[25] The effects those experiments had on his writing style in German call for further research, but their lyrical consequences in Romanian are evident in a literary work that, though limited quantitatively, is by no means negligible. Had he written only "Poem pentru umbra Marianei" and the prose poem that begins with the words "Erau nopţi," he would still have deserved to be included in an ideal history of Romanian poetry as a prominent figure, next to other names that have become famous in Europe, since he cultivated the language of Eminescu and Arghezi with passion and talent, albeit only for a while.

I quote below the entire prose poem mentioned above, in order to allow it to reveal the importance of Celan's texts in Romanian:

Erau nopţi când mi se părea că ochii tăi, cărora le desenasem mari cearcăne portocalii, îşi aprind din nou cenuşa. În acele nopţi, ploaia cădea mai rar. Deschideam geamurile şi mă urcam, gol, pe pervazul ferestrei, ca să privesc lumea. Copacii pădurii veneau înspre mine, câte unul, supuşi, o armată învinsă venea să-şi depună armele. Rămâneam nemişcat şi cerul îşi cobora steagul sub care-şi trimisese oştile în luptă. Dintr-un ungher mă priveai şi tu cum stăteam acolo, nespus de frumos în nuditatea mea însângerată: eram singura constelaţie pe care n-o stinsese ploaia, eram Marea Cruce a Sudului. Da, în acele nopţi era greu să-ţi deschizi vinele când flăcările mă cuprindeau, cetatea urnelor era a mea, o umpleam cu sângele meu, după ce concediam oştirea duşmană răsplătind-o cu oraşe şi porturi, iar pantera de argint sfâşia zorile care mă pândeau. Eram Petronius şi din nou îmi vărsam sângele între trandafiri. Pentru fiecare petală pătată stingeai câte o torţă.

Ţii minte? Eram Petronius şi nu te iubeam.

There were nights when it seemed to me that your eyes, under which I had drawn big orange circles, lighted up their ashes again. On those nights, rain fell less frequently. I would open the windows and climb, naked, up onto the window sill, to look at the world. The trees of the forest would march toward me, one by one, obedient, a defeated army came to surrender its weapons. I would stand still and the sky would lower its flag, under which it had sent its armies into battle. From a corner, you too would look at me, as I was standing there, unspeakably beautiful in my bloodstained nudity: I was the only constellation the rain had not obliterated, I was the Great Southern Cross. Yes, on those nights it was hard for you to open your veins when the flames enveloped me, the citadel of urns was mine, I would fill it with my blood after dismissing the enemy army, rewarding it with cities and ports, while the silver panther tore the dawn that was watching me. I was Petronius and, once more, I was shedding my blood among roses. For each stained petal, you blew out a torch.

Do you remember? I was Petronius and I was not in love with you.

Few prose poems included in Mihai Zamfir's anthology can appear next to this gem Celan gave to the Romanian literature. But the poet's gift is not limited to a gem or two, and, although Celan wrote relatively little in Romanian, it is necessary and worth our while to know this "little" in order to better understand his entire work.

In the summer of 1970—the summer of his death—*L'Éphémère* published, on a whole page, the manuscript text of this apothegm formulated by the poet a year earlier: "La Poésie ne s'impose plus, elle s'expose."[26] This apothegm was included in the massive, but criticizable and criticized, edition in five volumes of Celan's works published in 1983 by Suhrkamp.[27] Being perhaps the only apothegm he wrote in French, it was granted the prestige automatically ascribed to all of Celan's texts, except those he wrote in Romanian. Let us admit that Celan's texts in Romanian are more interesting and more substantial than the pun he formulated in French—otherwise ingenious and valid.

To sum up: apart from the seven poems (plus a fragment of an unfinished poem) and the eight prose poems he wrote in Romanian, Celan also translated into Romanian a number of texts from Russian literature (Chekhov and Lermontov, mainly) and from German literature (four parables by Kafka). Undoubtedly, there were other poems he wrote in Romanian apart from those I have kept—not to mention the Surrealist games, of which I have retained only an example from Questions and Answers. It is, perhaps, too pretentious to claim that these texts in their entirety constitute an oeuvre in themselves, but it seems unquestionable to me that they complete Celan's oeuvre and shed unwonted light on it.

Before leaving Romania, Celan wrote, among other things, a prose poem in which he speaks of "the adolescence of a farewell." If we interpret this metaphor *ad litteram*, should we not regard the poet's Romanian texts as a sort of supreme and superb farewell, destined to preserve its adolescence forever?

# 5

# Rebuilding the Bridges

Our life wears on under the sign of change.
—RILKE[1]

So, Paul Celan left Romania toward the end of 1947, heading for Vienna, via Budapest. Our paths then separated for a very long time—a time full of dull or quiet moments, as well as dramatic events, at both ends. Apart from the typed poems that would be included in his first little book of poems, *Der Sand aus den Urnen*, Paul had also taken with him from Bucharest a letter from Margul-Sperber to Otto Basil, the editor of the Viennese monthly *Plan*, the first-ever Surrealist publication in German. This letter is a rarely encountered example of perspicacity and, above all, of generosity, that recalls the words with which, on another meridian and in a different historical age, Emerson saluted in Walt Whitman the emergence, at last, of a great poet in America. Here is how Margul-Sperber recommended Celan to Otto Basil, an influential literary critic at the time:

> Without meaning to anticipate your competent judgment, it gives me great pleasure to tell you that Paul Celan is the poet of our Southern-Eastern landscape whom I have been expecting for half a lifetime and who is fully rewarding my faith. Celan spent his time here in Romania in an exclusively non-German linguistic environment. But his poetry shows brilliantly that there is such a thing as an illumined spirit of language, which does not depend upon the familiar language of direct, everyday use. In my opinion, of all the manifestations of the younger generation of German-language poets, his work has the most unmistakably unique style

> and possesses the brilliance of utmost originality; it is not an easy read, to be sure, and calls for affectionate sincerity, preparation, and devotion. As far as I am concerned, I believe, in all modesty, that *Der Sand aus den Urnen* is the most important book of poems of the last few decades, the only poetic counterpart to Kafka's prose.[2]

In its last issue, the journal *Plan* published a fragment of this letter as a comment on the seventeen poems by Celan included in its pages. At about the same time—that is, in the spring of 1948—I received a message from my friend in the form of an expensive edition of Joyce's masterpiece *Ulysses*, with the following dedication on the frontispiece, written in Romanian: "Lui Petrică, cu gândul la ce va fi mâine. Paul. Viena, Martie 1948" (For Petrică, with thoughts of what tomorrow will bring. Paul. Vienna, March 1948).

And soon afterward a letter dated March 12, 1948, which had, on all of its three pages, as well as on the envelope, the stamp of Austrian censorship ("Österreichische Zensurstelle. 495"). The text of this letter requires certain clarifications regarding both the people to whom it refers and the emotional state Celan was in when he wrote it. The letter is full of puns but hides a much more serious emotional state:

> Dragul meu Petrică,
>
> Între ceea ce numeşti tu o tăcere nesemnificativă şi ceea ce ar putea fi o semnificaţie tacită, mai creşte o iarbă, care e mai mult decât un calambur. De când am realizat ceea ce ne-a propus acel vers al lui Fundoianu, răsucit pe neînţelesul tău şi al meu, am avut câteva zeci de ocazii, oferite de tot atâtea absenţe sau prezenţe înregistrate cu pumnii la tâmple, pentru a mă gândi la tine şi la ceilalţi. . . .
>
> Ce aş putea să-ţi spun despre acest tărâm, despre care mă întrebi şi care nu e un tărâm, ci o râmă cu toate atributele pe care le poate implica trecerea de la masculin la feminin plus pierderea capului? Petrică, frate, noi ăştia cu profilul mai mult sau mai puţin

levantin (cum îţi şade bine să-l defineşti) şi cu un sejur mai mult sau mai puţin îndelungat (cum îmi permit să mă consolez) în oraşul lui Matei Caragiale, suntem nişte adevăraţi titani. Păcat de noi, Petrică. Păcat şi de acel prea scurt anotimp care a fost al nostru, cette belle saison des calembours, care cine ştie când va mai reveni, acum când nu mai jucăm Question-Réponse în vecinătatea domnului bibliotecar şi ne spunem drăgălăşenii cu ochii închişi. . . .

My dear Petrică,

Between what you call insignificant silence and what could be a silent significance, another blade of grass grows, which is more than a pun. Since I accomplished what that verse from Furdoianu suggested us, a verse twisted for your and my incomprehension, I've had a few dozen opportunities, offered by as many absences or presences borne with my fists upon my temples, to think of you and the others. . . .

What, since you ask me, can I tell you about this country, which is not a country but a worm with all the attributes implied in the shift from masculine to feminine, plus the loss of the head?[3] Petrică, brother, we who have this more or less Levantine profile (as you like to define it) and after a more or less prolonged stay (as I allow myself to console myself) in Matei Caragiale's city,[4] we are true titans. What a pity about us, Petrică. A pity, too, about that all too brief season that was ours, cette belle saison des calembours, which will return who knows when, now that we no longer play Questions and Answers and we no longer tell each other sweet nothings with our eyes closed.

The letter ended: "Al tău sincer prieten şi trist poet de limbă teutonă, Paul" (Your sincere friend and sad poet of the Teutonic language, Paul). I do not recall what I wrote in reply, or whether I replied to my friend at all; probably not. Looking back, I feel ashamed of my timorous attitude, which I might be able to explain by the objective circumstances and conditions I was living in, but which remains cowardly nonetheless. Moreover, I was absorbed in many projects:

I was preparing both my baccalaureate and my degree in letters at the same time, I was working on various journals and in two editorial offices—at the Cartea Rusă publishing house and at the *Agerpress* news agency—I was newly married, and I had to work hard to earn my living. Why should I lie? I was doing fairly well, and I could share, up to a point, the enthusiasm and the illusions of many of my fellow youths. We had entered, unknowingly, "the obsessive decade,"[5] but at the time not even a lucid spirit such as Marin Preda's could have included in that expression any of the regrettable events that took place during that period, especially since they were accompanied by others, gladdening and long wished for. What the English so eloquently call "hindsight" (translatable into Romanian as "the understanding that comes after the event") cannot compensate for the lack of vision people reveal when they experience events that later can amaze or confuse them.

In *Imposibila întoarcere* (The Impossible Return), Marin Preda gave a by now classic explanation of the phenomenon, which he considered then (in 1971) irrevocably classified:

> Never before, perhaps, has the primal aggressive spirit had a more solid foundation of ideas than in this half century. Considering the meaning it acquires for me in the contemporary context, I apply the phrase "primal aggressive spirit" to this notion, this mindset, or this devastating force of nature that emerges during periods of heightened social tension and that tends to contest the values of the spirit. In order to replace them with what? With nothing! One can lead a better and easier life without them.[6]

Preda was referring, first of all, to the forms in which "the primal aggressive spirit" was manifesting itself in the West: the events of May 1968, still fresh in the memory of the time, prompted the Romanian writer to publicly condemn the "contesting" intellectuals who had served this spirit "through a continuous attack on all the so-called bourgeois values." He was referring to Sartre in particular, but I think that, through his example, Preda wanted, rather, to criticize a whole category of intellectuals who had a negative influence on Romanian culture:

> We, too, have experienced this phenomenon, under different conditions, and in different colors, in a culture which was far from having reached its peak. The values were, in similar fashion, subjected to incessant attack, for a decade, while classical and contemporary writers who had not grasped the import of this peasants' revolt or that workers' manifesto were brought to trial. . . . Artistic creativity was brought down to the level of the most vulgar form of thinking, and literature was ascribed, by default, a popular character and romanticism that were meant to prevent, in the name of a vision of the future, a lucid scrutiny of the present, whose description was proclaimed only in theory.[7]

Preda dotted the i's and crossed the t's when he observed, further on, that the writers of his generation gained recognition "by fighting, sometimes without the most elementary weapons, against the primal and demagogic spirit that was feasting ostentatiously after grabbing many key positions, from where, grinning cynically, it kept a close eye on all manifestations of creativity."[8]

In his part of the world, Celan was not sheltered from this "primal aggressive spirit," which was manifesting itself there in different forms, of course, but had, in effect, similar results. Although he had been relatively well received by the intellectual circles in Vienna, and encouraged to publish, it is clear that he did not feel at ease in that "metropolis of German literature" of which he had dreamed so long. I find no other explanation for the way in which he described the beautiful city on the banks of the upper Danube in the abovementioned letter. Perhaps Paul intuited, during his brief sojourn in Vienna, the sad but real paradox formulated by Milo Dor shortly after the poet's death: "Paul Celan's fate is yet another proof that Austria only has dead or exiled poets."[9]

Before leaving Austria for good, only six months after his arrival in Vienna, Celan had nonetheless found time to submit his poems for publication and make some friends. I found out about these things from Margul-Sperber, to whom Paul continued to write up to his departure from Vienna. In a letter dated February 1948, he wrote to his mentor ("Mein lieber guter Herr Sperber" [My dear, good Mr. Sperber]) that he had met the Surrealist painter Edgar Jené, who might become "mein hiesiger Sperber—oh, gewiß ein kleinerer als Sie" (my local Sperber—oh, of less importance than yourself, certainly). "He comes from the Saarland, lived in Paris for many years, was encouraged, in his youth, by Paul Westheim[10] in Berlin and certainly lacks any prejudice. Here he is, so to speak, a 'pope' of Surrealism, of which I am now the most influential (and only) cardinal."

Celan also informed Margul-Sperber that his little book of poems, *Der Sand aus den Urnen*, was being published, at his own expense (4,600 shillings, obtained with the help of some friends) at the press of a certain Erwin Müller, and asked him to send him as soon as possible any suggestions he might have for the contents of the book.[11]

In a letter dated April 21, 1948, he sent Margul-Sperber a poem he had written the day before: "Apart from you, I don't know anybody who could tell me whether it is truly beautiful." In the same letter, he communicated to his mentor that, in about a month's time, he would be leaving Vienna for Paris, "which is no easy matter," asking him in a postscript to send him the exact address of "Mr. Philippide," to whom he was sending his "best wishes."

The letters sent to Margul-Sperber clearly show Paul's loyalty to his Romanian friends, as well as his desire to remain spiritually in contact with them. The praise he brought to Margul-Sperber as the only person capable of telling him whether his poems were "truly beautiful" was not a gratuitous compliment: he really missed Margul-Sperber, even though in the meantime he had found in Vienna a "local Sperber" in the painter Edgar Jené, one of whose merits being that "he certainly lacks any prejudice" (that is, racial prejudice, as can be inferred from the context).

Jené was one of the five editors of the journal *Plan*, in whose last issue (spring 1948) Celan's poems were published. Jené was preparing a special issue of the journal dedicated to Surrealism, for which André Breton, Julien Gracq, and others had announced their contributions, but the journal would be discontinued. As in Romania, but for different reasons, the cultural climate in Austria was not favorable to poetry. Paul was also irritated by the delay in the publication of his debut volume, which was still waiting for an editor to distribute it. In the letter he sent to Margul-Sperber on April 21, 1948, Paul confessed to a growing detachment from this volume, stating that it was more important for him to write new poems than to see his old ones published.

Through his interactions with the Viennese Surrealist circle, the lesson learned in Bucharest from Gherasim Luca, Paul Păun, and all the others became more profound and complex. In a programmatic text written specially for an album dedicated to Jené titled *Edgar Jené: Der Traum vom Traume* (Edgar Jené: The Dream of Dreams), Celan reiterated some of the aesthetic principles of Surrealism in a manner rather similar to that adopted in the pamphlets and manifestos of Trost, Gherasim Luca, and so on. The rhythm acquired in Bucharest had thus been preserved.

Celan's frequent and assiduous interactions with the Viennese Surrealists might account for his drastic revision of his views on his own poetic creation up to that point. Uwe Martin thinks so, and not entirely without reason: "After his conversations with his Surrealist friends and colleagues, certain doubts emerged in Celan, namely whether, given the success he wanted to obtain, it was a good idea to include in his first volume of poetry the early poems influenced by Trakl and Rilke."[12]

Uwe Martin's theory was that Celan withdrew the five hundred copies of *Der Sand aus den Urnen* from circulation (eventually published in Vienna in August 1948, after his departure for Paris)[13] not so much because of the typing mistakes as because of a stricter lyrical exigency that would manifest itself clearly in *Mohn und Gedächtnis* (Poppy and Memory), the volume he published in 1952. Indeed, comparison of the two volumes reveals the absence from *Mohn und Gedächtnis* of many poems still included in the little volume published in Vienna. The volume from 1952 opens with a cycle titled *Der Sand aus den Urnen*, which contains only a part—the most valuable part, in Celan's view—of his early poetry, the latter being much more amply represented in the little book published under the same title in Vienna in 1948.

Yet, why did Paul decide to leave the Austrian capital, where such an evolution was in no way impeded?[14] It is not as if he did not have a circle of friends there of the same aesthetic orientation: apart from Edgar Jené and his wife Erika—a writer, who signed with her maiden name, Von Lillegg—there was also the young poet Klaus Demus, "ein sehr begabter Mensch" (a very talented man), as Paul described him in a letter to Margul-Sperber in the summer of 1948. And there were others, too—Paul had retained the ability to make friends very quickly. But it seems that the friendship with the "pope" of Austrian Surrealism started to grow cold at a certain point, then, for reasons still unknown, was definitively broken. What is certain is that the poem dedicated to Jené, "Erinnerung an Frankreich" (Memories of France) would appear in the volume *Mohn und Gedächtnis* without the initial dedication to the Austrian painter.

Erika Jené sent Margul-Sperber a letter, dated July 21, 1948, in which she expressed her fond appreciation of Celan's old mentor, adding:

> You are, it seems, the first person to have realized that Paul is a poet. You sent him to us and he came, bringing himself and his poems. . . . Paul is in Paris now, and he is doing well, for the time being. Full of worry and concern, we squint at Fate, and hope that it will treat him kindly. His poems are with the press, at last; unfortunately, everything moves very slowly here. The first copy is for you, so he said to me, and as soon as it is ready, I will send it to you.[15]

Fate did not treat Paul very kindly in Vienna, since he left it in July 1948, and did not prove very generous to him in Paris, either, particularly at the beginning—as I was to find out later. As a matter of fact,

I had no news from Paul for almost a decade, and Margul-Sperber was no longer in correspondence with him, either. Besides, Margul-Sperber had started to write "occasional poetry," like so many others. Similarly, Nina Cassian, especially after her debut volume *La scara unu pe unu* (On a Scale of One to One), became the subject of virulent criticism in the press, due to the formalist and decadent features that apparently characterized her poetry. The list of those who accepted compromise with their own vocation is very long and contains illustrious names, as well as obscure ones, such as mine.

I do not remember exactly how I started to hear about Celan again, or how I acquired his address in Paris: 29 bis, Rue de Montevideo. Many years had passed since our last exchange of letters; now it was the summer of 1957, and I felt it was time to resume our correspondence. So I suggested to Nina Cassian that we should write a letter together (it seemed less . . . risky this way). To our surprise and joy, Paul wrote back quite quickly, in perfect Romanian and in the same state of mind as the one that prompted us to write to him after so many years: "Dragul meu Petrică, m-am bucurat mult, nespus de mult, citindu-vă scrisorile, a ta şi a Ninei" (My dear Petrică, I was so happy, unutterably happy, to read your letters, yours and Nina's)—thus his answer began, continuing with a sort of survey of the decade that had passed since our last written dialogue:

> Zici că au crescut depărtările—nu, Petrică, n-au crescut chiar aşa, dimpotrivă. Tăcerile sunt aceleaşi, cuvintele, scoase de *aici*—cum nu s-ar asemăna, rostite dincolo sau dincoace? Cine nu e singur? Cine nu e năpădit de tot felul de spaime, atomice şi altele? N-am devenit nici mai european, nici mai occidental. Nu prea am prieteni. Acea "faimă" despre care-mi vorbeşti—ai putea să-i pui câteva ghilemete în plus. Trăiesc şi eu, scriu şi eu versuri uneori, am tradus câteva cărţi neesenţiale, am fost un timp traducător la Geneva (*Bureau International du Travail*), în ultimul an am fost lector de limba germană la École Normale. Din când în când, sunt invitat în Germania pentru a ceti versuri. N-am rămas nereperat de anti-semiţi. Mai important: m-am însurat acum cinci ani, nevasta

> mea e (şi ea) pictoriţă. . . . Primul nostru copil l-am pierdut o zi după naştere—a fost greu, greu, greu. Avem un băiat, Éric, a avut doi ani în iunie, suntem trei, singuri, *voici notre monde*. . . .
>
> You say that the distances have grown—no, Petrică, they haven't grown that much, on the contrary. The silences are the same; the words, originating from *here*—how can they not resemble, whether uttered there or here? Who isn't lonely? Who isn't invaded by all sorts of fears, atomic and so on? I've become neither more European, nor more Western. I don't have many friends. The "fame" you mention—you could add some extra quotation marks to it. I live as best I can, too, sometimes I, too, write poems, I've translated a few inessential books, I worked as a translator in Geneva for a while (*Bureau International du Travail*) and I've been working as a German-language lecturer at the École Normale for a year now. Every now and then I'm invited to Germany to read poems. I haven't been able to escape the anti-Semitic radar. More importantly: I got married five years ago, my wife (too) is a painter. . . . We lost our first child the day after its birth—it was hard, hard, hard. We have a son, Éric, he turned two in June, we are a family of three, alone, *voici notre monde* [this is our world]. . . .

After asking me to tell "master Philippide" how happy he was that he had not forgotten about him, Paul added the following thought: "Mi-am spus uneori, şi i-am spus-o şi Margaretei, cât e de nedrept că tocmai eu am fost favorizat de o limbă 'cu circulaţie mondială.' Dacă, cel puţin, aş putea, într-o zi, să-i traduc pe ceilalţi!" (I've sometimes told myself, and told Margareta, too, how unfair it is that it was I who had the advantage of a major language of the world. If only I could at least translate the others some day!).

This intention of his would be realized only to a small extent, through the translation of a few poems by Gellu Naum and Virgil Teodorescu[16]—another indication of Paul's attachment to Surrealism—but, if he had had the time, he would have translated much more Romanian poetry. I know that, at a certain point, he wanted to translate substantially from Arghezi's work (he had translated two poems of his in Bucharest[17]) and that Arghezi, when in Switzerland, sent his daughter Mitzura to Paris to talk with Celan about the prospect of publishing a representative edition of Arghezi's poems in German.

The next letter from my friend that I have kept is dated February 17, 1958; it is written in French, which would from then on be (with very few exceptions) the only language Paul used in his letters to me. In the meantime, various changes occurred at both ends of this correspondence: in Paris, Paul's move to a new house (78 Rue de Longchamp) and in Bucharest a (brief) return to an oppressive atmosphere he himself suggested in the letter dated February 17, 1958: "My dear Pierrot, what can I say, how can I answer you? I had sent you the two volumes of my poems—they were returned the other day with the mention 'Denied.' (Maybe I should have sent them to the Writers' Union address?)."

The bridges were still fragile and would remain so for a while yet. Nevertheless, the first step had been taken, and neither Paul nor I wanted to let silence settle between us again. Rereading my own letters to him (I have kept only some of them or, rather, their drafts), I realize the reticence and hesitations that crisscross them and that stood in the way of absolute sincerity. To be sure, I was trying hard to be as "correct" as possible, in order not to irritate who knows whose eyes; for this reason I sometimes adopted an upbeat tone when I spoke about my work and that of others, without mentioning the difficulties we were experiencing.

For example, in my answer to Paul's letter, which constituted a renewal of our correspondence, I sketched the following self-portrait:

> My biography has nothing sensational in it. As you know, there was a grand adventure in my life, an unfortunate and pathetic one, a sort of minor equivalent of Rimbaud's descent to the tropics. Having survived it, I've become a wiser person. . . . So I've grown wiser, and the wise, like happy peoples, have no history. That doesn't mean that I'm entirely happy. Sometimes I feel very lonely, just like you. But I possess a milder temperament and I get

> over it. My moments of impasse in the company of Melancholy are brief—and I escape from them by traveling and working, living and watching. . . . I like traveling, it gives me the opportunity to discover the world and get enthusiastic about the diversity of its aspects. I've come to the conclusion that I don't know my own country very well, so I've traveled a lot lately to several places, especially in Dobrogea[18]—in order to fill the large gaps in my knowledge. I guess you still remember some of the beauty of the Romanian landscape.

In general, I did not have many reasons to call myself happy. But it seems that Celan, about whom his Romanian friends were starting to get news, had even fewer. Between March 1958 and February 1962, there was a gap in our correspondence—a "historical" gap (filled with the wars in Lebanon and Algeria), but also one marked by many personal events. For Celan, this hiatus was linked to the name of Claire Goll, the widow of the Expressionist poet Yvan Goll.

In a long and heartrending letter sent on July 30, 1960, to Margul-Sperber, who had also resumed his correspondence with Paul, the latter informed him about a series of quite incredible but unfortunately real events regarding the accusation of plagiarism leveled by Claire Goll against our mutual friend. The "prehistory" of this accusation—reactivated several times—was, according to Paul, the following:

> I contacted the Golls at the end of fall 1949 to convey your good wishes to them. On this occasion, I offered them, as a gift, a copy of my volume of poems published in Vienna, *Der Sand aus den Urnen* (editor A. Sexl, Vienna, 1948).
>
> Goll was very impressed. Until his death (in March 1950), I often visited him, and during those visits I showed and read to him and his wife some texts published only in journals or—colossal imprudence—yet unpublished. Yvan Goll hadn't written anything in German for years, and the fact that he then returned, shortly before his death, to German is owed mostly—please don't take this as a sign of vanity on my part!—to his acquaintance with me

> and my poems. Goll also asked me to translate his French poems; I promised him I would. . . .

After Yvan Goll's death, Paul started, in effect, to translate his poems, preparing three volumes of them. "While I was engaged in the translation, the widow found everything entirely admirable; but she had other intentions which, credulous and trusting as I was, I didn't suspect." In short, Mrs. Goll would have liked to publish Celan's translations under her own name, which she eventually did, in fact, with the complicity of a Swiss editor.

"But this theft was not enough for her," Paul went on.

> The widow started to edit "the posthumous work" of the deceased. In 1951, the first volume of this "posthumous work" came out, in German, titled *Traumkraut*. It's obvious that the author or, rather, the authoress of this publication was perfectly familiar with my little book of poems published in Vienna—with all its many typos that made me put an end to its distribution. This volume of Goll's had no impact—I must stress this fact, because it's significant. In 1952, my volume of poetry *Mohn und Gedächtnis* came out; as you know, it represents, in large part, a new edition of my Viennese book. *This* volume was much appreciated.

Then, the abusive widow proceeded to attack: with the help of some "Germanist gangsters" from the United States, she spread, in the press, on the radio, and through the letters she sent to some individuals, the slanderous accusation that *Mohn und Gedächtnis*—published in 1952—was allegedly a plagiarism of Goll's 1951 volume. Celan was called "a rogue, a plagiarist and a fraud" ("Indeed, my dear Alfred Margul-Sperber").

This plot, hatched in 1953, assumed even more sinister connotations in time, related to a certain recrudescence of Nazism in the German Federal Republic. It reached a point where Paul was accused of having "fabricated" "the *legend* of his parents' being killed in such a tragic manner by the Nazis!"

But what hurt Celan most was the fact that, "so far, there has been nobody to protest or at least utter a word of indignation." "Oh, if only you knew!" he exclaimed at the end of the letter. "I've often wondered whether it wouldn't have been better if I had remained among the beech trees of my native country . . ." (Ich habe mich schon oft gefragt, ob ich nicht besser bei den Buchen meiner Heimat geblieben ware . . . ).[19]

In the many letters he sent to Margul-Sperber and to me during the immediately following period, "the plagiarism affair" recurs with obsessive insistence, explainable by the diabolical assiduity with which Claire Goll repeated her defamatory and unfounded allegations. Paul was exaggerating in only one respect: he was not as alone as he thought. There were, in fact, some Austrian and German writers who stood up for him: Marie-Luise Kaschnitz, Ingeborg Bachmann, and Klaus Demus had firmly rejected the accusation in a statement published in the *Neue Rundschau* (3 [1960]), as had Georg Maurer, in *Die Welt* (December 31, 1960) and Walter Jens, in *Die Zeit* (24 [1961]). The extremely thick file of the lawsuit initiated by Claire Goll against Celan in 1960 is under lock and key in the Academy of Darmstadt and will probably lie there for a long time to come. If I raise this issue, it is because I am trying to explain—to explain to *myself*—the gloomy letters I received from my friend. For the same reason, I have read Claire Goll's volume of memoirs, published in Paris in 1976 and titled *La Poursuite du vent* (Pursuit of the Wind[20])—a beautiful title, but one that conceals so many vicious calumnies!

The widow of the great poet Yvan Goll claimed that Paul had once taken advantage of her husband's hospitalization and tried to . . . rape her (Paul being, at the time, about twenty-eight years old, while Mrs. Claire was at least twice that!). According to the same author, Paul asked her to forgive him for the attempted rape, performed, supposedly, "in a state of somnambulism," and to swear that she would never reveal "what happened" that night. "I swore," says Claire Goll, "and, despite the polemic he initiated against me, I never made that episode public. But because he plagiarized Goll, he became so scared of his own shadow as well as mine that he never opened the door without asking first: 'Have you seen Claire Goll?' In order to escape his regrets or anguish, he ended up by throwing himself into the Seine."[21]

There are several absurdities that strike the reader of this account, written by Mrs. Goll so late, at the age of eighty-five. First of all, there is the connection, by no means evident, between the so-called attempted rape and the supposed plagiarism, both presented as certain, undeniable facts. Secondly, there is the statement according to which it was Paul who initiated the polemic, not herself—an absurd statement, if we think that an author accused of plagiarism has no interest in provoking a self-disclosing polemic: silence is of much greater advantage in such cases, although it cannot prevent the eventual exposure. Thirdly—but no less important—what is striking here is the cruelty with which Claire Goll, at her venerable age (which should have been the age of wisdom), "explains" the poet's suicide by his desire to "escape his regrets and anguish" caused by the unfortunate episode, supposing it had taken place in reality, not only in the inflamed imagination of the old lady. As an aside, I would like to point out that her entire book is constructed on the scaffold of venomous gossip, from which not even the men she esteemed or loved are spared, from Rilke to Yvan Goll, as well as Malraux, Picasso, Joyce, and many others. In his review of the volume *La Poursuite du vent*, Bertrand Poirot-Delpech, the literary columnist of *Le Monde*, rightly observed that "the poet Yvan Goll's widow extends indiscretion to the limit of gossip, and malice to the point of senile dispute," adding:

> Unable to discern the remarkable, unique qualities of the geniuses she encountered during her eighty-five years of artistic life, she clung to the obvious fact that, in their private lives, these geniuses are no different from ordinary people, though they might have . . . an extra measure of selfishness and cowardice. Why did she not choose, instead of their company and, sometimes, their advances, the company and advances of less exceptional people, more of her level? There can be only one excuse for the profoundly

> vexed snobbishness of this pain in the neck (ce snobisme dépité d'emmerderesse): the need to avenge her long, miserable existence, that of a failure, of a persecuted little girl, a wife without fame or money, an offended mistress—offended and, apparently, also frigid . . . [22]

After this necessary—in my view—parenthesis, which only serves to *situate* the problem by referring to this report in order to illustrate the character of the person directly responsible for the allegation of plagiarism brought against Celan, I return to the poet's letters during the period when the accusation started to circulate again, among certain scandalous publications in the West. The year is 1962 when this moving correspondence reaches a high point, and it is difficult to ignore it because it constitutes a human document with profound implications, indispensable for an understanding of Celan's destiny and his relations with the surrounding world, with the past, the present, and his poetry itself. What emerges, above all, from the letters he sent during 1962 to his Romanian friends—to Margul-Sperber, Nina Cassian, and myself—is an acute sense of loneliness, of isolation in a hostile world. Overwhelmed by the moral suffering caused by the fact that his honor as a poet had been tainted, Paul turned to his faraway friends of yore, desperately clinging to their image, still intact in his memory. After Margul-Sperber's reply to one of his letters regarding "the plagiarism affair," he sent him his wholehearted thanks for the simple fact that he did send him an answer at all: "Now we are no longer alone! (Because we have nobody, neither in the Federal Republic nor here)." He wrote to me in almost the same terms around the same date (March 8, 1962): "Thank you—from all my heart I thank you. We thank you, you and Yvonne. We are no longer alone, you say it's impossible that we have no friends here in France, but you see . . . it *is* possible. . . ."

In a letter to Margul-Sperber (dated March 9, 1962), one can easily detect another leitmotif of the entire correspondence of that period: the desire "to return home." For example, Paul emphasized that, in his speech on receiving the Büchner Prize (in 1960), "I said, among other things, that I was back where I started from" (habe ich u.a. auch gesagt, ich sei wieder da, wo ich angefangen habe).

In another letter to Margul-Sperber, on his birthday, Paul sent him a letter of praise that in fact reiterates the idea of "the impossible return":

> Your name is where it has always been: at that beginning which allowed me to choose the path I have taken, with words, with the words of our language, yours and mine. You, my dear Alfred Sperber, have always been a model for me. I've never forgotten how much I owe you. . . . In a sense, my path parallels yours . . . [23]

Celan also evokes "the mountains and beech trees of our homeland" (unserer heimatlichen Berge und Buchen), which have ensured his affection for the Carpathians forever. Under the pressure of his bitter disillusionment, the poet turns to his native Bukovina, toward which he impotently directs the antennae of his tormented soul. The idealization of the lost country acquires touching undertones and goes hand in hand with a violent negation of his immediate surroundings. As if it were black dandruff, Celan shakes off the fifteen years he lived in the West. Both in the letters he sent to Margul-Sperber and in those addressed to me, he vehemently attacks a civilization that he at that time regarded as built on false values and, moreover, as threatened by the danger of a resurgence of fascism. The image he conveys of Adenauer's Germany is a nightmarish one, undoubtedly exaggerated but not lacking in a certain real basis. In a letter dated April 25, 1962, responding to some perplexities of mine, Paul asked me to trust him:

> *I stand by everything* I've told you, Petrică, and I hope that one day I'll have the opportunity to show you, black on white, that I haven't invented anything. (Besides, all this goes beyond my personal case, obviously.) There's only one thing I would like to stress here: I've always *taken a stand against* Nazism, wherever I saw it raising its head. Always. But neo-Nazism is quite a complex

> phenomenon: it has assumed, among other things, the mask of a certain nonconformism. In the Federal Republic, there's a rebirth of nationalism, with its old myths, adapted to the requirements of the moment. Disguise is reigning, in literature and elsewhere. This is the time of depraved reality, the time of mythomaniacs, the time of distortions, the time of the so-called *Männerbunde*,[24] very Germanic, very Western, the time of projections and of retrospective alibis. The time of *all* ambiguities, of *all duplicities*, the time of *Ersatzes* of all kinds.

With his acute sensitivity, wounded by the tragedy of his parents' death, Celan sensed even the least perceptible signs of neo-Nazism and neofascism. His spiritual barometer, gravely shaken by so many inner storms, was by no means defective. Moreover, he was keenly aware of the danger that a reemergence of Nazism represented for his vocation: "You know what it means for a German-language author, who had also lived through the Nazi terror, to find himself separated, for the second time, from his mother tongue," he wrote to me on September 5, 1962, after he tried to explain to me why he had agreed to resume his association with the S. Fischer publishing house in Frankfurt for the publication of a school edition of his poems.[25] At the time, I did not quite understand what made Celan regret having granted the publishing house permission to publish that collection, which included "a quite useless bibliography" containing the titles of some translations he had made while in Romania, as well as the title of my translation of the "Todesfuge" into Romanian, which had been published in *Contemporanul*. (At Paul's request, I myself had furnished this information to the German publishing house.) I realized, however, that it was a matter of an extremely profound spiritual crisis:

> But one can't reach an agreement with bad faith, so here I am alone again. My nerves are just my nerves, and they collapsed—the causes were very real, very objective—so I found myself offering those who didn't even expect it the alibis they will not hesitate to make public at once.

In this context, for me a rather confusing one, Paul also confessed that he was "consumed by a burning desire" to find his Romanian friends again, adding: "This hope is still alive." In the last letter of our rich correspondence during 1962, dated September 12, Paul reiterated that the collection of his poems was to be a school edition ("This means making myself posthumous, in a way; however, I hope I'll survive") and ended with the statement quoted above, about his "poet-friends" in the Bucharest of 1945–47.

I have kept a draft of my answer to Paul's admirable letter, a draft from which I will quote a few paragraphs that show the perplexity I and his other friends felt about the bitter confessions of a poet we, after all, could not understand: despite the calumnious campaign launched against him, Celan had become a "name," his books were being published, he was receiving prizes, and so on. For example, in April 1962, in about the same period when he was writing to me with barely controlled anger about the situation in the German Federal Republic, he was received as an extraordinary member of the poetry department of West Berlin's Art Academy, together with Ingeborg Bachmann, Max Rychner, and Carl J. Burckhardt. Seen from far away—from the distance that separated us—the prizes and other honors Celan received were misleading, since they were, in fact, covering over the very complex reality of a fame for which our friend paid a very high price. Here is how I saw the situation:

> As regards your tribulations as a German-language poet, trust me, *I* understand you and support you with all my heart, even though certain details (for instance, those related to the "school edition" of your poems) elude my comprehension (that is to say, I don't understand why such an edition necessarily means *te rendre un peu postume* [make you somewhat posthumous]). A few days ago I had the great joy of seeing, in a recent number of *Lettres Françaises*, two poems by Paul Celan, published in top position on a page dedicated to German poetry from the East and West (Paul Celan, "*un des meilleurs poètes qu'ait révélés l'après-guerre*" [one of the best poets that the postwar period has given us], states the journal's bio-bibliographical note!) . . . You will perhaps tell me

> that this doesn't mean all that much to you. Be that as it may, I was very happy to see it, dear Paul.

Neither I nor Paul's other friends could truly comprehend his drama, which was very real, despite the successes he had attained. The letters we received from him confused us,[26] mainly because of the political views he formulated in them—the poet seemed to have found again a radicalism that was impossible for us to understand, since we did not have a clear and ample image of his inner motivations. At any rate, amidst a serious crisis such as the one he was going through in 1962, it was natural for him to appeal to the images, ideals, or even myths of his youth in order to be able to deal with the attacks of certain enemies (not all of them imaginary!) with right-wing political views. This endeavor—at once spiritual and ideological—made him exaggerate things and see a sort of universal conspiracy against him, where there was perhaps nothing more than a campaign of calumnies orchestrated by the perfidious Mrs. Claire Goll and her lawyers. What might be considered surprising in a poet like Celan, whose work is so entirely devoid of any element pertaining to immediate political reality, are the words he used in his letters: "the cancer of fascism," "my hope is in the East," "mon vieux coeur de comuniste," and so on. All these expressions do not seem to characterize very well the poet who, during the same period, published the volume titled *Niemandsrose*, dedicated to the memory of Mandelstam. Some statements from the correspondence of those years may appear even more bizarre, such as the statement that Marc Chagall was a "decadent," which seems to be borrowed from the propagandistic arsenal of the proletkult—all the more bizarre, as Paul had always loathed such simplistic formulas, and he was using them now of his own free will, without being constrained to do so.

They were doubtless a manifestation of the despair he felt, a despair to which he was condemned by the very condition of his self-exile: living in Paris, writing in a language associated with his parents' killers and used widely again to spread hatred and calumny—all these aspects could not have been beneficial to his peace of mind. Celan's dread of seeing himself "separated, for the second time," from his mother tongue perhaps took exaggerated forms, but that fear was not groundless. The tendency to turn back to the ideals and visions of his youth and even to a certain type of language was part of an understandable spiritual process, as was his "burning desire" to be among his Romanian friends once again. The problem was that those Romanian friends were in a situation that made it difficult for them to understand him properly, overwhelmed as they were by many worries and troubles, of a different kind, to be sure, but no less oppressive. Celan was returning, spiritually and intellectually, to a past from which he retained only, and exclusively, its ideal side. He was seeking the absolute both in poetry and in politics, while his Romanian friends had no choice but to be content, in general, with smaller victories, achievable only by applying the principle of relativity in their field of activity. Those who yearn for the absolute encounter, in their search, much more suffering than ordinary people, accustomed as the latter are to the small but stubborn steps of gradual progress.

In order to illustrate this statement, I resort to my own case again: in a letter from the beginning of March 1962, I confessed to Paul my sincere indignation about "the sinister conspiracy" against him and advised him to find some allies: "It's hard to believe that you can't find any, though you say that 'there is no man' around you! That's impossible!" To which I added: "As for me, I'm doing well. I continue to write poetry and translate from the classics."

Leaving aside the slightly condescending, though well-intentioned, tone adopted toward my friend in giving him such advice, I cannot help being bewildered and embarrassed by the mistake I made when I expressed a complacency that was entirely artificial and out of place. What need was there for my friend to hear about my philistine self-satisfaction when he was struggling in a desert of such vastness?

In the fall of 1962, our correspondence came to a halt and I thought that my letters and those from his other Romanian friends had eventually irritated Paul. It was only in the second half of December 1963 that I received from him an explanation for his prolonged silence, an explanation which had nothing to do with my suppositions: Paul had had a breakdown!

> My dear Pierre,
>
> Here I am writing to you again, after a long silence, not very loquacious now either, that's true, but present nonetheless. Last year, around Christmas, I went through a period of very serious depression, but I managed to recover my equilibrium and resumed my work at the École Normale at the end of January. Since then, I've been going up the slope, there are still highs and lows (des hauts et des bas), sleeping proves difficult, but I work and carry on. . . .

The letter ended with these words: "The cultural exchanges between Romania and France are intensifying—could they not bring you to Paris one day? I do hope so. All our best wishes to you both! Your brother-friend, Paul."

Until the fulfillment of Paul's hope, and mine—which was even stronger—another three years would pass, during which our correspondence became less frequent, interrupted by long silences. The year 1962 remains "the terrible year" of capital confessions, made to some friends who were incapable of comprehending them fully and who were too far away from him to be able to help him effectively. Beyond their indisputable value as documents regarding the profound crisis Celan was going through in that period, his letters shed some light on his poetic work as well. One might say of Paul's correspondence what Marthe Robert said about Kafka's:

> His letters become, on a small scale, what his novelistic work was, on an almost infinite scale: a battlefield between literature and reality, on which, however, he does not fight alone anymore. . . . Kafka imposed on his letters a dual task, one almost impossible, almost inhuman, almost incomprehensible to others—that of effectively putting an end to his isolation, and at the same time of preserving for him the essence of his solitude.[27]

Like Kafka, Celan rarely speaks about his literary work in his correspondence, but when he does he offers interpretive keys that are much more precise than those assembled by critics preoccupied exclusively with the words on the page. An example: in the letter he sent to Margul-Sperber in March 1962, Celan illustrates his statement "I'm right back where I started from" with one of his poems, "Shibboleth," in which he intercalated the famous slogan of the Spanish republican combatants—"*No pasaran.*" "The gentlemen in West Germany cannot forgive me for this either," he added.

The poem's title is a Hebrew word, related to an episode from the book of Judges (12:6) about the war between two Semitic tribes, the Gileadites and the Ephramites: whenever somebody from Ephraim tried to escape by crossing the fords of Jordan conquered by the Gileadites, the latter would ask him: "Art thou an Ephraimite?" If the fugitive denied this, they would tell him: "Say now Shibboleth," a word the fugitive could not pronounce correctly. "Then they took him, and slew him at the passages of Jordan."

Celan's poem would make no sense outside this biblical text, which helps us decipher not only the meaning of this or that word but also the very source of inspiration for the poem: the acute awareness of his precarious status as a German-language poet, a status threatened by a reemergence of anti-Semitism, always ready to question the ability of a foreigner like Celan to pronounce German words correctly.

Toward the end of the 1950s, such foreign and bizarre words begin to invade Celan's poetry, and they appear in his correspondence as well. A letter he sent to Margul-Sperber (on March 9, 1963) bears the signature "Paul," followed, in brackets, by the words: "Russkij poiet in partibus nemetskich infidelium" (Russian poet in the land of German infidels), an imaginative combination of Latin and Russian, invented by a mind excessively preoccupied not so much with the exactness of the terms as with suggesting a complex and dramatic existential truth.

Soon afterward, I received from Paul the volume of poems by Serghei Esenin that he had translated, with the following dedication in four languages: “Für Petre Solomon, na dobruiu pamiat, frăţeşte, din inimă, Paul Celan, Lutetiae Czernowitiorum, 25.4.1962.” Such combinations become more and more frequent in Celan’s poetry, which, on the one hand, as mentioned above, contracts and, on the other, shatters, allowing all sorts of foreign linguistic elements to penetrate its fissures. Certainly, this phenomenon has not escaped the critics’ attention, but it was not very well grasped, being used mainly as a pretext for semiotic or “semanalytic” exercises, with no connection to the existential drama of the poet.[28] One of the few critics to have made this connection was the American professor John Felstiner. In his presentation at the Celan conference held in Cerisy in the fall of 1984, Felstiner observed: “By the late ’50s, the European Jewish catastrophe seems to have overtaken Celan a second time, with distinct effects on his writing. Two things strike me about the poems of this period collected in *Die Niemandsrose* (The No-One’s Rose, 1963): they are expressed with polyglot energy, and they turn repeatedly to Jewish themes.” Although the American translator interprets this explosion of “polyglot energy” exclusively from the perspective of a return to Judaism, he describes the phenomenon accurately:

> We hear in these poems—along with Celan’s odd compounds and fractures, disruptive syntax, repeated or truncated syllables, and his arcane, archaic, technical, playful, and neologized German—we encounter the words “Baobab,” “Menhir,” Friedrich Hölderlin’s babble, “Pallaksch,” “Kannitverstan”; a nonsense title, *Huhediblu*; or others, such as *Radix*, *Matrix*, *Havdalah*, and *Mandorla*; we find *Pneuma*, *Anabasis*, and *Benedicta*. We see three poems with French titles and more with French quotes in them, others with Latin, Spanish, English, Russian, Hebrew, and Yiddish.

After he points out the abundant presence of names of people and places in Celan’s poetry, Felstiner advances the following explanation:

> Certainly he found himself seeking out new verbal resources because he felt the lyric vocabulary was inadequate, exhausted. What’s more to the point, the seven or eight other languages

> migrating into his verse call into question the German around them; they render the mother tongue problematic.[29]

Celan was descending toward his past in Bukovina and Bucharest, in a desperate attempt to regain his spiritual equilibrium, shaken by his ordeals with a Germany that was still averse to him. But his spiritual state forced him to descend even deeper, toward an archaeological stratum, as it were—the stratum of the biblical history of the Jewish people, victims of the Nazi Holocaust. This archaic level was less tangible than the Bukovinian layer, which was connected to a relatively recent history.

Together with the many other layers from his past, Celan was also regaining his appetite for wordplay, manifested in his Bucharest period; only that now, given the crisis he was going through, the act of playing with words turned into "un jeu de massacre."[30] The poet was subjecting the German language—"this German language of mine, et qui reste douloureusement mienne" (and which remains painfully mine), as he confessed in a letter—to pressures that were equivalent, in a sense, to the moral pressures and humiliations he himself endured. It was a personal conflict with his mother tongue, but this struggle had, paradoxically, some beneficial effects on the massacred language: just like Rimbaud in *Illuminations*, Celan broke through the limits of a linguistic medium he considered inadequate, allowing lexical and syntactical elements from other languages to operate freely within it. This, too, was a form of searching for the absolute, undertaken, of course, for different reasons than those that made Rimbaud or Mallarmé revolutionize the French language.[31]

As a rule, such seekers for the absolute are complex people and they end badly, often in madness. Celan's correspondence betrays certain signs of madness, too, but of a madness whose causes are, as he himself says, "very real, very objective." Because of the paroxysm that seemed to have dictated them, the letters from 1962 in particular represent a veritable temperature chart of a seriously ill person, on the verge of collapse. Like Hölderlin—another seeker of the absolute—Celan suffered from cyclothymia, a nervous disorder in which periods of exhaustion alternate with fits of anger, but which does not prevent those afflicted by it from being clearheaded or from telling the truth. The authors of a study of Hölderlin draw attention to the following danger, which applies to Celan's critics as well:

> A judgment formulated about a poet who ended in madness can be falsified in two ways; first, by his adversaries, who, since the onset of madness is rarely specified, can interpret everything he had done before as already marked by madness, as already corrupted and devastated; secondly, that judgment can be falsified because of some bad friends—people who will interpret the entire work of the ill person as being itself sick. Such an interpretation functions, so to speak, in a distorted manner, backward, by extending the madness throughout the period of health, toward its origins. . . . Hölderlin was not exempted from these misfortunes, particularly the second. To many men of letters, he is, above all, the mad poet.[32]

Preparing myself to leave for Paris in the fall of 1966, I was feeling very emotional and nervous at the thought of seeing Paul again. I knew he had been seriously ill, but his latest letters justified a certain measure of hope, although one of them, dated August 29, 1966, informed me that Paul "had spent seven months in clinics": "You will soon be in Paris and we'll talk to our heart's content, but don't tell anybody about it. I hope you'll agree to stay, as our guest, two or three weeks longer than your invitation from the PEN Club[33]. . . ."

# 6

# Twenty Years Later and Abroad

Poetry, that instance when losing metamorphoses into winning. And the genuine poet chooses to lose to the point of dying, in order to win.

—JEAN-PAUL SARTRE[1]

*I* am trying to remember as accurately as possible the significance of my departure for Paris in the fall of 1966, which was possible thanks to a conjunction of favorable circumstances. About a year and a half earlier, in Bucharest, I had met a few French writers, members of the French PEN Club—Yves Gandon, Paul Vialar, Jean de Beer, and Solange Fasquelle—and had become friends with them during a trip in my country. Given the relaxed atmosphere of the time, cultural exchanges were intensifying, making much-desired trips abroad possible. Having received an official invitation from Jean de Beer, the general secretary of the French PEN Club, with the specification that this international institution would "pay all the expenses" involved in my stay in Paris, I contacted the Writers' Union of Romania, which helped me obtain the necessary passport. Zaharia Stancu,[2] the new president of the Union since February 1966, was most understanding. Besides, trips to the West were no longer such rare occurrences. Some of my friends had been ahead of me in this respect—Nina Cassian and Crohmălniceanu, for example. The latter had met Paul Celan in Paris in 1964, when he had been invited by the board of COMES, a recently created organization to help promote contacts between writers from the east and those from the west. Maria Banuş, A. E. Baconsky, and Marin Preda had also met Paul in the French capital. After his return to Bucharest, Baconsky[3] told me about this meeting with great enthusiasm—I had given him Celan's address and they spent an entire night talking and walking on the banks of the Seine. Together with Victor Eftimiu,[4] Eugen Jebeleanu,[5] and Alexandru Balaci,[6] Marin Preda left for Paris in the spring of 1965, at the invitation of the same PEN Club, and through him I sent Paul some of the Surrealist texts I had kept for him.

These "antecedents" gave me encouragement: I was looking forward to seeing my friend again and, to be honest, I did not give too much thought to the suffering he had been through, hoping with all my heart that it belonged to the past. As for me, I was in a euphoric mood: apart from the fact that I finally had the chance to visit Paris, I had recently become a father, so I was thinking of my son Alexandru all the time (Paul, too, congratulated me in a letter).

I left Bucharest by train on the evening of November 14, 1966, and arrived in Paris in the morning of November 16. Shortly after settling into one of the PEN Club guest rooms, on the fourth floor of a "Proustian" building on 66 Rue Pierre Charron—a stone's throw from the Champs-Élysées—I called Paul to let him know I had arrived. Later that day, I found at the concierge's a parcel that my friend had left for me containing a guide to Paris and a copy of *Le Flâneur des deux rives*, Apollinaire's lyrical account of the Paris of bygone days, reprinted by Gallimard. Inside the book, there was a little card, on which Celan had written: "Bine ai venit, Petre. Ton ami Paul. 16.IX.66."[7]

The following day, on Tuesday November 17, I visited him in the modest apartment in which he lived with his wife, Gisèle Lestrange, and their son, Éric, on 78 Rue de Lonchamp, on the fifth floor of an old building that had no elevator. I have found in my travel diary this brief note on Celan: "Changed, of course, after so many years, but not unrecognizable: he has a very high forehead, an impression caused by his hair—thinned out and graying. Slightly stooped in posture and looking a little weary. He speaks in French with me, though he hasn't forgotten Romanian completely. He has a verbal tic: *n'est-ce pas?*" We quickly resumed our friendship, finding again, without much difficulty, the thread that had been interrupted for so many years—the thread that connects through direct contact, not through correspondence, which can substitute for it only to a small extent. Paul's illness, about which he had written to me many times, had left its marks on him, as had the years, but he seemed to be on the road to recovery.[8] At any rate, he was very happy to see me again, and kept asking me about his Romanian friends, especially Margul-Sperber and Philippide. He knew that Margul-Sperber had been ill and regretted that, over a year before, he had reproached him for I don't remember what joke related to the plagiarism allegations. Paul's face clouded every time we talked about this matter, which, in his view, was far from being a "closed case." He even offered to show me the archive of documents he kept at his country house in Normandy, but I tried to avoid this embarrassing subject as much as I could, so in the end he stopped bringing it up. But I realized then that the attitude of some of his Romanian friends puzzled him: they congratulated him on his successes (in 1964 he had won another prize, the North Rhine-Westphalian State Prize for the Arts), interpreting them as proof of the fact that "the plagiarism affair" might have been a figment of his imagination rather than something that had really happened. He told me about a conversation he had had on this topic with Maria Banuş, whom he otherwise held in high esteem.

Paul allowed no confusion between his "fame," a term he used in quotes, and the real and serious state of affairs in the German Federal Republic, although the fact that Willy Brandt's Social Democratic Party had just become part of the governing coalition reassured him a little, giving him some reason for hope. He showed the same intransigence toward other, seemingly insignificant, matters. For example, during his visit in 1964, Crohmălniceanu had told Paul that a former editor-in-chief of *Scânteia*—from the time when Paul worked on that newspaper—had "developed a nervous disorder." Crohmălniceanu thought that this piece of news might please Celan, because that man had fired him from the editorial team of the newspaper.[9] But Paul was not pleased to hear the news at all, and he particularly disliked the light, cheerful tone in which Crohmălniceanu communicated it to him; not only, due to his morbid sensitivity, did he react strongly to any allusion to his nervous breakdown, but he felt solidarity with other people and their suffering, even if they happened to be his former enemies. It was an old character trait of his, now exacerbated by his illness.

Could it be that Paul had lost his sense of humor? To a certain extent, yes, which was not surprising considering the difficulties he was facing. I don't recall hearing him laugh in Paris as I had heard him doing in Bucharest, in our youth. He no longer played with words, either, as he used to. In this Paris, which had become a veritable Monte Carlo of word games and where you were assaulted at every turn by commercials based mainly on puns, Celan put on a sad and bitter smile. What had happened to him? To say simply that he had grown old or that he was mad is to utterly simplify things and to choose the easiest path, one of superficial understanding. I believe that Paul's acute, even morbid sensitivity made it possible for him to perceive "the madness of the century" more accurately, the symptoms of which were multiplying on the entire planet at an alarming rate: the wars that had recently broken out in various parts of the world, the increasingly large amounts of money spent on armaments, the intensification of terrorism, the Cultural Revolution in China, and many other things. On the other hand, the early 1960s were also marked by the launching into space of the first man, the Soviet Russian Yuri Gagarin (in April 1961), a landmark event, but one that might have been interpreted by a poet not only as a triumphant proof of mankind's urge to progress, but also as a sign of a desire to desert the planet.

In literature, the 1960s started in France with a series of unsettling and, at the time, symptomatic manifestations, which were a sort of climax to tendencies emerging during the previous decade. Under the influence of the *Tel Quel* group (whose journal had started to come out in 1960), the concept of *literature* itself was being abandoned, to be replaced by that of *writing* (écriture), through which notions such as *work*, *creation*, or even *author* were discredited, rendered obsolete.

Language had long been the major obsession of writers, philosophers, and, of course, linguists, and now it was being perceived especially as a means of producing a *text*, irrespective of its quality or meaning. Regarded, ever since Saussure, as "a system of signs," language was turning against literature precisely when the audio and visual media were striking serious blows at it.

I will not list here the innumerable phenomena that illustrate what I would call the will of modern man to give up on language in favor of other means of expression or communication. I would only like to mention some of the most important ones in order to evoke the climate in which Celan, a genuine poet, saw the very grounds and instruments of this vocation, words, threatened. In 1961, Raymond Queneau (an otherwise remarkable writer) had established, with François Le Lionnais, the so-called OULIPO group (*Ouvroir de littérature potentielle*) (Workshop of Potential Literature), with the view of applying mathematics to experimental writing. Shortly before, Queneau had published the volume *Cent mille milliards de poems* (One Hundred Thousand Billion Poems), in which he had suggested that ten sonnets constructed with the same rhymes and following the same grammatical structure could be rewritten in an almost infinite number of combinations. In 1965, Philippe Sollers, the editor-in-chief of *Tel Quel*, published a novel titled *Drame*—the drama being that of language: the novel consisted of sixty-four "songs," in analogy to the sixty-four black and white squares of a chessboard. Also in 1965, Georges Perec, another novelist who was very popular in the 1960s, published *Les choses* (The Things), which consisted of a huge inventory of objects and was awarded the Renaudot Prize. Three years later, in 1969, he would publish the novel *La disparition* (The Disappearance), the subject of which being . . . the disappearance of a vowel.

The 1960s also represented a sort of golden age for the language sciences, from semiotics to "grammatology," as Jacques Derrida titled his 1967 study, in which he proposed a way of evading the limits imposed by traditional culture, based on speech. In the seminar he was holding at the École Pratique des Hautes Études, Jacques

Lacan was developing his psychoanalytical system, also centered on the question of language: according to him, the human unconscious itself was structured like a language; thus, psychoanalysis was a form of linguistic analysis.

In the field of literary criticism, intertextuality was triumphing, supported as it was by a literature that, since James Joyce, had offered abundant material for such tautological, nonreferential interpretations. After a long period in which structuralism prevailed and was still referring to reality, Jacques Derrida, Roland Barthes, and others were now placing the literary text in front of a mirror that only reflected other texts back.

At first sight, all these phenomena should have been to the poet's liking, since they were crowning a long struggle for the independence of the word, but in reality the autonomy of language was obtained at the very high price of losing its importance and its power to stir feelings and emotions. The famous *langagier* festival, held in Paris and in other Western capitals (in Eastern European countries, language was being subjected to a process of devaluation, different in essence, but with somewhat similar results), was taking place at a time when *the word* had lost almost all its authority: television, bombarding viewers with images from all over the world, marginalized it effortlessly.

The 1960s also constituted a glorious time for another extralinguistic phenomenon: the so-called happenings, a sort of hybrid performance in which dance, music, and film dispensed with great ease with any contribution by words. The extraordinary diffusion of rock music during the same decade (marked by the proliferation of such bands as the Beach Boys, the Kinks, and the Byrds) is related to this context, too, a context defined by George Steiner in terms of a considerable narrowing of the sphere of language: "Large areas of meaning and praxis now belong to such non-verbal languages as mathematics, symbolic logic, and formulas of chemical or electronic relation. Other areas belong to the sublanguages or anti-languages of non-objective art and *musique concrète*. The world of words has shrunk."[10]

A genuine poet has no reason to feel very happy in such a world, in which his only instrument (or weapon) is relegated to the status of a museum relic. There are also, undoubtedly, poets who resign themselves to this situation and try to adapt to it—the 1960s offer us numerous examples of poets who repudiate "the Gutenberg galaxy": Gerhard Rühm, Ernst Jandl, and many others, of various nationalities, abandoned "the galaxy" in order to practice concrete, phonetic, sonorous, mechanical, spatial, and even electronic poetry, often enjoying widespread promotion (especially on the radio), access to which poets still faithful to their vocation were denied.

This was another reason why Celan, who was living in Paris in the midst of these evolutions or revolutions, felt more and more isolated. Surrounded by so much experimentalism, he was delighted to rediscover Heine, about whom he wrote to Nina Cassian (on April 25, 1962): "I have often re-read Heinrich Heine, here, in Paris. Do you know his little poem 'To Edom'?" Of course, his admiration for Heine also involved a feeling of identification with the destiny of the great German poet of Jewish descent, self-exiled—like himself—to Paris, where, for several decades, he fought an unequal battle against the philistinism of his fellow countrymen, as the poem "An Edom!" (1824) shows:

Ein Jahrtausend schon und länger,
Dulden wir uns brüderlich,
Du, du duldest, daß ich atme,
Daß du rasest, dulde Ich.

Manchmal nur, in dunkeln Zeiten,
Ward dir wunderlich zu Mut,
Und die liebefrommen Tätzchen
Färbtest du mit meinem Blut!

Jetzt wird unsre Freundschaft fester,
Und noch täglich nimmt sie zu;
Denn ich selbst begann zu rasen,
Und ich werde fast wie Du.

To Edom

For more than a millenium
We have tolerated each other in brotherhood:
You, tolerating the fact that I am breathing,
I tolerating your fits of rage.
Very occasionally, in dark times,
You would behave strangely,
Tinting your sweet
Little pious claws with my blood.

Now our friendship is firmer,
Growing day by day—
For I, too, began to rage
And I am becoming almost like you.

The Heine case offered Celan yet another analogy, to which he specifically referred in a letter to Margul-Sperber, on February 8, 1962, when he was on the heights of the spiritual crisis caused by "the plagiarism affair" and by what our friend regarded as a deliberate attempt at "rendering him anonymous": "You remember Will Vesper, the one who wrote the *anonymous* 'The Lorelei.' I myself am—literally, my dear Alfred Margul-Sperber!—*the one who doesn't exist.*"[11]

It is interesting to note another analogy between Celan and Heine—perhaps even an influence the latter exerted upon his successor: in his cycle of *Hebrew Melodies*, written toward the end of his life, Heine introduced some Hebrew words into the German language, thus setting a classical precedent for Celan.

In both cases, we encounter an act of doing violence to language for existential rather than aesthetic reasons, though the consequences at the level of lyrical expressivity are by no means negligible. At any rate, Celan's modernity does not derive from a desire to keep up with the times, and the mere mention of Heine in this context betrays a will to return to the past rather than an avant-garde impulse. Celan is modern by virtue of his firm anchorage in contemporary history, through his painful experience of its dramas and problems, even though the expression these find in his work is often enigmatic and obscure—ostensibly similar to much of the poetry of our time. I am referring here to authentic poetry, not to its many surrogates, for which Celan felt nothing but contempt. How could he have appreciated, for example, the "biopsies" that, starting in 1966, were being recorded on tape by Bernard Heidsieck, a German poet settled, like Celan, in Paris? Or the so-called *cri-rythmes* and *mégapneumes*—recordings of squeaks and mewls made by François Dufrêne and Gil J. Wolfman, friends and followers of Isidore Isou?

Paul Celan was very annoyed by such experiments, and this became very clear to me when I mentioned to him my intention to meet Isidore: "Don't go to him, he's a fraud," he told me. But, as he did not insist on it, I went to see Isou anyway, out of curiosity. I found "the father of Lettrism" in a hotel room on Saint-André-des-Arts in the Latin Quarter. Isou remembered me and seemed to be glad to see me again, but he immediately started to play his usual mediocre role.

Accordingly, he took me to a café at the corner of the street, where he was awaited by some of his dedicated admirers, among whom, I believe, was Dufrêne. The Lettrist group was preparing to choose a candidate for . . . the presidential elections, which were approaching; they were therefore intensifying their activity, especially in the academic world. Also present were two or three students, whom Isou lectured at for a couple of hours, looking at me every now and then out of the corner of his eye as if to say, "See what an important personage I have become?" At a certain point, he suggested I should become his representative in Romania! He told me that in Yugoslavia and Czechoslovakia he already had many followers, so it was high time his native country converted to Lettrism, too. But I remained as reluctant as I had been two decades earlier, when he showed me his aberrant manifesto.

I told Paul about my meeting with Isou, and I think that was one of the few moments when he laughed heartily, even though he seemed, at the same time, to be scolding me for my foolishness. His reaction to Lettrism seemed symptomatic to me. It should not be interpreted as indicative that he was losing his sense of humor but, rather, as a fully justified rejection of excessive experimentalism, which was threatening to stifle true innovation. At that time, Lettrism was not even the most aggressive artistic experiment: as a matter of fact, it had become "classicized," far outstripped as it was by other experimental forms, much louder and with grander pretensions, but wholly lacking in humor. Celan's statement that "la poésie ne s'impose plus, elle s'expose" refers precisely to these experiments, which were proliferating at an alarming rate.

In an essay included in a recent anthology of avant-garde literature, Ian Wallace describes eloquently the situation created by the emergence of concrete poetry:

> Recent movements in literature, concrete poetry explicitly, treat language as an opaque medium, which throws content back into the realm of literature as "something to say," rather than "what is said" . . .
>
> Gorged with experience, the "something to say" given by literature is no longer needed, or rather, the preservation and accumulation of "great works" renders contemporary works into pathetic clichés of greatness. An even more tragic condition—the rare works of contemporary genius that do exist, those that do have something to say, are powerless to affect the dominating forces of our society, which are not spiritual or of the imagination, but rather are technological and economic.
>
> So now we have nothing to say. That this is true is indicated by the fact that when literature does maintain an attempt to say something of importance, it inevitably talks about its own emptiness.[12]

Celan, who had so much to say and who desperately believed in poetry, would have agreed with this analysis, which also contains an explanation for his relative lack of humor. In Paris, in 1966, this poet who had once played so passionately with words no longer enjoyed puns, which had become excessive. I call it "his relative lack of humor" because humor continued to be a feature of his spirit. During our long walks in "Panam" (as he informally called Paris), Paul was very relaxed. Despite having many obligations—as a lecturer at the École Normale and as head of the family (his son, Éric, was eleven years old at the time, and required nurturing)—Paul wanted to show me *La Ville Lumière* (The City of Light) and share with me his observations, usually in an amused tone.

Thanks to him, I learned how to travel by bus and by metro, a challenging lesson for somebody from Bucharest who was accustomed to trolleys. But we walked a lot, Paul preferring this means of transport for short distances. From his place we quickly reached the Place du Trocadéro, where there was the imposing equestrian statue of Marshall Foch. From there, we walked to the immense terrace situated between the two wings of the Palais de Chaillot to look at the Eiffel Tower, the Champ de Mars, and the bridges over the Seine. The Passy district, where Paul lived, was relatively quieter than other districts and stimulated a desire for walks. I cannot reconstruct the route of those promenades with any precision, but I do remember that, at my friend's suggestion, I visited Balzac's house on the Rue Raymond in Passy. From there we went to the neighboring district of Auteuil on the Rue La Fontaine, where Marcel Proust had been born and where, according to the book by Apollinaire that Paul gave me, the shoemaker-poet Alexandre Treutens used to go. The latter "wrote vaguely humanist poems, which he read in bars, to diggers and sailors," wrote Apollinaire, adding that the old shoemaker would wander the Paris suburbs and ask the respective mayors for special authorizations. "I saw with my own eyes an authentic document, issued by the town hall of Enghien, for Alexandre Treutens, which granted him permission to exert his profession as a *wandering poet* in the village of Enghien for *one day*."

Paul knew many such stories, from books or hearsay, and he enjoyed recounting them, amused, punctuating them with deep sighs. We often walked on the banks of the Seine, too, stopping in front of the stalls of the famous bouquinistes, much more numerous in those days. On one of these walks, Paul taught me to throw a ten- or twenty-centime coin into the river as a token of good luck to return to Paris.

Apart from being my guide, Paul was very generous with his practical and even political advice, telling me, for example, to avoid this or that former legionary whom I might have run into. "Paris is a city full of traps," he would warn me, worried about what might befall me. At the same time, he tried to soften the shock that most foreign visitors felt upon their first contact with Paris—that sensation of astonishment generated by the vastness and kaleidoscopic variety of the French metropolis. The "bewilderment syndrome" caused by the sight of such abundance of goods in shop windows or by the Parisian elegance, would have affected me as well, as it did so many of my fellow countrymen, had I not had Celan's lucidity of mind, which filtered the images I was registering and corrected my impressions. Although in love with "Panam," Paul retained his powers of critical discernment, knowing how to distinguish between appearance and reality. The Paris of opulence and elegance was foreign to him because he had remained a modest man, with frugal, almost austere habits. Every time he invited me to dinner, he bought some things from a local store—cookies or salami—to add to the menu prepared by his wife. Gisèle worked in an engraving studio in Montmartre and got home late: like most Parisians, the Celan family ate together only in the evening, but Paul wanted to adjust their schedule to suit mine, so he sometimes invited me to lunch, too.

He had long ago given up smoking, and he only drank a glass of red wine every now and then. His austerity was dictated not only by the nervous disorder that afflicted him but also by his modest income. Because of this, he could not afford, for example, to frequent luxury restaurants. Yet he insisted on offering me "a truly Parisian evening" at the famous restaurant Au Lapin Agile, which Philippide had warmly recommended to me: during his student years in Paris, the Romanian poet had often eaten in that restaurant, which had been named after the sign painted by the graphic artist A. Gill—hence the name Au Lapin Agile (à Gill). Under its former name of Cabaret des Assassins, the restaurant had enjoyed an even more resounding fame, being the meeting place of many writers and artists: Francis Carco, Pierre Mac Orlan, Vlaminck, Picasso, Utrillo, and others.

I went there with Paul and Gisèle on the evening of December 11, 1966, two days before my departure, so that was, in fact, my farewell evening. I don't remember either the words or the silences we exchanged on that occasion. Paul was rather melancholy, and so was I, but he nonetheless made an effort to appear cheerful—he, too, I think, was amused by the restaurant he was entering for the first time. At a certain point, the pop singer Yves Mathieu appeared among the tables, a fellow with bushy eyebrows and thick lips, who sang some typically Parisian songs, very poetic and relaxing. Another singer followed, Pierre-André Douket, who, accompanying himself on guitar, just like Georges Brassens, sang a few songs composed by himself. As a souvenir of that evening, Paul bought me a record with four of Mathieu's songs and wrote on the sleeve the words "En souvenir de Panam, de Montmartre, du Chevalier de la Barré," signing underneath this, in Cyrillic characters, "Pavel Pavlovici Ţelan."

The allusion to "the knight of La Barre" makes me think that we talked about politics, too, since that knight was a quasi-legendary character from the eighteenth century, martyr of the struggle for freedom against the monarchy, very popular in the Montmartre district, where a street bears his name to this day. Celan was still a man of the Left, without affiliation to one party or another, but with evident sympathies for socialism and, at any rate, with an irrepressible aversion to fascism. Let us recall that Paris was then, in a way, on the eve of the events of May 1968, which were prefigured by growing political and social tension. In my euphoric state I was, naturally, less attentive to these aspects; moreover, I was moving in different circles, which involved exhibitions and shows (the DADA retrospective exhibition organized by the Modern Art Museum, the exhibition *In Vermeer's Light* at the Orangerie, and the Picasso retrospective at the Grand Palais and Petit Palais—these were the great artistic events at which I had the good fortune to be present). Also, busy paying various visits, I was becoming a very sociable, even snobbish person, frequenting illustrious personalities such as Graham Greene, Eugène Ionesco, Pierre Seghers, André Maurois, the Duchess of La Rochefoucauld or . . . Isidore Isou.

Talking to Paul about these meetings, some planned, others entirely accidental (I had met Maurois at a book sale exhibition organized by the PEN Club at the Palais Galliera), I realized that my friend was leading an extremely isolated life in the Parisian metropolis. He did not belong to any literary coterie and knew very few French writers, mainly solitary figures like himself, such as Henri Michaux—a poet of exceptional discretion and modesty who, shortly before, had refused the Grand prix national des Lettres. Celan had translated into German a substantial collection of Michaux's poetry, recently published in Frankfurt.[13] His own lyrical work was virtually unknown in France, where, not long before, Maurice Nadeau's journal *Les Lettres Nouvelles* had published a few poems by Celan in a special issue dedicated to "German writers of today" (December 1965–January 1966). Also in 1966, *La Nouvelle Revue* published a few other poems by Celan, translated into French. Although my friend had translated a considerable number of French poets—Rimbaud, Nerval, Mallarmé, Apollinaire, Éluard, Valéry, Desnos, Supervielle, Michaux, Réne Char, and so on—Celan was not a "name" in Paris.

To draw him out of his isolation, I thought I should introduce him to the poet André Frénaud, an admirable man whom I had befriended in Bucharest a few years earlier during his visit to Romania as a guest of the Writers' Union of Romania. Frénaud was also a solitary man, although at that time he seemed very active in his role as promoter of East-West relations within the COMES organization—one of the cultural institutions created in that period of relative relaxation. Paul asked me to invite him to dinner at his place on the Rue de Longchamp; thus, the two Parisian poets met and talked. Gisèle prepared a copious dinner for us with plenty of wine, and Paul was in a rare mood of vivacity. But I also remember an embarrassing moment, caused by a conversation about political matters: talking about the dogmatism of the 1950s, Paul seemed to be reproaching us, me and other Romanian writers he knew, for being somehow resigned to this phenomenon. I remember that Frénaud spoke in my defense, making the necessary distinctions. We departed as friends, of course: such discussions, if held in good faith, could not spoil our mutual trust. Still, Frénaud left a bit embarrassed, telling me on the way out, "Il a un côté fou, votre ami" (He's a bit crazy, this friend of yours). What bothered the French poet was precisely the passion with which Paul had discussed the matter: Paul judged things from an absolute perspective, including me as well in the exigency of this absolute. More realistic—more attentive to any sign of change—Frénaud was glad about the turn for the better that had taken place in Romania during those years. The two poets would never meet again, so my attempt to break Paul's isolation was unsuccessful.

Soon after that dinner, I had the opportunity to see my friend in an environment where he felt less lonely: the Goethe Institute on the Avenue d'Iéna had scheduled an evening in homage to the poet Nelly Sachs, who had turned seventy-five and had received the Nobel Prize for Literature. Paul Celan had been invited to read some poems written by the venerable poet, with whom he was friends and to whose work, marked by the tragic destiny of the German Jews, he could relate. In the not-very-full hall of the Goethe Institute, Paul's trembling voice resounded solemnly, lending special resonance to Nelly Sachs's poems.[14]

The reading of these poems crowned an evening of recollections to which Professor Beda Allemann, too, brought his contribution, having come from Bonn specially for the gathering. At the end of the program, Paul introduced me to the distinguished professor who would later edit his works. On this occasion, it became clear to me that my friend was, in fact, quite well known; he should not have used the word "fame" in quotes. In the Federal Republic of Germany, studies and articles on his poems were being published all the time, and they were not only laudatory but also very insightful; in them, Celan's poetry was recognized as of exceptional value—as perhaps the supreme poetic oeuvre of the postwar years. The thorough critical analyses of such scholars as Walter Jens, Beda Allemann, Karl Krolow, Siegbert Prawer, and many others, especially after 1960, had the effect of securing Celan's place in the West German critical awareness. But this recognition was perhaps too late in coming. Although he enjoyed it, in a quiet way, the poet continued to feel fragile and vulnerable, as if he couldn't trust not so much the praise he received but their ability to definitively change his status as an immigrant to German literature. In his full glory, Paul Celan continued to be dominated by his complexes, such as the ghetto syndrome, which he carried inescapably within himself and which pushed him toward a tragic form of Judaism.

On the evening of December 11, Paul took me to Au Lapin Agile, as I mentioned above. My visit to Paris was drawing to its end. I could have stayed longer, enjoying Paul's hospitality (he had already prepared for me the room on the sixth floor that Gisèle used as her studio), but my one-month visa was about to expire. Also, I was missing my family. So I left Paris, heading for Bucharest, on the evening of December 13, 1966. Paul insisted on accompanying me to the Gare de l'Est, so we had one more opportunity to exchange a few words and silences. He also brought me a last present—a superb edition of John Keats's poems, which I wanted, then, to translate into Romanian. Before saying goodbye, he told me that he was hoping "nothing bad would happen" upon my return to Romania and suggested, should anything unpleasant occur, to write to him, asking him, for example, if his son, Éric, "is still collecting stamps." I never had the opportunity to use this code, which was quite naïve after all.

In the summer of 1967, I had the chance to see Paul again, for the last time. I was in Paris with a group of poets—Radu Boureanu,[15] Gellu Naum, Geo Dumitrescu, and Victor Felea.[16] I had received, from the Minister of Flemish Culture of Belgium, a prize for my translation of an anthology of Flemish poems into Romanian. Many things had happened since we last met, not only in Paris but also in Bucharest—not to mention the grave events taking place in the world (the war in Vietnam, aggravated by the intervention of American troops; then, toward the end of June, the Six Day War in the Near East). In Bucharest, Alfred Margul-Sperber died at the beginning of January: he had barely had the chance to hear the relatively good news about Paul that I had given him.

Shortly after I communicated the sad news to him, in a letter in which I enclosed the obituary published in the press, Paul replied, in a grieving tone (I am quoting his answer in the original, written as it was in a French sprinkled with Romanian and English words):

> Je le savais. Samedi, dans un journal allemand, *Die Welt*, une notice dite culturelle: le nom, l'âge, la langue, le pays. J'étais dans la rue, il faisait froid et, comme cela m'arrive de temps en temps, je cherchais un peu mon nord (qui est, décidément, un peu à l'est).
>
> Alors, ce fut, encore, avec le gel et mon soufflé, "l'heure de Sperber," son heure, si j'ose dire, totale. *Mi-era a năduşeală, a lacrimă.*—A-weeping.—Puis j'ai pensé que je pourrais prendre un avion. Puis j'ai remarché.
>
> Je trouve le nécrologue de l'Union des Écrivains tres digne et je ne suis point insensible au fait que les coordonnées de cette existence—un peu anachronique, un peu catachronique, comme toute existence de poète—y paraissent, nues, claires, sous leur nom.
>
> I knew about it. On Saturday, in a German paper, *Die Welt*, a piece of so-called cultural news: the name, the age, the language, the country. I was on the street, it was cold and, as it sometimes happens to me, I was in a way looking for my north (which, decidedly, is a little to the east).
>
> It was then, again, with the freezing cold and my breath, "the hour of Sperber," his total hour, if I can call it so. *Mi-era a năduşeală, a lacrimă.*[17]—A-weeping.—Then I thought I could catch a flight. Then I continued my walk.
>
> I find the obituary written by the Writers' Union very dignified and I can't ignore the fact that the coordinates of his existence—a little anachronistic, a little catachronistic, like the existence of any poet—seem bare, clear, under their name.

Soon afterward, Paul fell seriously ill, as I would find out much later from his reply to a letter I had sent him from Belgium, in which I informed him of my arrival. He had been hospitalized in February and, although he resumed his activity as a lecturer at the École Normale Supérieure, he continued to follow I don't know what course of treatment. Also, it was clear that he no longer lived at his old address, because he asked me to send my letters to École Normale, 45 Rue d'Ulm, Paris V-ème, so we could meet.

As soon as I settled in at the shabby hotel in Paris, on the Rue de l'Exposition (Hôtel de Talma), in a room I was sharing with Geo Dumitrescu and Victor Felea, I wrote to Paul at the address he indicated. A few days later, he came to my hotel to see me. He was a profoundly changed man, grown old prematurely, taciturn, sullen. In a letter I sent my wife, I described Paul thus: "On Monday morning, Paul came to my hotel; poor man, he is suffering from profound depression, of which he is aware and which has got worse since his separation from Gisèle. Now he 'lives' at the clinic where he is under treatment and never goes home anymore."

In fact, sometimes he slept at the École Normale in the little room next to the somewhat larger one in which he held his classes, on the ground floor of the huge university building. Once, when I went there to see him, he had just finished a class he had conducted with four or five students. The rest of the nights, he slept at the clinic. "They're doing experiments on me," he once told me, in a faded voice, interrupted by those sighs that were caused, perhaps, by the electric shocks and the tranquilizers the doctors administered to him. What could I say to that? I was dumbfounded—because of the stupor, and the scorching heat (it was an uncommonly torrid summer!)—and I wished I could help him somehow, but I did not know how. Paul had become like Hölderlin: a victim of doctors, since his illustrious predecessor, too, had much to suffer because of the treatments he had been subjected to (at the clinic where he had been hospitalized before finding an oasis of peace in the house of the good-hearted carpenter Zimmer, from Tübingen).

The comparison with Hölderlin might seem farfetched, of course, like all comparisons, although there are certain analogies regarding their destinies as well as their work. Even though Hölderlin praised the light of day and Greek antiquity while Celan's poems were dominated by the dark of night and contemporary history, both were great solitaries—isolated and misunderstood. Writing, each in his own way, profoundly personal poetry, disregarding the fashions and models offered by their respective contemporary ages, both of them evolved toward a lyricism that aspired to silence, under the unbearable pressure of certain inner constraints caused by the world around them.[18] Living the life of a recluse for over thirty years in a little tower suspended above the River Neckar, Hölderlin wrote awkward poetry in a language that was at times simple, or even perplexing sometimes, a sort of enigmatic babble, studded with bizarre images. Paul Celan did not have such a tower that could make his tormented existence bearable, and where he could allow his poetry turn into babbling. His madness, less serene than Hölderlin's, would throw him into the Seine three years later.

Our last meeting left me with a very bitter taste, but it offered me no clues about such an end. Despite his depressive state, Paul was trying hard to be helpful: whenever he had a little free time, he walked with me in the city and invited me for a snack—a sandwich or a cup of coffee. Once, he took me to a German bookshop to inquire about a book by Klee, which my wife needed for her doctoral dissertation. The bookshop owner, an old German scholar, knew Paul well and promised him he would order the book, *Das bildnerische Denken.*

Paul was not depressed all the time: he had moments of great joy—very brief, admittedly, and punctuated by nervous, shrill, convulsive laughter. I have found, among my papers, a note in which he asked me to postpone our meeting at the École Normale for the following day. The note ended thus: "Vive le jambon infini et ses Joachims!—Paul" (Long live the infinite ham and its Joachims!—Paul).

He remained nostalgic for "the beautiful season of wordplay," although he had not played with words for a long time. What impressed me in him now was his silence—a heavy and tenacious silence, at times interrupted by such statements as "They're doing experiments on me" or "Women find it hard to live with geniuses" (this latter remark, by which he tried to explain to me, in a tone of bitter self-irony, his separation from Gisèle, lingers vividly in my memory). We said goodbye to each other on the sultry morning of July 6. I went to the École Normale again, looking for him. We walked together in silence in that beautiful old Parisian district, Place de la Contrescarpe.

Around lunchtime, we entered a small restaurant to have something to eat, then resumed our silent walk. On the Rue Descartes, number 39, Paul showed me the house in which Verlaine lived for a while and died—a house of five floors with a bookshop on the ground floor called Verlaine. We continued our walk to the bus stop, we waited together a little, then I got on to go to the center, while Paul, stooped and downcast-looking, started to walk back to the École Normale, waving his tired hand at me. For a few more hours, I walked aimlessly in Paris before boarding the plane for Bucharest. My heart heavy, I kept thinking of the wretched figure of my friend.

If anybody believes that Celan's existential drama is foreign to his poetry—and there are plenty who refuse to see the connection between them—that person is dreadfully mistaken. He did not hesitate to admit this connection whenever he had the opportunity to do so. In his answer to the good thoughts and wishes I sent him, as usual, for his birthday—November 23—he described that "festive" day thus:

> The 23rd isn't over yet, it's 9pm, I'm at the Rue d'Ulm, at my desk; I've just written a poem that ends with the words: *Kaltstart, trotz allem,/mit Hämoglobin*, which means, roughly: starting (or, rather, *racing*), despite everything that has happened, with the help of hemoglobin. Éric came to congratulate me on my birthday, I took him to see my modest lodgings, a stone's throw from here, on the Rue Tournefort. After twenty years of Parisian life, to end in a furnished studio with a kitchen, and no room for my books . . .

In the same letter, he drew my attention to a poem from *Atemwende*, his most recent volume (published in the autumn of 1967):

> On page 68 of *Atemwende*, there is a sort of anamnesis of Mangalia; on page 79, the Wallachian buffaloes that Rosa Luxemburg caught a glimpse of through the prison bars converge with three words from Kafka's "A Country Doctor" and with the name

ROSA. I coagulate, I'm trying to make it coagulate. Paris—where is it, I wonder?

We have here the very formula of Celan's poetry. At first sight, it invites an intertextual reading, offering its readers mirrors in which they can contemplate the tormented face of the text. But what seems much more important to me is the poet's appeal to have his words read through an existential grid, in which each of them acquires profound meanings and becomes a wound, an open wound, with the blood about to coagulate.

In an age dominated by orientations and practices that place language at the center of concern in philosophy and literature—though, on the other hand, language loses in importance and relevance as it gains more autonomy—such poetry risks being regarded by many as a linguistic performance, capable of being appreciated by semioticians and other text deconstructionists. It is clear that Celan's poetry, too, is inscribed in the general movement of modern poetry, which, since Mallarmé and Rimbaud, has ceaselessly proclaimed its independence from both everyday language and the real world, fiercely searching for its own language and reality. But, in this constraining context, which involved not only a determined gesture of distancing from the "real world" but also a certain undeniable enrichment of the means of expression, Paul Celan impresses with a life experience and tragic vision that cannot be reduced to "the words on the page." The spectacles of "signifiers" devouring their "signified" until everything becomes insignificant is not his specialty. With him, every word bears the mark of the profound drama it emerges from, even though he does not communicate its "message" in a direct and pedestrian manner. As Michael Hamburger observes, "the darkness in Celan's poems, their leaps and bounds, their haltingness and their silences, all these are inseparable from their authenticity and their fascination."[19]

Apart from this, Celan's poetry, difficult as it is, always aspires to a new form of communication, to an ideal dialogue, ardently desired until the last moment. Let us recall what he himself said in 1958, in his speech upon receiving the Bremen Literature Prize:

> Das Gedicht kann, da es eine Erscheinungsform der Sprache und damit seinem Wesen nach dialogisch ist, eine Flaschenpost sein, aufgegeben in dem—gewiß nicht immer hoffnungsstarken—Glauben, sie könnte irgendwo und irgendwann an Land gespült werden, an Herzland vielleicht.

> A poem, as a manifestation of language and thus essentially dialogue, can be a message in a bottle, sent out in the—not always greatly hopeful—belief that somewhere and sometime it could wash up on land, on heartland perhaps.[20]

As I have already pointed out, starting with the volume *Sprachgitter* (1959), Celan's poetry becomes sparser, increasingly contracted, aspiring toward silence in a more poignant manner. Yet the yearning for dialogue does not vanish from it, the pronoun *du* remaining one of its constant elements in a lexical landscape otherwise devastated by violent storms. The poet does not cease to proclaim, to the very end, his longing for dialogue, for union, even though, under the pressure of his illness and solitude, he might appear resigned to the idea that "es sind / noch Lieder zu singen jenseits / der Menschen" (there are still songs to be sung beyond humanity), as he so beautifully put it in a poem from the volume *Fadensonnen*.

Among the poets who could be invoked in an attempt to situate Celan in a spiritual family—from Hölderlin to Trakl and Rilke—I would also name the Italian poet Giuseppe Ungaretti (and Paul translated some poems by him). Hermetic like Celan—for similar reasons, perhaps: the organic antifascism and the irrepressible need to confess in a language unpolluted by the miasmas of tyranny—Ungaretti titled five of his collections of poems *Vita d'un uomo*. About the first of them, *L'Allegria*, he said: "This old book is a diary. The author has no other ambition (and believes no great poets have, either) than to leave behind a beautiful biography of himself."[21]

In an essay on Ungaretti from 1956, Gäetan Picon pointed out that the great Italian poet did not have the fortune of a proper translation in France:

> A sort of *determination towards dislocation* separates, in my opinion, the admirable French poetry since Mallarmé and Rimbaud to this day from the confused totality of experience. From the moment when he begins to write, every French poet is already settled within poetry: the trajectory he adopts is not from life to poem, but from poetry to his own poem . . . I have always found it puzzling that a literature like ours, gripped as it is by a sort of logical anger and dominated, from Racine to Rimbaud, from Malherbe to Mallarmé, from Flaubert to Breton, from Pascal to Valéry, by a passion for extremes, should be defined in terms of reason and measure . . . Ungaretti speaks to us in a different language: that of the man dumbfounded by his human destiny, which he assumes in all its confused and torn totality.[22]

In the last two or three years of his life, Celan had the satisfaction of being adopted by a group of French poets gathered around the journal *L'Éphémère*: André du Bouchet, Yves Bonnefoy, Michel Deguy, and others. Without meaning to generalize, let alone to make value judgments, one can observe that all these poets, endowed with talent in different measures, have—or perhaps had—in common the search for a linguistic absolute, after Mallarmé's supreme example. "A poem hides, rather, the metaphor of its own existence, in its breath and argumentation," said Michel Deguy, for example (in a text titled *Actes*), adding: "A poem never ends in knowledge."

This view of poetry as self-referential, as a text devoid of any horizon existing outside itself (as well as outside other texts), has also influenced the translations of Celan's poems by some members of the group, which prompted Henri Meschonnic to speak of "a massacre of Celan's poetry," imputable to the group's ideology. This ideology forced André du Bouchet, for example, to translate *Atemwende* as *détour du souffle*, which, Meschonnic says, "means turning Celan into a display figure, within a dated ideology of Parisian writing à la Blanchot, which theorizes a different experience." Celan wrote *tournant du soufflé*, which means "turning point of the breath": "Writing is that which swerves and causes swerves, crossroad-change, thus transforming both the writing and existence itself."

Meschonnic also protests against those who state (again following Maurice Blanchot[23]) that Celan's voice "rises and, at the same time, becomes silence, in order to tell us the Word is dead." There is no "difficulty of utterance" as such, Meschonnic points out: "It [the difficulty] is different every time," and in Celan's case, it is precisely his own personal way of expressing "a situation without hope"[24] that has been ignored.

Celan's poetry seems to evolve, along with much modern poetry, toward the silence that necessarily follows excessive meditation on language. But it remains profoundly personal, in a context that favored depersonalization and dissolution into anonymity. To illustrate the difference more clearly, it is sufficient to compare any of Celan's poems (of the last phase, which draws nearest to silence) with any of those written in the same period by the many practitioners of concrete, phonetic, or electronic poetry—for example, those written by Ernst Jandl, its most famous representative. Among others, Jandl wrote an untitled poem in which he suggests that the German vowel ö (o with an umlaut) was born thus:

e
ee
eee
ooooooo öööö ooooooo.

Such "poems" abound during that period and unfortunately represent a widespread phenomenon, classified as such by an elegant anthology of concrete poetry published in the United States, in which the Austrian poets Ernst Jandl and Gerhard Rühm appear next to the Brazilian brothers Augusto and Haroldo de Campos (founders of the poetic group *Noigandres*), the German poets Helmut Heißenbüttel and Claus Bremer, the Czechs Joseph Hiršal and Bohumila Grögerová, Emmett Williams and Aram Saroyan from the United States, and the Japanese Seiichi Niikuni and Fujitomi Yasuo.[25] Nothing, or almost nothing, differentiates these late successors to Marinetti (and to Apollinaire in his *Calligrammes*) except their names, which are the only elements that betray their belonging to different cultures. Though called concrete, this type of poetry is, in fact, very abstract, its equivalent in the visual arts being abstractionism, devoid as it is, in its turn, of precise indications and dominated by the same universalistic ambition. It is interesting to note that one of the most aggressive reactions against abstractionism took place in the German Federal Republic in the 1960s, through the group *Fluxus*, animated by Joseph Beuys. Renewing the connection with the Expressionist tradition, the painters who belonged to this still very active group returned to figurative art, an art of strident chromatism, and were determined to express the tensions and obsessions of the age in a "referential" artistic language.

Celan's poetry, too, in its last phase, follows (or perhaps inaugurates) this direction. It attains universality through a profoundly personal language, full of references to the poet's tragedies and to the tragedies of the times, and not through their negation. Precisely because it is *lived*—authentic, grounded in experience—this poetry becomes communicable, despite the difficulties and the perplexities it creates. As his good friend Alexandru Philippide observed, "Paul Celan's obscurity is the antipodes of any kind of mediocrity. His poetry can even serve as an antidote to convenient banalities. It is the result of intense anxiety, in which the agitated life of humanity in our century is reflected."[26]

Undoubtedly, such profound, solemn poetry finds it difficult to penetrate the consciousness of people at the end of the century, dominated as it is by the cult of speed and numbers. But it abundantly rewards one's efforts to decipher it.

Criticism of Celan's work has mainly highlighted those elements that place it within a certain wave of modernity—that which flows toward silence—by emphasizing, for example, that in *Atemwende* "poetry remains in a no-man's-land, between language and non-language,"[27] or that, in the same volume, "poetry is not defined through language, or as a particular form, however obscure, of it, but as silence only: the negation of speech, as the most radical criticism of language."[28]

I do not believe that Celan's poetry can be reduced to that—to a radical critique of language. On the contrary, it might represent, in the last analysis, an affirmation of the power of the word, that is, of poetry, in a world that seems to be willing to give up on language or to replace it with images, mathematical calculus, or electronics. Even during the years of utmost despair and absolute solitude, Celan continued to hold on to the word as if it were an impossible lifebuoy. The poems collected in the few posthumous volumes—*Schneepart*, *Lichtzwang*, *Zeitgehöft*—can be and have been read especially in the lugubrious light of his tragic end in the waters of the Seine. Indeed, they contain a premonitory element: many of them speak about water and fish ("das schwimmende Wort/hat der Dämmer,"[29] thus a poem from *Lichtzwang* ends, while another one begins with the line "Schwimmhäute zwischen den Worten" [web(bing)] between the words),[30] but many others proclaim a moving desire to live or—as he emphasized in the previously mentioned letter—to start again, be it with the help of "hemoglobin." A poem dedicated to his son (one of two included in the posthumous volume *Schneepart*) speaks better than I possibly could about what happened to the poet and to the times he lived in:

In der Flüstertute
buddelt Geschichte,

in den Vororten raupendie Tanks,

Unser Glas
füllt sich mit Seide,
wir stehn.[31]

In the megaphone
history is grubbing away,

in the suburbs the tanks are caterpillaring,

Our glass
fills up with silk,
we stand.

Such lines, quite numerous in the posthumous volumes, have a sort of clarity that contradicts the current impression of Celan as a "master of darkness," as Rainer Gruenter described him.[32] We should not allow ourselves to be deceived by the fact that, in the poet's later poems, there is also a process of "atomization" of language, of semantic disintegration of the German words or of their coupling with words from other languages. The act of extending the German lexicon toward other linguistic horizons reveals, beyond the poet's wish for "revenge,"[33] a will to speak and to engage in dialogue, that is, to remain within language, not to distance himself from it.

There is a type of metaphor that is often encountered in Celan's poems—the metaphor based on the points of the compass: "als brennende Gäste vom Süden" (as burning guests from the south), from the poem "Spät und tief" in the volume *Mohn und Gedächtnis*; "am Südwall des Herzens" (at the south wall of the heart), from the poem "Im Spätrot" in the volume *Von Schwelle zu Schwelle*; "in den Flüssen nördlich der Zukunft" (in the rivers north of Future), from a poem published in the volume *Die Niemandsrose*; "vom Osten gestreut, einzubringen im Westen, gleich-ewig" (scattered by the east, gathered in the west, at once eternal), from a poem included in the volume *Fadensonnen*, and so on. The obsession with the four points of the compass is evident in the poet's correspondence as well: "I was on the street, it was cold, and, as sometimes happens to me, I was somehow searching for my north—which is, decidedly, a little bit to the east." This obsession has its own profound meaning and assumes the status of an organizing principle in some of Celan's metaphors. Personally, I see it as a sign of his openness to a universality understood as the sum of all compass points, without excluding any of them. What in some of Celan's poems may appear to be doing violence to the German language in fact expresses his desire for the coexistence of various cultures, which he himself integrated into a personal and original vision. Perhaps this is precisely the "secret message" of Celan's poetry of the last phase, and not the silence he seemed to be reaching toward and which he gave the impression of mimicking, like so many contemporary poets.

It is a message that is interwoven with the poet's entire existence, with his biography, so complex and paradigmatic in its own way, even though it distinguishes itself through its tragic dimension, which renders it so singular. Before becoming an affluent of the Seine, Paul Celan crossed the contemporary geography and history of the European continent like a poetic river full of contrary or complementary energies. Their burden was perhaps too heavy to be borne by a single man, besieged by so many adversities. Perhaps his final gesture had been, from the beginning, inscribed in his destiny as a deracinated poet. Perhaps . . . Perhaps . . . It is hard—and would also be indecent—to say what exactly drove him to throw himself into the Seine on a black day at the end of April 1970. He must have accumulated too many sorrows, past and present, caused by his inner turmoil and by external events.

But I believe that Henri Michaux was closest to the truth when he wrote, shortly after the poet's death:

> C'était trop grave en lui, ce qui était grave. Il n'eût pas permis qu'on y pénétrât. Pour arrêter, il avait un sourire, souvent, un sourire qui avait passé par beaucoup de naufrages.
>
> Nous faisions semblant d'avoir avant tout des problèmes touchant le verbe.
>
> . . .
>
> La cure, venue de l'écriture, ne suffisait pas, n'a pas suffi.
>
> . . .
>
> Il s'en est allé.[34]

> It was too grievous in him, that which was grievous. He would not allow access to that. In order to prevent it, he often wore a smile, a smile that had survived many a shipwreck.

> We pretended that our problems were, above all, related to words.
>
> . . .
>
> The solace offered by writing was no longer enough.
>
> . . .
>
> So he left.

His departure raised many questions, and the answers cannot be easily found. What is certain is that, through his tragic destiny itself, Paul Celan draws attention, in the most eloquent manner, to the difficulties poetry encounters in its attempts to exist in the contemporary world. The answers he offered to tormenting questions—which troubled not only him but his contemporaries all over the world as well—can be found, and deserve to be understood, in his exemplary work, meant to survive the passage of time.

*Notes*

*Index*

# Notes

## On Paul Celan

1. The time Paul Celan spent in Bucharest right after the war (1945–47) has generally received little attention from his biographers and critics. The first three chapters of this book contain Solomon's account of Celan's stay in the Romanian capital—his work as a translator at the Cartea Rusă Publishing House, the friendships he developed there (most notably with Alfred Margul-Sperber, who marked his debut and remained, like Solomon, a lifelong friend), as well as his contact with the very active Romanian Surrealist group of the time. [T.N.]

2. *Paul Celan, Nelly Sachs: Correspondence*, trans. Christopher Clark (Rhinebeck, NY: Sheep Meadow Press, 1995), 17.

3. Celan wrote seven lyric poems and eight prose poems in Romanian. See chapter 4 ("The Adolescence of a Farewell"), in which Petre Solomon discusses Celan's Romanian texts, their stylistic particularities, and contextual details, as well as their place in Celan's oeuvre. The English version of Celan's Romanian texts was first published in 2015 in Nina Cassian's translation (*Romanian Poems by Paul Celan*, Rhinebeck, NY: Sheep Meadow Press). [T.N.]

4. John Felstiner, *Paul Celan: Poet, Survivor, Jew* (New York: W. W. Norton, 1995), 253, 181.

5. *Selected Poems and Prose of Paul Celan*, trans. John Felstiner (New York: W. W. Norton, 2000), 329.

6. Hans-Georg Gadamer, epilogue to *Gadamer on Celan*, trans. and ed. by Richard Heinemann and Bruce Krajewski (Albany: State Univ. of New York Press, 1997), 142.

7. Michael Hamburger, introduction to *Poems of Paul Celan* (London: Anvil Press, 1988), 18.

8. Felstiner, *Paul Celan*, 254.

9. Hans Egon Holthusen, quoted in Felstiner, 79.

10. Paul Celan, *Collected Prose*, trans. Rosemary Waldrop (Rhinebeck, NY: Sheep Meadow Press, 1986), 16.

11. Theodor Adorno, "Cultural Criticism and Society," in *Prisms*, trans. Samuel Weiber and Shierry Weber (London: Spearman, 1967), 34.

12. *Selected Poems and Prose*, trans. Felstiner, 395.

13. Felstiner, *Paul Celan*, 161. A word of caution is called for. We have only Celan's account of the meeting. What Celan reports does not square with what Buber had written seven years earlier: "They [our persecutors] have so radically removed themselves from the human sphere . . . that not even hatred, much less an overcoming of hatred, was able to arise in me. And what am I that I could presume to 'forgive'!" Quoted in Maurice Friedman, "Paul Celan and Martin Buber," *Religion and Literature* 29, no. 1 (1997), 46.

14. Felstiner, *Paul Celan*, 131, 133.

15. *Selected Poems and Prose*, trans. Felstiner, 245; *Glottal Stop: 101 Poems*, trans. Nikolai Popov and Heather McHugh (Hanover and London: Wesleyan Univ. Press, 2000), 19.

16. Felstiner, *Paul Celan*, 226.

17. *Selected Poems and Prose*, trans. Felstiner, 261.

18. *Selected Poems and Prose*, trans. Felstiner, 307.

19. Felstiner, *Paul Celan*, 268.

20. Felstiner, *Paul Celan*, 327.

21. Recalling his visit to Celan in Paris in 1966, twenty years after they had last seen each other, Petre Solomon noticed with bitter sadness the changes in his friend. What most impressed Solomon was Celan's silence, "a massive, tenacious silence," broken only by remarks such as "They're doing experiments on me." See chapter 6. [T.N.]

22. Felstiner, *Paul Celan*, 243, 330.

23. Quoted in Felstiner, *Paul Celan*, 287.

24. *Selected Poems and Prose*, trans. Felstiner, 396.

25. Philippe Lacoue-Labarthe, *Poetry as Experience*, trans. Andrea Tarnowski (Stanford: Stanford Univ. Press, 1999), 38, 122. Lacoue-Labarthe's book was first published in 1986.

26. Lacoue-Labarthe, *Poetry as Experience*, 33.

## Argument

1. Pierre-Jean Jouve, *Les Noces, suivi de Sueur de Sang*. Paris: Gallimard, 1966, with an introduction by Jean Starobinski. [T.N.]

2. See Walter Benjamin's essay "The Task of the Translator" (1923), in *Illuminations*, trans. Harry Zohn, ed. and intro. Hannah Arendt (New York: Harcourt Brace Jovanovich, 1968), 69–82 (esp. 79–80). [T.N.]

3. "Speech on the Occasion of Receiving the Literature Prize of the Free Hanseatic City of Bremen," in Celan's *Collected Prose*, trans. Rosmarie Waldrop (Rhinebeck, NY: Sheep Meadow Press, 1986), 34. English translation slightly modified. [T.N.]

4. T. S. Eliot, "Tradition and the Individual Talent" (1919), in Eliot, *Selected Essays, 1917–1932* (New York: Harcourt, Brace, 1932), 7–8. [T.N.]

5. In a letter to George Sand, dated Dec. 1875, Flaubert wrote: "According to the ideal of art that I have, I think that the artist should not manifest anything of his own feelings, and that the artist should not appear in his work any more than God in nature. The man is nothing, the work is everything." *The George Sand–Gustave Flaubert Letters*, trans. Aimée L. McKenzie, intro. Stuart P. Sherman (London: Duckworth, 1922), 213. [T.N.]

6. Roland Barthes, *Le Degré zéro de l'écriture* (Paris: Éditions Gonthier, 1964), 36, 44–45. [A.N.]

*Writing Degree Zero*, trans. Annette Lavers and Colin Smith, preface by Susan Sontag (trans. 1967; New York: Hill and Wang, 1968), 48. [T.N.]

7. *Language Mesh*. Michael Hamburger's translation, in *Paul Celan: Selected Poems*, trans. Michael Hamburger and Christopher Middleton, with an introduction by Michael Hamburger (Harmondsworth: Penguin, 1972), 50. [T.N.]

8. Protesting against some French versions of Celan's poems, Meschonnic stated that the poet "writes in the language of those who killed him, and he kills it" (écrit dans la langue de ceux qui l'ont tué, et il la tue). See Henri Meschonnic, "On appelle cela traduire Celan," *Les Cahiers du chemin* (La Nouvelle Revue Francaise, Jan. 15, 1972), 115–49. [A.N.]

9. See Michael Hamburger's introduction to *Paul Celan: Poems. A Bilingual Edition* (New York: Persea, 1980). [A.N.]

10. See George Steiner, "An Enclosure in Time," *Times Literary Supplement* (Feb. 4, 1977), 132. [A.N.]

11. Paul Celan, "Du liegst im großen Gelausche" (Dec. 1967), in Celan, *Schneepart: Gedichte* (Frankfurt am Main: Suhrkamp, 1971), 8. [T.N.]

12. See Jean Bollack's foreword to *Celan-Studien*, by Peter Szondi (Frankfurt am Main: Suhrkamp, 1972). [A.N.]

13. Gaëtan Picon, *L'Usage de la lecture* (Paris: Mercure de France, 1979), 7–8. [A.N.]

14. Picon, *L'Usage de la lecture*, 15–16. [A.N.]

15. Eugen Simion (born 1933) is a Romanian literary critic and historian, editor, essayist, and member of Academia Română (the Romanian Academy). In his book *Întoarcerea autorului* (The Return of the Author) (Bucharest: Univers Enciclopedic, 1981; repr. 2013), he discusses the biographical approach to literary criticism (as elaborated by Sainte-Beuve) and Proust's absolute rejection of it in

the latter's essay "Contre Sainte-Beuve." Simion analyzes the mysterious relation between a text and its writer, emphasizing the dimension of self-discovery involved in the process of literary creation. [T.N.]

16. "Rose, oh reiner Widerspruch, Lust, / Niemandes Schlaf zu sein unter soviel Lidern" (1925) (Rose, oh pure contradiction, desire, To be no one's sleep under so many lids), in Rainer Maria Rilke, *Sämtliche Werke*, ed. Rilke-Archiv, with Ruth Sieber-Rilke and Ernst Zinn (Frankfurt am Main: Insel, 1955–66), 3:185. "Rose, oh reiner Widerspruch," as determined by the poet in his will, is the epigraph on Rilke's tombstone. [T.N.]

17. George Steiner, "The Scandal of the Nobel Prize," *New York Times Book Review* (Sept. 30, 1984), in which he deplores, among other things, the fact that Paul Celan did not receive the prize. [A.N.]

18. For the full text of this prose-poem, see chapter 4 (pp. 112–14). [T.N.]

19. Pierre Joris offers a slightly different translation of the first line: "As Partisan of Erotic Absolutism, reticent megalomaniac even among divers, and simultaneous messenger of Paul Celan's halo." In Paul Celan, *Paul Celan: Selections*, ed. and intro. Pierre Joris (Berkeley: Univ. of California Press, 2005), 41. [T.N.]

20. Urmuz (1883–1923), a Romanian writer, was the author of *Pagini bizare* (Bizarre Pages), which has been translated into many languages. He is considered a leading representative of the avant-garde (alongside, most notably, Tristan Tzara and Ilarie Voronca) and a precursor of Surrealism. His writings are defined by irony, humor, and parody. Since his style seems to challenge literary conventions and to undermine the literary act itself, his texts have been compared to those of Kafka or Beckett. The "perfect unreality" in which Urmuz's characters live and the complex combination of ridicule and the tragic that characterizes them spring from Urmuz's own obsessions with death, the irrationality of life, and the irrepressible need to find independence from the abyssal spectacle of existence. For an English edition of his work, see Urmuz, *The Complete Works*, trans. Miron and Carola Grindea (London: Atlas Press, 2007). [T.N.]

21. Milo Dor, "Paul Celan" (1970), in *Über Paul Celan*, ed. Dietlind Meinecke (Frankfurt am Main: Suhrkamp, 1973), 281. ("Er kam buchstäblich aus dem Nichts" is Milo Dor's terrible statement in the German original.) [A.N.]

22. Horst Bienek, "Narben unserer Zeit" (1959), in *Über Paul Celan*, ed. Meinecke, 46. [A.N.]

23. See Beda Allemann's afterword to Paul Celan, *Ausgewählte Gedichte* (Frankfurt am Main: Suhrkamp, 1969), 163. [A.N.]

24. Israel Chalfen, *Paul Celan: Eine Biographie seiner Jugend* (Frankfurt am Main: Insel, 1979). [A.N.]

English edition: *Paul Celan: A Biography of His Youth*, trans. Maximilian Bleyleben (New York: Persea, 1991). [T.N.]

25. For example, Chalfen affirms that Paul wrote "for his friend Petre Solomon" a series of poems and prose texts in Romanian and gave them to me, as a present. Equally false is the statement that I was the one who introduced Paul to Maria Banuş, a non-Jewish poet, or that Gellu Naum was Jewish. See Chalfen, ibid. (English edition), 148–49. [A.N.]

26. See Uwe Martin's foreword to the texts of the Celan conference in Bucharest, Oct. 1981, in *Zeitschrift für Kulturaustausch* (Journal of Cultural Exchange) 3 (Stuttgart, 1982). [A.N.]

27. See *Neue Literatur* (Bucharest) 11 (1980–82). [A.N.]

28. Alfred Margul-Sperber (1898–1967) was a German-language poet, translator, and journalist, born, like Celan, in Bukovina. He was the most influential Bukovinian poet at the time Celan lived in Bucharest, and he played an important role in the latter's early career. [T.N.]

29. Jules Supervielle, *Le Corpse Tragique* (Paris: Gallimard, 1959). [T.N.]

30. Alexandru A. Philippide (1900–1979) was a Romanian writer, poet, essayist, and translator. His poetry was influenced by the German Romantics, particularly Novalis, whom he admired greatly. He translated works by Goethe, Schiller, Shakespeare, Voltaire, Chekhov, Novalis, Lermontov, and others. Celan called him "master Philippide" (pp. 33, 132). [T.N.]

31. Nina Cassian, a lifelong friend of Paul Celan, was a Romanian poet, essayist, translator, and composer. Of Jewish origin, she lived in Romania until 1985, when she settled in the United States after being granted asylum due to the political situation in her country. Her first volume of poetry, *La scara unu pe unu* (On a Scale of One to One), was published in 1947, when Celan was still in Bucharest. English editions of her poetry include *Lady of Miracles: Poems*, sel. and trans. Laura Schiff (Berkeley: Cloud Marauder Press, 1982); *Life Sentence: Selected Poems*, ed. and intro. William Jay Smith (New York: W. W. Norton, 1991); *Take My Word for It: Poems* (New York: W. W. Norton, 1998); *Continuum: Poems* (New York: W. W. Norton, 2009); and the posthumous collection of poems and drawings *The Avant-garde Doesn't Die and Never Surrenders* (New York: New Meridian Arts, 2016). She was the translator of *Romanian Poems by Paul Celan* (Rhinebeck, NY: Sheep Meadow Press, 2015). [T.N.]

32. Vladimir Colin (1921–91), of Jewish origin like Nina Cassian (his wife until 1948), was a Romanian translator and writer of short stories, fantasy novels, and fairy tales, and was regarded as the master of science fiction in Romanian literature. His work has been translated into several languages. In English, see *Legends from VamLand*, adapted by Luiza Carol (London: Center for Romanian Studies, 2000). [T.N.]

33. Horia Deleanu (1919–98), a good friend of Celan's, was a Romanian playwright, theater critic, and translator. In his volume *Întâlniri memorabile*

(Memorable Encounters) (Bucharest: Hasefer, 1995), he dedicates a chapter to "Paul Celan, poetul îndurerat" (Paul Celan, the Anguished Poet), in which he writes about his friendship with Celan. [T.N.]

34. Ovid S. Crohmălniceanu (1921–2000) was an important Romanian literary critic and historian. [T.N.]

35. It was thanks to Kraft that a volume containing almost one hundred poems Celan wrote in Czernowitz during 1934–44 was published in 1985: *Paul Celan, Gedichte. 1938–1944*, intro. by Ruth Kraft (Frankfurt am Main: Suhrkamp Verlag, 1985). This volume, which was admirably edited and contains facsimiles of the original texts written by the young poet himself for Ruth Kraft, sheds an unwonted light on the early poetry of Celan, although some of them had been published before in various journals or even in the debut volume *Der Sand aus den Urnen*. What appears particularly important to me is the fact that the volume goes beyond the recently imposed limits upon Celan's work, enriching it with early pages that had remained outside the "canon." I would also like to mention the publication, also in 1985, of the volume *Antschel Paul—Paul Celan*, by Barbara Wiedemann-Wolf (Tübingen: Max Niemeyer Verlag, 1985), a doctoral dissertation on the early work of Celan, including what he wrote in Bucharest. [A.N.]

36. Solomon alludes here to the aforementioned observation (p. 12) made by Jules Supervielle, according to which "memories are [made] of wind, they invent clouds." [T.N.]

## 1. Bucharest in the Time of Paul Celan

1. Valéry Larbaud, "Des villes et encore des villes," in *Les Poésies de A. O. Barnaboot* (Paris: Gallimard, 1966). [A.N.]

2. Paul Morand, *Bucarest* (Paris: Librairie Plon, 1935), 285–86. [A.N.]

3. Morand, *Bucarest*, 291. [A.N.]

4. Grigore Ionescu, *Bucureşti. Ghid istoric şi artistic* (Bucharest: Historical and Artistic Guide) (Bucharest: Fundaţia Regală pentru Literatură şi Artă, 1938), 51. [A.N.]

5. Morand, *Bucarest*, 124. [A.N.]

6. Constantin Bacalbaşa (1856–1935) was a Romanian journalist, memorialist, and politician. He wrote *Bucureştii de altădată* (The Bucharest of Yore) in four volumes between 1927 and 1932. He was the author of another volume of memoirs, *Capitala sub ocupaţia duşmanului* (1921) (Bucharest in the Time of the German Occupation), in which he described the atmosphere in the Romanian capital in 1916, after the arrival of the German troops. It is regarded as an important testimony to the World War I experience. [T.N.]

7. Constantin Bacalbaşa, *Bucureştii de altădată* (Bucharest: Editura Ziarului Universul, 1935), 1:64. [A.N.]

8. A small-time Romanian industrialist, Valentin Alexandrescu, who had helped many Jews from Czernowitz to escape deportation, offered to hide the Antschel family in his little factory, but Paul's mother refused. Convinced that his parents would join him later, Paul went to that hiding place alone. When he returned home, he found that his parents had been deported. See Israel Chalfen, *Paul Celan: A Biography of His Youth*, 147. [A.N.]

9. Chalfen, *Paul Celan: A Biography of His Youth*, 159. [A.N.]

10. Ibid., 157. [A.N.]

11. Marcel Aderca (1920–2008), a Romanian writer and translator, worked for Cartea Rusă between 1945 and 1948. [T.N.]

12. Felix Aderca (1891–1962) was a Romanian novelist, playwright, poet, journalist, and critic. An important figure in Romanian modernism, he opposed narrow traditional approaches to literature (increasingly popular after World War II), anti-Semitism, and the impositions of the Communist regime. [T.N.]

13. Allusion to Simone de Beauvoir's autobiographical book *La force de choses* (Paris: Gallimard, 1963). English edition: *Force of Circumstance*, trans. Richard Howard (London: Penguin Books, 1968). This idea is reiterated in Petre Solomon's autobiographical volume, published posthumously and titled precisely *Un Personaj care-mi poartă numele. Colaj memorialistic 1923–1947* (A Character that Bears My Name. A Collage of Memoirs 1923–1947) (Bucharest: Humanitas, 2016). Although writing in the first person, Petre Solomon specifies at the beginning that the person he used to be is like a character hiding beneath the written pages, and confesses to be very much intrigued by him. Solomon also cites Rimbaud's famous dictum *Je est un autre*, under whose sign he writes his volume of memoirs. Solomon, *Un personaj*, 10. [T.N.]

14. Antonescu's regime lasted from 1940 to 1944, when Romania, caught between Hitler's Germany and Stalin's Russia, became an ally of the former. Ion Antonescu (1882–1946) was appreciated by Hitler for his skills in military strategy. He is considered by some to be a war criminal and by others to be a national hero who managed to preserve the sovereignty of the Romanian state during World War II. He sent tens of thousands of Jews to death camps in Transnistria, but he also prevented the deaths of thousands of others (the number of Jews who survived under his rule is higher than in any of the other Axis powers). In 1946, he was convicted of war crimes and executed. For more on this controversial figure, see, for example, Dennis Deletant, *Hitler's Forgotten Ally: Ion Antonescu and His Regime, Romania 1940–1944* (Hampshire: Palgrave Macmillan, 2006). [T.N.]

15. Ury Benador (1895–1971), a Romanian playwright and novelist, was the secretary of the State Jewish Theater during 1950–55. [T.N.]

16. Of Jewish descent, Alexandru Graur (1900–88) was one of the most important Romanian linguists. Between 1941 and 1944, the anti-Semitic policies forbade students and teachers to attend public schools and universities, so he founded the Jewish Private High School. He received several national and international prizes for his research and activity in linguistics. [T.N.]

17. Mihail Sebastian (1907–45) was a Romanian playwright, journalist, and novelist. His *Journal* (originally published as *Jurnal. 1935–1944* [Bucharest: Humanitas, 1995]) is a masterly testimony to the dark decade of anti-Semitism in Romania. It is a chronicle of personal experiences as well as of the social and political life in Bucharest in the years 1935 to 1944. The passages that quote the anti-Semitic discourses of intellectuals he had admired (as was the case, for example, of Nae Ionescu) are particularly poignant. In recent years, his writings have gained international recognition. For English editions, see *For Two Thousand Years*, trans. Philip Ó Ceallaigh (London: Penguin, 2016); *Journal 1935–1944: The Fascist Years*, trans. Patrick Camiller (Chicago: Ivan R. Dee, 2000), or *The Accident*, trans. Stephen Henighan (Windsor: Biblioasis, 2011). [T.N.]

18. Ovidiu Constantinescu (1914–93) was a Romanian novelist and translator. [T.N.]

19. Eugen Lovinescu (1881–1943), an important representative of Romanian modernism, was a literary critic and historian, playwright, and novelist. His critical ideas greatly influenced approaches to literary criticism in Romania in the twentieth century. [T.N.]

20. Ahasuerus is the name that, in several biblical texts and legends, refers to "the wandering Jew." [T.N.]

21. Of Jewish origin, Saşa Pană (1902–81) was a Romanian avant-garde poet, novelist, and short story writer. [T.N.]

22. Tudor Arghezi (1880–1967) is one of the most appreciated poets in Romania. His poetry is often a lyrical rendering of the spiritual problems of the twentieth century. He has been translated into many languages and received several national and international prizes. Among his translators were Neruda, Rafael Alberti, and Quasimodo. Paul Celan translated into German two of his poems, "Între două nopţi" (Between Two Nights) from the volume *Cuvinte potrivite* (Fitting Words), and "Transfigurare" (Transfiguration) from the volume *Versuri de seară* (Evening Verses). For an English edition of his poetry, see *Selected Poems of Tudor Arghezi*, trans. Michael Impey and Brian Swann (Princeton: Princeton Univ. Press, 2015). [T.N.]

23. George Călinescu (1899–1965) was one of the most important literary critics in Romania. [T.N.]

24. Geo Dumitrescu (1920–2004) was a Romanian poet and translator. [T.N.]

25. Mihail Sadoveanu (1880–1961), a prolific novelist, short-story writer, and journalist, was one of the most appreciated representatives of realism in Romanian literature. He was a heavily built man, hence Solomon's allusion to the creaking wood. [T.N.]

26. Traian Cerbu (1898–1949) was a Communist militant and manager of Cartea Rusă. [T.N.]

27. Armand Popper (1916–76) was a founding member of the Jewish Democratic Committee in 1945, manager of Cartea Rusă from 1950 onward, and later vice-president of the State Committee for Arts and Culture. [T.N.]

28. Dolfi Trost (1916–66) was a Romanian Surrealist poet and theorist. He was one of the founders of the Bucharest Surrealist group, which included poets such as Gherasim Luca, Gellu Naum, Paul Păun, and Virgil Teodorescu. He created entopic graphomania, a drawing method that consists of marking a sheet of paper with dots where it appears to have impurities, then linking these dots in order to obtain the drawing. [T.N.]

29. Of Jewish descent, Paul Păun (1915–94) was a Romanian avant-garde poet who wrote in both Romanian and French. He joined the Surrealist group in the late 1930s and contributed to various literary journals. After Communism came to power, he found himself persecuted by the Communist censors, so he left for Israel, dedicating the rest of his life to his medical career, with only sporadic returns to literature. He died in Israel in 1994, two months almost to the day from Gherasim Luca's suicide in Paris. [T.N.]

30. Silvian Iosifescu (1917–2006), a Romanian literary critic and translator, wrote some twenty-five books of criticism and translated from French and English literature. [T.N.]

31. Petre Solomon seems to allude here to Urmuz, a writer much appreciated by Celan, whose *Bizarre Pages* contains many instances of antagonistic confrontation between characters. [T.N.]

32. Cezar Petrescu (1892–1961), a novelist, translator and journalist, was one of the most important literary figures in the interwar period in Romania. [T.N.]

33. Andrei Oțetea (1894–1977) was a Romanian historian. He edited *The History of the Romanian People*, published in English in 1970 by Twayne Publishers. [T.N.]

34. Alexandru Rosetti (1895–1990) was one of the most important philologists and linguists in Romania. His major work was *Istoria limbii române* (The History of the Romanian Language), and he made a considerable contribution to the development of the "linguistics school" in Bucharest. [T.N.]

35. Iorgu Iordan (1888–1986) was a Romanian philologist, journalist, linguist, and diplomat (he was the Romanian ambassador to Moscow during 1945–47).

Along with Alexandru Rosetti and others, he promoted the development of the field of linguistics in Romania. [T.N.]

36. Otilia Cazimir (1894–1967) was a Romanian poet and prose writer. She published over sixty volumes of poetry and received several literary prizes. She is particularly well known for her poems for children. [T.N.]

37. George Lesnea (1902–92) was a Romanian poet and translator. [T.N.]

38. Ion Biberi (1904–90) was a Romanian prose writer, essayist, and literary critic. Having encyclopaedic knowledge in several fields, he practiced and promoted an interdisciplinary approach to literature. [T.N.]

39. Radu Tudoran (1910–92) was one of the most popular novelists of the twentieth century in Romania and a translator of Russian writers. [T.N.]

40. Ion Călugăru (1902–56) was a Romanian novelist, journalist, and critic. [T.N.]

41. Octav Şuluţiu (1909–49) was a Romanian writer and literary critic. His prose was written in the confessional style practiced by other writers of the time, such as Max Blecher or Mihail Sebastian. [T.N.]

42. Eugen Schileru (1916–68) was a Romanian art and literary critic, essayist, and translator. [T.N.]

43. See pp. 124–25.

44. Chalfen, *Paul Celan: A Biography of His Youth*, 67–68. [A.N.]

45. In a short essay, Horia Deleanu recounts his memories of Celan: their first encounter during the war, their student years at the University of Czernowitz, the horror of the war experience, how Celan saved Deleanu's mother by sending her a letter in which he stated that Deleanu was alive, their reunion in Bucharest, and the time they spent together reading the Russian masters (Dostoevsky, Pushkin, Gogol), by whom Celan was fascinated. Deleanu confesses that what has always impressed him in Celan was the latter's "ability of not allowing horror to obscure the importance of poetry; on the contrary, the horror which was accumulating in the world at that time and which possessed Celan, too, more than once, became, under the transformative power of his talent, fascinating poetic images, thus adding intense subtlety to the value of his writing." Horia Deleanu, "Paul Celan, poetul îndurerat" (Paul Celan, the Aggrieved Poet), in *Întâlniri memorabile*, 184–85. [T.N.]

46. Benjamin Fundoianu (1898–1944), more widely known as Benjamin Fondane, was a Romanian poet, critic, and philosopher who wrote in Romanian and French. He moved to Paris in 1923 but continued to collaborate with Romanian avant-garde journals. His exile was marked by the difficulty of writing in French. He was deported from Paris and died in the gas chambers of Auschwitz-Birkenau in 1944. His friend Emil Cioran dedicated to him an "exercise in admiration," in which he offers the contours of his intellectual and spiritual profile. Emil Cioran,

*Exercitii de admiratie. Eseuri si Portrete* (Exercises in Admiration. Essays and Portraits), trans. Emanoil Marcu (Bucharest: Humanitas, 2003), 157–65. He was much appreciated by writers such as Benedetto Croce, Miguel de Unamuno, Miguel Angel Asturias, Jean Cocteau, Jean Cassou, Marcel Raymond, and Raymond Aron. His life and poetry (especially the poems about rural life in Moldavia) had a powerful impact on Paul Celan. For English editions, see, for example, *Ulysses*, trans. Nathaniel Rudavsky-Brody (Syracuse: Syracuse Univ. Press, 2017), or *Existential Monday*, trans. Bruce Baugh (New York: NYRBC, 2016). [T.N.]

47. Of Jewish origin like his friend Benjamin Fundoianu/Fondane, Ilarie Voronca (1903–46) was an avant-garde poet who wrote in Romanian and French. His work was neglected during the anti-Semitic regime in the 1930s and the early 1940s. Starting in 1945, both Voronca and Fundoianu received much attention in the literary circles Celan frequented during his stay in Bucharest. Too much aggrieved by having lost many relatives and friends in the Holocaust, Voronca committed suicide in France in 1946. [T.N.]

48. Alexandru Philippide, *Scrieri* (Writings), vol. 4 (Bucharest: Minerva Publishing House, 1978), 291. [A.N.]

49. The Aeolian harp was a much-used motif in Romanticism (see, for instance, Coleridge's poem "The Eolian Harp," 1796). The expression also recalls Walter Benjamin's famous essay "The Task of the Translator," where Benjamin, referring to Hölderlin's translations, observes that "in them, the harmony of the languages is so profound that sense is touched by language only the way an Aeolian harp is touched by the wind." Walter Benjamin, *Selected Writings. Volume I 1913–1926*, ed. Marcus Bullock and Michael W. Jennings (Cambridge: Belknap Press of Harvard Univ. Press, 2002), 262. [T.N.]

50. Mihai Eminescu (1850–89) was a Romanian poet, novelist, and journalist. He is the national poet of Romania and the last great Romantic poet in Europe. For English editions of his poetry, see, for example, Mihai Eminescu, *Poems*, trans. Corneliu Popescu (Bucharest: Cartea Românească, 1989), or *The Legend of the Evening Star*, trans. Adrian George Sahlean (Newton: Prospero Press, 2014). [T.N.]

51. Alfred Kittner (1906–91) was a German-language poet and prose writer, born, like Celan, in Czernowitz. [T.N.]

52. Here, as elsewhere, Petre Solomon does not include reference to the original text from which the quotation is taken. [T.N.]

53. Petre Solomon alludes here to a volume of poetry by Benjamin Fundoianu/Fondane titled *Privelişti* (Sights), published in 1930, which revolutionized the Romanian poetic sensibility, and which Celan admired. [T.N.]

54. Ioana Postelnicu (1910–2004) was a Romanian novelist and short story writer. [T.N.]

55. Eusebiu Camilar (1910–65) was a Romanian writer and translator and a member of the Romanian Academy. [T.N.]

56. Eugen Barbu (1924–93) was a popular Romanian novelist and controversial political figure. [T.N.]

57. Ion Barbu (1895–1961) was a poet and mathematician, and one of the most important representatives of the Romanian literary modernism, along with Tudor Arghezi, Lucian Blaga, and George Bacovia. [T.N.]

58. As Georges Bataille observes, the inquiry was opened by the Communist weekly *Action* shortly after World War II and was entirely unanticipated—no previous articles or comments had led to such a question. The name of the paper itself recalls one of the fundamental communist principles: the idea that a change in the world can be effected only through action—purposeful, authoritative action. Existential problems, doubts, or deformities are to be completely ignored in this pursuit of achieving goals through action. Kafka's writings are at the opposite pole of communist logic. See Bataille, "Kafka," in *Literature and Evil*, trans. Alastair Hamilton (London: Calder and Boyars, 1973), 125–45. [T.N.]

59. Tudor Vianu (1897–1964) was an important literary critic and historian who wrote extensively on stylistics, aesthetics, and the influence of (Western) philosophy on Romanian culture. [T.N.]

60. Ion Marin Sadoveanu (1893–1964) was a Romanian novelist and playwright. [T.N.]

61. Oscar Walter Cisek (1897–1966) was a Romanian writer, art critic, poet, and essayist who wrote both in Romanian and in German. [T.N.]

62. Iţic Manger (1901–69) was a Jewish writer considered to have revolutionized Yiddish literature in the interwar period. Born in Czernowitz, like Celan, he lived in many countries, among them Romania, Poland, the United States, and Israel. For an English edition, see, for example, Itzic Manger, *The World According to Itzic: Selected Poetry and Prose*, trans. and ed. Leonard Wolf (New Haven: Yale Univ. Press, 2002). [T.N.]

## 2. The Poet's Friends and Lovers

1. ". . . But I had, long ago, poet friends: it was between '45 and '47, in Bucharest. I will never forget them." [T.N.]

2. Reference to the quotation from Paul Morand in chapter 1 (p. 17). [T.N.]

3. The equivalent of "derilious" is the nonce word *derilă*, which does not exist in the Romanian language; this is probably Celan's playful anagrammatic softening of "delirious." It could also be a playful construction of the opposite of "sane," namely "derailed." [T.N.]

4. "De–a—d," *Zeitschrift für Kulturaustausch* (Journal of Cultural Exchange) 3 (1982): 213. [A.N.]

5. Constantin Stere (1865–1936) was a Romanian writer, politician, and jurist. [T.N.]

6. Gib Mihăescu (1894–1935) was a Romanian novelist and playwright. His novels and short stories are characterized by sharp psychological analysis. His last novel, *Donna Alba* (1935), is largely autobiographical and describes the writer's experiences during the First World War. [T.N.]

7. Eugen Simion, *Scriitori români de azi* (Contemporary Romanian Writers) (Bucharest: Cartea Românească, 1984), 3:585. [A.N.]

8. Simion, *Scriitori*, 585. [A.N.]

9. A diminutive of Petre Solomon's first name. [T.N.]

10. Siegbert Prawer, *Über Paul Celan*, ed. Meinecke, 143. [A.N.]

11. John Felstiner, "The Biography of a Poem," *New Republic*, April 2, 1984. [A.N.]

Reprinted in John Felstiner, *Paul Celan: Poet, Survivor, Jew* (New Haven: Yale Univ. Press, 2011), 28. [T.N.]

12. Heinrich Stiehler, "Die Zeit der Todesfuge," *Akzente* (Munich, Feb. 1972). [A.N.]

13. John Felstiner, "Paul Celan: The Strain of Jewishness," *Commentary* 79(4) (Apr. 1985): 44–55. [A.N.]

Reprinted in Felstiner, *Paul Celan: Poet, Survivor, Jew*, 28–30. [T.N.]

14. The word used in the original text is *dor* ("muzică de dor"), which is difficult to translate into English, since it does not have a suitable equivalent. The Romanian philosopher Constantin Noica emphasizes the primordial significance of this word in Romanian language and culture. *Dor*, Noica points out, encompasses opposite feelings—pain/sorrow and pleasure, seeking and nonfinding. These opposing terms combine to form the word *dor*, which denotes a sort of unexplainable "rational harmony." This word is a synthesis, the result of fusion, of blending, and not of composition, of joining together of two or more words, as is the case with other languages such as Greek or German. Constantin Noica, *Sentimentul românesc al ființei* (The Sense of Being in Romanian Culture) (Bucharest: Humanitas, 1996), 54–56. *Dor* denotes a complex spiritual experience, one that involves profound longing, the sorrow caused by the unfulfillment of that longing, as well as the acute awareness of the impossibility of that fulfillment. This bundle of seemingly contradictory feelings is marked by a tinge of pleasure, derived from the longing itself. It is often employed in a context of nostalgically summoning up, in one's mind, a temporally or spatially remote sense of well-being, a loved person, now absent, or some other previous experience of joy or bliss. Etymologically, the

word derives from the Latin *dolus*, which means "pain." The verb *a dori* (to want/ to desire) derives from *dor*.

Noica (1909–87) was one of the most important Romanian philosophers. Under Communism, he was arrested in 1958 and sentenced to twenty-five years of forced labor at Jilava. He served six years of his sentence before his release in 1964. He made a major contribution to the development of philosophy in Romania, influencing thinkers such as Gabriel Liiceanu and Andrei Pleşu. He wrote many philosophical studies—on Descartes, Kant, Hegel, Plato, and others—as well as a series of treatises on the characteristics of Romanian philosophical thought and on the ontological perspectives inherent in the Romanian language. [T.N.]

15. In his presentation at the 1981 Celan conference in Bucharest, Crohmălniceanu would confess, among other things, that the acceptance of Celan's poem for publication "was a real surprise for our small group, because we knew that he frequented Gherasim Luca and Paul Păun and did not hesitate to use Surrealist imagery." Since the first question the editorial board of *Contemporanul* asked about any poem was "What does the author mean?" Crohmălniceanu explains the acceptance of Celan's poem thus: "Maybe its success was due to the direct confession it contained about a horrid reality . . . Or maybe he was thought to be some kind of stranger, one of the few survivors of the Nazi camps. Whatever the reason, I have not heard the usual observations about the obscurity of poetry." (see *Zeitschrift für Kulturaustausch*, 213). [A.N.]

16. See Felstiner, "Paul Celan: The Strain of Jewishness." [A.N.]

17. In 1921, Alexandru Buican (Arnoldi) was one of the militants who, in Bucharest, formed the executive committee of the Romanian Socialist-Communist Party. He and thirteen other militants of Bessarabian and Bukovinian origin participated as delegates at the Third Congress of the Comintern, held in Moscow between June and July the same year. See Vladimir Tismaneanu, *Stalinism for All Seasons: A Political History of Romanian Communism* (Berkeley: Univ. of California Press, 2003), especially chapter 2, "A Messianic Sect: The Underground Romanian Communist Party, 1921–1944," 37–85. Later, Buican graduated from the International Lenin School in Moscow in the 1930s, fought in the French resistance, and was a survivor of the Nazi camps. After the war, he was appointed vice president of the Institute for Cultural Relations with Foreign Countries. He was one of the most active supporters of the Soviet propaganda in Bucharest, infiltrating it into all possible media, including *Scânteia*, the newspaper of the Romanian Communist Party. Before starting work as a translator for Cartea Rusă publishing house, Celan worked at *Scânteia* for a short period of time. His job consisted of translating from the Russian propagandistic periodicals *Pravda* and *Izvestia* into Romanian. Celan—who had left Czernowitz because it had become Communist under Soviet Union domination—found it hard to endorse the

Communist propaganda, even indirectly. Dissatisfied with his work (and, probably, his non-Communist attitude as well), Buican fired young Antschel from *Scânteia*. Crohmălniceanu recalls how Buican—a very dark character, to say the least—developed a veritable hostility toward Celan, which persisted even after Celan no longer worked at *Scânteia*. When he found out that Celan was working at Cartea Rusă, he called the manager and warned him that he had hired an enemy of the working class. See Andrei Corbea-Hoisie, *Paul Celan: Biographie und Interpretation/Biographie et Interprétation* (Iaşi: Polirom, 2000), 70–71. [T.N.]

18. Quoted in John Felstiner, "Paul Celan: The Strain of Jewishness." [A.N.]

19. Sanda Movilă (1900–70) was a Romanian poet and novelist. [T.N.]

20. Veronica Porumbacu (1921–77) was a Romanian poet, prose writer, and translator of Jewish extraction. Especially in the 1950s, her work, of little aesthetic merit, supported the popular Communist topics of the time. [T.N.]

21. Baudelaire, in the chapter "L'Art romantique" in *L'École païenne*; see Œuvres, Pléiade, 1954, 980. [A.N.]

Here, Baudelaire deplores the emotional aloofness and the excessive preoccupation with form in the artists who belonged to the school of "art for art's sake"—to the detriment of morality, truth, even passion. Such an "immoderate taste for form" (le goût immodéré de la forme) leads to a sterile art. [T.N.]

22. Breton wrote in *L'Amour fou* (Paris: Gallimard, 1937): "Each love clarifies the image of the loved woman, the last of them being the outcome of a lifetime." The Surrealist poets exalted love with an obsessional insistence, visible in the titles of many of their works, such as *L'Amour et la poésie* (Éluard), *La Liberté ou l'amour* (Desnos), *Anthologie de l'amour sublime* (Benjamin Peret), and many others. [A.N.]

23. Matzo (Yiddish: *matsah*; Hebrew: *matsa*), part of Jewish cuisine and a key element of the Passover festival, is the name given to an unleavened flatbread. [T.N.]

24. George Rafael (1920–85) was a Romanian theater director. He staged many plays written by important playwrights of the time, such as Eugene Ionesco and Mihail Sebastian. [T.N.]

25. Mihail Petroveanu (1923–77), called "Milo" by Celan in the letter he sent to Petre Solomon from Vienna, was a Romanian literary critic and historian. [T.N.]

26. The Iron Guard (also called the Legionnaire movement) was a radical political organization that promoted its radical agenda of nationalism, anti-Semitism, and anti-Communism by combining its political ideology with religious fanaticism. It was founded in 1927 by "Captain" Corneliu Zelea Codreanu, and was in power for a short period of time (Sep. 1940–Jan. 1941), which was marked by "a frantic attempt to carry out, using murderous violence, what the historian Eugen Weber called the archangelic revolution." Vladimir Tismaneanu, *The Devil in History:*

*Communism, Fascism, and Some Lessons of the Twentieth Century* (Berkeley: Univ. of California Press, 2012), 224–25. [T.N.]

27. See chapter 5 (p. 128). [T.N.]

28. Quoted by Bianca Rosenthal, in her presentation at the Celan Conference in Bucharest 1981. See *Zeitschrift für Kulturaustausch* 3 (1982), 230. [A.N.]

The title of Rosenthal's essay is "Quellen zum frühen Paul Celan: Der Alfred Margul-Sperber-Nachlass in Bukarest." [T.N.]

29. I have kept from those years a copy of the splendid poem "Heaven," by the English poet Rupert Brooke (1887–1915), a copy transcribed by Celan's hand. He had a good knowledge of English poetry, which was my field, but I was more interested in "social poetry." Celan got me acquainted with other aspects of English literature. [A.N.]

30. Ion Pillat (1891–1945) was an important Romanian poet, essayist and anthologist. [T.N.]

31. Alexandru Philippide, *Considerații confortabile* (Comfortable Considerations) (Bucharest: Eminescu Publishing House, 1970), 223. [A.N.]

32. Sașa Pană, *Născut în '02* (Born in '02) (Bucharest: Minerva Publishing House, 1973), 620. [A.N.]

33. Apart from the already mentioned translations from Chekhov, Lermontov, and so on, I would like to mention an article published under the name "Paul Ancel" in *Revista Literară* 5 (1947), under the heading "The Review of Reviews." In that article, Paul presented some news from Russian literature: a recent study of Dostoevsky, written by the critic V. Alexandrov, commended by Paul because "it throws a somewhat new light" on Dostoevsky's literary work, presenting it as that of a sometimes "lucid, clear-sighted and prophetic utopian" but also of a man whose eyes are often clouded by the prejudices, ill will, and ignorance of the people around him; a volume of poetry by S. Marsak; and an essay published in the journal *Zvezda*, celebrating the 125th anniversary of the birth of Nekrasov, "a fierce adversary of the apologists of pure art in last century's Russia." Although the presentations are kept within the limits of the views formulated by the respective authors, the emphasis placed by Paul Celan illustrate some of the convictions he held at that time. [A.N.]

34. Chalfen, *Paul Celan: Eine Biographie seiner Jugend*, 147–48. [A.N.]

35. Ion Caraion (1923–86) was an important Romanian poet, essayist, and translator. With Virgil Ierunca, he founded *Agora*, where Celan published some poems during his stay in Bucharest. He died in Switzerland, where he had emigrated in 1981 due to persecution in Romania. Some of his work has been translated into French, German, and English. [T.N.]

36. An old Romanian ballad, one of the most important ballads in Romanian folk poetry. [T.N.]

37. Lucian Blaga (1895–1961) was one of the most important figures in the Romanian culture of the interwar period. A poet, philosopher, playwright, and novelist, he suffered persecution by the Communist regime because he refused to support its ideology and practices. His work has been extensively translated into English; see, for example, *Complete Poetical Works of Lucian Blaga, 1985–1961* (Unesco Collection of Representative Works), trans. Brenda Walker and Stelian Apostolescu (London: Centre for Romanian Studies, 2001). [T.N.]

38. Quoted by Uwe Martin in a long and well-documented article on Celan's first volume of poetry: "*Der Sand aus den Urnen.* Zu Paul Celans erster Gedichtsammlung," in *Cahiers d'études germaniques* (Université de Provence, Centre d'Aix) 7 (45) (1983): 46–67. [A.N.]

## 3. The Beautiful Season of Wordplay

1. André Breton, "Premier Manifeste," *La révolution surréaliste* 2 (1929). [A.N.]

2. Roman Jakobson, *Essais de linguistique générale* (Paris: Éditions du Minuit, 1963), 86. [A.N.]

For the English version of Jakobson's discussion of puns, see Roman Jakobson, "On Linguistic Aspects of Translation," in *Selected Writings II: Word and Language* (The Hague: Mouton, 1971), 266. [T.N.]

3. Pierre Guiraud, *Les Jeux de mots (Que sais-je?)* (Paris: Presses Universitaires Françaises, 1976). [A.N.]

4. Guiraud, *Les Jeux de mots*, 87–91. [A.N.]

5. Ibid., 113–19. [A.N.]

6. Oscar Lemnaru (1907–68) was a Romanian journalist, novelist, and translator, of Jewish descent. [T.N.]

7. Geo Dumitrescu wrote the volume *Libertatea de a trage cu puşca* during the years 1940–43, but, because of certain petty judges whom circumstances had brought to power, it could not be published until 1946, in a limited edition. As the poet himself specifies on the cover of a later edition (1966), these poems were a form of protest against injustice and horror, of resistance to the dictatorship and its odious war, as well as a reaction against the literature of the time, which extolled the virtues of fascism. They represent, Dumitrescu confesses, "the message of young impatience, anxious for communication," and the result of "an immediate cry in search of an echo." Here are the first two stanzas of the poem that gave the volume its title: "În groapa neagră, poate chiar într-un cimitir, / oamenii, prietenii mei înarmaţi, îşi ascultau propriile şoapte—/ toţi erau murdari, slabi, şi patetici ca în Shakespeare, / îşi numărau gloanţele şi zilele şi nădăjduiau un atac peste noapte. // Atunci a ieşit luna, fără cască, de undeva din bezna ghimpată; / dar oamenii

n-au căzut cu fețele la pământ, / ci au aprins țigările, discutînd despre libertatea de a trage cu pușca, / rezemați comod în groapa neagră sau poate chiar pe cîte-o piatră de mormânt" (In the black hole, or rather, perhaps, in a graveyard, / the people, my armed friends, were listening to their own whispers—/ they were all dirty, emaciated, and pathetic as in Shakespeare, / counting their bullets and their days, hoping for an attack during the night. // At that moment, from somewhere in the thorny darkness, the moon came out, without a helmet; / but the people did not fall with their faces to the ground, / they lit their cigarettes, talking about the freedom to shoot a gun / leaning comfortably in the black hole or rather, perhaps, against some gravestone). Geo Dumitrescu, *Nevoia de cercuri. Libertatea de a trage cu pușca* (Bucharest: Editura pentru literatură, 1966), 170–71. [T.N.]

8. In a preface to the posthumous volume of essays by Robert Klein, André Chastel, who had worked with him in Paris for many years, emphasizes the competence and intellectual passion of the essayist from Romania, comparing him with Walter Benjamin—"a Benjamin who, early on, would find in Husserl the decisive stimulant, which the other had found in Marx." André Chastel, in his introduction to Robert Klein, *La Forme et l'intelligible* (Paris: Gallimard, 1970), 21. Like Celan, whom he knew, Robert Klein left Romania in 1947. An unsettling similarity between the two destinies: Klein committed suicide in Italy, in the spring of 1966; like Celan, he was almost fifty years old. [A.N.]

9. Isidore Isou (1925–2007) was a Romanian-born poet, film critic, and artist of Jewish origin. He moved to Paris in 1945, later becoming a naturalized French citizen. He was the founder of Lettrism, an artistic movement that was inspired by the principles and practice of Dada and Surrealism. Kaira M. Cabañas observes: "If Dada reduced poetry to phonemes (the smallest sound unit that forms meaningful contrasts between utterances), the Lettrist endeavor hinged on the question of bodily intonation, explored as a means by which to divide a phoneme's articulation internally. The Lettrists proposed a manner for the production of such sounds, by way of tongue clicks, hiccups, coughs, growls, and lisps." Cabañas, *Off-Screen Cinema: Isidore Isou and the Lettrist Avant-Garde* (Chicago: Univ. of Chicago Press, 2014), 10–12. The basic principle of Lettrist poetry consists of the fact that the propositional content of language is displaced by the physicality of the utterance and the immediacy of aural sensation. [T.N.]

10. A "language" created by Nina Cassian, in which certain words or syllables are Romanian, but many others are invented by herself; thus, the lines escape the construal of any recognizable meaning. [T.N.]

11. The pseudonym of the leader of the Dada movement (born Samuel Rosenstock) derives from the Romanian expression *trist în țară* (sad in my country). [T.N.]

12. This pun is based on the polysemy of the Romanian word *somn*, which means both "sleep" and "sheatfish." Literally, it would translate thus: "I want to sleep.—Sleep or sheatfish?" [T.N.]

13. In 1935, Salvador Dalí wrote a poem titled "Je Mange Gala" (Gala being his wife). Maybe Celan was not thinking of the famous Surrealist painter but was simply employing a common way of speaking in Romanian, in which the verb "to eat" also denotes visual pleasure and attraction. [A.N.]

14. "L'image est une création pure de l'esprit. / Elle ne peut naître d'une comparaison mais du rapprochement de deux réalités plus ou moins éloignées. / Plus les rapports des deux réalités rapprochées seront lointains et justes, plus l'image sera forte—plus elle aura de puissance émotive et de réalité poétique"; Pierre Reverdy, *Nord-Sud* (Mar. 1918), quoted by André Breton, *Manifeste du Surréalisme* (1924; Paris: Gallimard, 1963), 31. [A.N.]

15. Marin Mincu, *Avangarda literară românească* (Bucharest: Minerva, 1983), 52. [A.N.]

16. Quoted by Marin Mincu in the introduction to *Avangarda Literară Românească*, from a text by Breton, "Devant le rideau," in *Le Surréalisme en 1947* (Paris: Éditions Pierre-à-feu, 1947), 15. Marin Mincu also quotes Jean-Louis Bédouin, who praised the Romanian Surrealists for their contribution to the International Exhibition in Paris, 1947, a contribution defined in relation to their effort to invent "new desires." [A.N.]

17. The death of Surrealism had been foretold by Saşa Pană, a representative of the "first wave," as early as 1945, when he published his *Poeme fără imaginaţie* (Unimaginative Poems), a title that he would explain later by the fact that "reality was more extraordinary than poetry" (see Pană, *Născut în '02*, 664). Even Maurice Nadeau, in his famous *Histoire du surréalisme*, considered that the movement had reached its end. [A.N.]

18. Gherasim Luca (1913–94) was a Romanian poet of Jewish descent. In the early 1950s, he moved to Paris, where he continued to write, in French, for the rest of his life. He was one of the founders of the Romanian Surrealist group (together with Gellu Naum, Paul Păun, Virgil Teodorescu, and Dolfi Trost). Like his friend Celan, he committed suicide by jumping into the river Seine, on March 10, 1994, leaving behind a last message (on the night of February 9), saying that he chose to leave "this world, because there is no place for poets in it." Although most of his texts are available in Romanian and French, some works by the Romanian Surrealist poet Gherasim Luca have recently been translated into English, enjoying widespread acclaim. See, for example, the volume *Self-Shadowing Prey*, trans. Mary Ann Caws (New York: Contra Mundum Press, 2012), or *Inventor of Love and Other Writings*, trans. Julian and Laura Semilian (Boston: Black Widow Press, 2009). [T.N.]

19. Gellu Naum (1915–2001), a Romanian essayist, translator, poet, playwright, and novelist, was one of the most important representatives of the Surrealist movement in Romania in 1941. After December 1947, due to the political situation in Romania (the press of the time published several articles against the Surrealists), the group dissolved, and many members of the group left the country. He continued to practice Surrealism until the end of his life. Of his work, Celan translated into German "Lanterna magică" (The Magic Lantern) and "Îmi place ca lupilor" (I Like It as Wolves Do). [T.N.]

20. Virgil Teodorescu (1909–87) was a Romanian poet, novelist, translator, member of the Romanian Surrealist group, and president of the Writers' Union of Romania (1974–78). [T.N.]

21. "The thought expressed in the stiff filaments of *silence* and *convulsion* precedes the impossible root, precedes it and follows it with the aid of a machine for lifting tons of glances and *all the fluid between the plants*." [T.N.]

22. Gilles Deleuze held Gherasim Luca's poetry in high regard and was fascinated by his theory of the "non-Oedipus." He compared Luca's poetry with the works of Kafka and Beckett. Together with Gilles Guattari, he studied closely the "non-Oedipal" approach to the Freudian conception of the dream, as elaborated by Luca and Trost (in their *First Non-Oedipal Manifesto*), as well as other Romanian Surrealist poets, who strove to find a form of expression that would resist Oedipal symbolism. Luca's poetry is filled with "non-Oedipal" references. [T.N.]

23. The passages from Gherasim Luca and Dolfi Trost are quoted here from the French text, published in Mincu's *Avangarda literară românească*, 625–34. [A.N.]

Luca and Dolfi's text was originally published as *Dialectique de la dialectique: Message adressé au mouvement surréaliste international* (Bucharest: Imprimeria Slova, Colecţia suprarealistă, 1945). [T.N.]

24. For more on cubomania, Gherasim Luca, and the Romanian Surrealist group in the 1940s, see, for example, Krzysztof Fijalkowski's essay "Cubomania: Gherasim Luca and Non-Oedipal Collage," *Dada/Surrealism* 20(1) (2015), DOI 10.17077/0084-9537.1301. [T.N.]

25. Chalfen, *Paul Celan: Eine Biographie seiner Jugend*, 150. [A.N.]

26. "non comme une nouvelle école artistique, mais comme un moyen de connaissance, en particulier de continents qui jusqu'ici n'avaient pas été systématiquement explorés: l'inconscient, le merveilleux, le rêve, la folie, les états hallucinatoires, en bref, l'envers du décor logique." Maurice Nadeau, "Deux documents intérieurs," in *Histoire du surréalisme* (Paris: Seuil, 1964), 43. [A.N.]

27. "L'humour, en tant que triomphe paradoxal du principe du plaisir sur les conditions réelles au moment où celles-ci sont jugées les plus défavorables, est naturellement appelé à prendre une valeur défensive à l'époque surchargée de menaces

que nous vivons." André Breton, "Limites non frontières du surréalisme," *La Nouvelle Revue Française* 25(281) (Feb. 1937): 205. [A.N.]

28. Breton, *Manifeste du surréalisme*, 42–43. [A.N.]

The original quote reads as follows: "Faites-vous apporter de quoi écrire, après vous être établi en un lieu aussi favorable que possible à la concentration de votre esprit sur lui-même. Placez-vous dans l'état le plus passif, ou réceptif, que vous pourrez. Faites abstraction de votre génie, de vos talents et de ceux de tous les autres. Dites-vous bien que la littérature est un des plus tristes chemins qui mènent à tout. Écrivez vite sans sujet préconçu, assez vite pour ne pas retenir et ne pas être tenté de vous relire. La première phrase viendra toute seule." [T.N.]

29. Gellu Naum and Virgil Teodorescu had published in Bucharest, in 1946, a chapbook titled *Spectrul longevității—122 de cadavre* (The Specter of Longevity—122 Corpses). [A.N.]

30. Marin Preda, *Delirul* (Bucharest: Cartea Românească, 1975), 172–94 passim. [A.N.]

31. Preda, *Delirul*, 192–93. [A.N.]

32. As Maurice Nadeau observed, "the Surrealist state of mind or, rather, the Surrealist behaviour, is eternal" (*Histoire du surrealism*, 4). [A.N.]

33. "Le surréalisme est le plus puissant explosif mental qu'on ait inventé. On peut dire, sans abuser des mots, qu'il tend à opérer dans le domaine du langage et des images, voire même des sensations, la plus fantastique réaction en chaîne." Michel Carrouges, *André Breton et les données fondamentales du surréalisme* (Paris: Gallimard/Nouvelle Revue Française, 1950), 139. [T.N.]

## 4. The Adolescence of a Farewell

1. Quoted in Constantin Noica, in his preface to his volume *Creație și frumos în rostirea românească* (Creation and Beauty in the Romanian Language) (Bucharest: Eminescu Publishing House, 1973). The quotation is from Eminescu's manuscript no. 2257, which is in the Romanian Academy Library. [A.N.]

2. See *Paul Celan: Selections*, ed. and intro. Joris, 149–54. [T.N.]

3. A. Alvarez, *Samuel Beckett* (New York: Viking Press, 1973), 40–41. [A.N.]

4. Speaking of Celan's relationship with the German language, Adrian Del Caro observes that his poetry "represents a watershed in the history of consciousness, because it ushers in a post-Holocaust consciousness. His German is antithetical to German nationalism and German nationalism's inherent Christian anti-Semitism, and it can be read as a style of German constantly at odds with German, as non-German rebuilding its home in German, as the effort to render German humane and not merely 'of and for Germans.' Celan's German cautions

us, at every turn, that a language may be hijacked, enslaved, and perverted by demagogues and ideologues, and this enslaved language may contribute to the genocide of those who are not 'of the Word.' Celan's German underscores the horrors inherent in language when it is divorced from humanity and elevated to the privileged discourse between mortals and God. Celan's mystic and surrealistic German alienates from the everyday in order to humanize speech, and the uncanny properties it displays are a deliberate, post-Holocaust strategy to address the fact that millions of innocent Jews and others will never have a resting place in the earth because of the fanatic hatred of a people bent by, and bent upon, having the last Word." Adrian Del Caro, "Paul Celan and the German of the Non-German," in *German Studies in the Post-Holocaust Age: The Politics of Memory, Identity, and Ethnicity*, ed. Adrian Del Caro and Janet Ward (Boulder: Univ. Press of Colorado, 2003), 119–20. [T.N.]

5. Constantin Noica, *Cuvînt împreună despre rostirea românească* (A Word Together about the Romanian Language) (Bucharest: Eminescu Publishing House, 1987), 268. [T.N.]

6. "Marianne" (*Der Sand aus den Urnen*, 1948), in Celan, *Gesammelte Werke in fünf Bänden*, ed. Beda Allemann and Stefan Reichert (Frankfurt am Main: Suhrkamp, 1983), 1:14. [A.N.]

7. George Steiner, *After Babel: Aspects of Language and Translation* (Oxford: Oxford Univ. Press, 1998), 166. [A.N.]

8. Steiner, *After Babel*, 167. [A.N.]

9. Ibid., 168. [A.N.]

10. Nina Cassian's bilingual volume *Romanian Poems by Paul Celan* contains an incorrect rendering: instead of *lacrima* (tear), Cassian's English version reads "crown," while in the original Romanian text, instead of the same word (*lacrima*), the word *crima* (crime) is wrongly used (pages 8 and 74, respectively). [T.N.]

11. Constantin Noica, *Sentimentul românesc al ființei* (The Sense of Being in Romanian Culture) (Bucharest: Eminescu Publishing House, 1996), 18–22. [A.N.]

12. Hugo Friedrich, *The Structure of Modern Poetry: From the Mid-Nineteenth to the Mid-Twentieth Century*, trans. Joachim Neugroschel (Evanston: Northwestern Univ. Press, 1974), 5. [A.N.]

13. Harald Weinrich, *Kontraktionen* (1968), reprinted in *Über Paul Celan*, ed. Meinecke (Frankfurt am Main: Suhrkamp, 1973), 216–17. [A.N.]

14. See Helmuth de Haas, "*Mohn und Gedächtnis*" (1953), in *Über Paul Celan*, ed. Meinecke, 32. [A.N.]

15. See Paul Schwarz, "Totengedächtnis und dialogische Polarität in der Lyrik Paul Celans" (1966), in *Über Paul Celan*, ed. Meinecke, 168–69. [A.N.]

16. Gellu Naum, *Castelul orbilor* (The Castle of the Blind) (Bucharest: Colecția suprarealistă, 1946), 18–26. [A.N.]

17. *Palatul Fermecat. Antologia poemului românesc în proză*, intro. and notes by M. Zamfir (Bucharest: Biblioteca pentru toţi, 1984), xiv–xviii. [A.N.]

18. Paul Celan, "A doua zi urmând să înceapă deportările," in *Antologia Poeziei Româneşti Culte de la Dosoftei până în 1993*, ed. Florin Şindrilaru (Bucharest: Teora, 1998), 532. [T.N.]

19. In the original Romanian text, Celan employs an unusual word order for this sentence, which would translate, literally, to "not this can be the sky," thus appearing to place emphasis on "this." [T.N.]

20. *The Diaries of Franz Kafka, Volume 2: 1914–1923*, ed. Max Brod, trans. Martin Greenberg with Hannah Arendt (London: Martin Secker and Warburg, 1949), 194 (Sunday, Oct. 16, 1919). [A.N.]

21. Friedrich observes that, in the twentieth-century poetry "dictatorial imagination . . . is the source of all transformation and/or destruction of the real world—and to such an extent that the products can be measured only heuristically rather than, in a definitive cognition, in terms of reality and the normal situation of mankind. Naturally, poetry has always blurred the distinction between 'it is' and 'it seems,' subjugating its material to the power of the versifying mind. But in the modern age, the world issuing from the creative imagination and sovereign language is an enemy of the real world." Friedrich, *Structure of Modern Poetry*, 161. [T.N.]

22. Elias Canetti, *The Tongue Set Free: Remembrance of a European Childhood* (Die gerettete Zunge: Geschichte einer Jugend), trans. Joachim Neugroschel (1977; trans. 1979; London: André Deutsch, 1988), 10. [A.N.]

23. Steiner, *After Babel*, 129–30. [A.N.]

24. Ibid., 132–33. [A.N.]

25. See, for example, Heidegger, who plays with all the semantic facets of German words to create new ones. Gabriel Liiceanu, who translated Heidegger into Romanian, observes that, through the German philosopher, "the entire language is brought to the level of philosophy and each word, however insignificant, is required to reflect and to mean, through the recovery of its original meaning, something different from what it normally means." Liiceanu, "Jurnal Heideggerian," *Secolul* 20 (1980), 234. "Pun-knowledge" takes the form, in Heidegger, of expressions, such as "das Dingsein des Dinges," "das Sich-ins-Werk-setzen," "Welt Weltet," "das Sich-zurückstellen," "das Hervorkommend-Bergende," "das Aufstellen der Welt und das Herstellen der Erde," etc. I have selected these examples from a study by the German philosopher, *Originea operei de artă* (The Origin of the Work of Art), translated into Romanian by Gabriel Liiceanu and Thomas Kleininger (Bucharest: Univers, 1982). The translators, often facing insurmountable translational difficulties, left the original expressions in brackets. Where they did not do so, the results were not the most felicitous. [A.N.]

26. "Poetry no longer imposes itself, it exposes itself." [A.N.]

27. Referring to this edition, *Gesammelte Werke in fünf Bänden*, Wolfgang Minaty wrote in *Die Welt* (Nov. 15, 1983) that it was not a critical edition, and wondered: "Do we have here everything about Celan? No. The letters are missing, for example, although they have been published several times, especially in fragments. The early poems in German and Romanian are missing as well. These were published once, somewhere far away. Finally, a commentary is lacking . . ." [A.N.]

## 5. Rebuilding the Bridges

1. Edward Snow translated this line as "Our lives pass in transformation" in Rainer Maria Rilke, *Duino Elegies: Bilingual Edition*, trans. Edward Snow (New York: North Point Press, 2001), 42, while William H. Gass offers a very different version: "Withinwards is everything," in "Rainer Maria Rilke: 'The Seventh Elegy,'" *Conjunctions* 32 (1999): 387. [T.N.]

2. Quoted by Milo Dor, "Paul Celan" (1970), in *Über Paul Celan*, ed. Meinecke, 282. [A.N.]

3. Here, Celan plays ingeniously with two Romanian words, *tărâm* (land), a noun with a masculine form in the singular, made up of two syllables (*tă-râm*), and *râmă* (worm), a feminine noun. By cutting off the first syllable of the word *tărâm* (the "head of the word," as he calls it further on), what remains is *râm*, to which he adds the feminine ending ă (hence the reference to "the shift from masculine to feminine"), obtaining the word *râmă*. Thus, in a bitterly playful way, he compares the country he is living in (Austria) to a worm, probably in order to convey the unpleasantness of his experiences there. [T.N.]

4. Mateiu Caragiale (1885–1936) was one of the most original of Romania's novelists. His most important work includes the novella *Remember* (Bucharest: Editura Art, 1921; rev. 2008) and the novel *Craii de Curtea-Veche* (Gallants of the Old Court), trans. Cristian Baciu (eLiteratura, 2013). [T.N.]

5. "The obsessive decade" is an expression coined by the Romanian novelist Marin Preda in an article of the same title, published in *Luceafărul* in 1970, later included in the volume of essays *Imposibila întoarcere* (The Impossible Return). In it, Preda shows how the literary works of the 1950s and even 1960s—belonging to the so-called genre of committed literature—reflect the political ideology of the time. One of the recurrent topics in that type of literature was that of class conflict, an idea artificially and deliberately promoted by Communist politicians and their supporters, with tragic consequences. The censorship of the time removed or modified certain paragraphs that were considered too dangerous. Although Preda uses the term "decade," his phrase can be extended to characterize the entire Communist period in Romania (1948–89). [T.N.]

6. Marin Preda, *Imposibila întoarcere* (Bucharest: Cartea Românească, 1971), 32. [A.N.]

7. Preda, *Imposibila întoarcere*, 34–35. [A.N.]

8. Ibid., 37–38. [A.N.]

9. Quoted by Milo Dor, "Paul Celan," in *Über Paul Celan*, ed. Meinecke, 285. [A.N.]

10. Paul Westheim (1886–1963) was a German art critic and historian associated with the Expressionist movement and known for his opposition to Nazism. [A.N.]

11. The correspondence between Paul Celan and Margul-Sperber was published in *Neue Literatür* (Bucharest, Jul. 7, 1975). [A.N.]

12. Uwe Martin, *Der Sand aus den Urnen*, in *Cahiers d'Études Germaniques* 7 (1983), 55. [A.N.]

13. The little book was published with a small Viennese publishing house, A. Sexl. [A.N.]

14. I owe Dr Victor Matejka, an Austrian journalist and historian, formerly responsible for cultural problems during the first postwar administration of Vienna, the information that Celan refused the job as librarian he had offered him. As anxious as he had been to arrive in Vienna, now Paul felt the urgent need to leave this metropolis, where he did not feel "in his element." [A.N.]

15. See *Neue Literatür* (Bucharest, Jul. 7, 1975): 55–56. [A.N.]

16. From Gellu Naum, Celan translated the poems "Îmi place ca lupilor" (I Like It as Wolves Do) and "Lanterna magică" (The Magic Lantern), and from Virgil Teodorescu "Castelana înecată" (The Drowned Chatelaine). [T.N.]

17. Celan translated from Arghezi "Între două nopți" (Between Two Nights) from the volume *Cuvinte potrivite* (Fitting Words), and "Transfigurare" (Transfiguration) from the volume *Versuri de seară* (Evening Verse). [T.N.]

18. Dobrogea is a region in the southeastern part of Romania, home to the Danube Delta. [T.N.]

19. This letter to Alfred Margul-Sperber was published in *Neue Literatür* (Bucharest, Jul. 7, 1975): 54–56. [A.N.]

Quoted in Felstiner, *Paul Celan: Eine Biographie* (Munich: C. H. Beck, 2000), 206. [T.N.]

20. The title recalls Ecclesiastes in the Bible, where the expression "pursuit of the wind" appears several times. [T.N.]

21. Claire Goll, *La Poursuite du vent* (Paris: Olivier Orban, 1976), 274. [A.N.]

22. See "Les racines de l'homme," a group review by Bertrand Poirot-Delpech of works by Claire Goll, Clara Malraux, and Patrick Modiano, *Le Monde* (Oct. 22, 1976): 15. [T.N.]

23. *Neue Literatür* (Bucharest, Jul. 7, 1975): 59. [A.N.]

24. The *Männerbund* (men's association) is a German term that originally referred to a group of male warriors in ancient Germanic tribes. This model of ritualistic brotherhood was used, in what appears to be a distorted interpretation, as the basis for the development of various groups and secret societies. Nazism, focusing on Männerbund-defining attitudes, such as masculine solidarity, manliness, and attitudes of superiority toward foreigners, used the cult as a model for the Sturmabteilung (a corporate militia of the German Nazi party) and for the Schutzstaffel (the SS). [T.N.]

25. Paul Celan, *Gedichte*, sel. Klaus Wagenbach and Paul Celan (Frankfurt am Main: S. Fischer Schulausgaben, 1962). An earlier, identically titled school edition issued by Fischer with exactly the same number of pages is also recorded for the year 1959. [T.N.]

26. In a letter he sent to Nina Cassian (dated Apr. 25, 1962, and written in French), Paul expressed his joy at "finding [her] again, after all these years": "Here I am, then, talking to you briefly . . . Believe me: everything I said about my 'case' is very true. But seen from afar, outside of its context, it must seem inconceivable to you. Still . . . I would like—the seasons passing by, as you say—to have the opportunity to talk to you face to face about all these things one day, to *show* you, to prove to you, black on white, that all these things are not a product of my imagination as a 'poet,' of my 'susceptibility as a solitary man.' Isn't Poetry progression towards Reality, which takes place amidst everything that surrounds and captivates us? To get involved—doesn't it mean, above all, to respond?. . . . Besides, I never knew how to *invent*—I literally lived everything I've ever written—and vice versa. I don't like metaphor, but I like talking to you, *addressing* these words to you. How can I make you believe that I'm not exaggerating? Please believe me, until you see it with your own eyes that this whole story—incredible as it may seem—is perfectly true. I hope your trust in me will endure . . ." [A.N.]

27. Marthe Robert, introduction to *Franz Kafka: Correspondance, 1902–1924* (Paris: Gallimard, 1965), 9. [A.N.]

28. Again, George Steiner is a notable exception here. He says, regarding this phenomenon: "All of Celan's own poetry is translated *into* German. In the process, the receptor-language becomes unhoused, broken, idiosyncratic almost to the point of non-communication. It becomes a 'meta-German,' cleansed of historical-political dirt and thus, alone, useable by a profoundly Jewish voice after the holocaust." Steiner, *After Babel*, 398. [A.N.]

Steiner's observation that Petre Solomon mentions here is formulated in the context of his discussion of Celan's translations of Shakespeare's sonnets (published in 1967). Steiner points out that his philosophy of translation is extremely complex, because he seeks to discover, in his translations, the means by which the original author conveys a meaning, the "topical 'means of his meaning.'" At the same time, Steiner observes, Celan tests his ability to create meaning through his translations. This aspect of his approach to translations is illustrative of his intricate relationship with his mother tongue, his "acutely paradoxical, unresolved, and finally self-destructive coexistence with the German language." Through translations, Celan displaces the German language into "a position of salutary strangeness. He could approach it with therapeutic dispassion as a raw material fatally his own yet also contingent and potentially hostile." *After Babel*, 398–99. [T.N.]

29. The French text of the presentation was made available to me by its author. [A.N.]

See the full text of Felstiner's Cerisy address, translated by Vivian Lehmann as "Langue maternelle, langue éternelle: La présence de l'hébreu," in *Contre-Jour: Études sur Paul Celan*, ed. Martine Broda (Paris: Le Cerf, 1986), 65–84. Published in English as "Mother Tongue, Holy Tongue: On Translating and Not Translating Paul Celan," *Comparative Literature* 38(2) (Spring 1986): 119, and developed further in Felstiner, "'Ziv, That Light': Translation and Tradition in Paul Celan," *New Literary History* 18(2) (1987): 611–31. [T.N.]

30. Allusion to Eugène Ionesco's play *Jeux de Massacre* (The Killing Games) (1974). [T.N.]

31. Rimbaud did the same thing, in a way, albeit in the opposite direction, when he introduced the German word *Wasserfall* into a text in *Les Illuminations*, a word that stirs a veritable semantic panic within the field of French words. "Je ris au wasserfall blond qui s'échevela à travers les sapins" (I laughed at the blond wasserfall that tousled through the pines), in "Aube" (Dawn) (1886). [A.N.]

32. *Hölderlin*, ed. Rudolf Leonhard and Robert Rovini (Paris: Seghers, 1963), 42. [A.N.]

33. PEN International (Poets, Essayists, and Novelists) is an association of writers with centers in over one hundred countries. The first PEN Club was established in London in 1921. [T.N.]

## 6. Twenty Years Later and Abroad

1. Jean-Paul Sartre, *Qu'est-ce que la littérature?* (Paris: Gallimard, 1948) (my translation). [T.N.]

2. Zaharia Stancu (1902–74) was a Romanian novelist, poet, and journalist who was president of the Writers' Union of Romania between 1966 and 1974. [T.N.]

3. Anatol E. Baconsky (1925–77) was a Romanian poet, novelist, and translator. [T.N.]

4. Victor Eftimiu (1889–1972) was a Romanian playwright, poet, and translator of Albanian origin. [T.N.]

5. Eugen Jebeleanu (1911–91) was a Romanian poet, journalist, and translator. [T.N.]

6. Alexandru Balaci (1916–2002) was a Romanian literary critic and historian who wrote extensively on Italian culture, including editing a multivolume history of Italian literature and compiling several dictionaries. [T.N.]

7. "Welcome, Petre. Your friend Paul. 16.09.'66." In the original, the first sentence is in Romanian and the second in French. [T.N.]

8. Cioran provides a similar account of his encounter with Paul Celan in the same year (1966), in a note from his *Cahiers*: "22 juin—Vu hier soir, P.C., sorti d'une clinique psychiatrique après six mois (ou davantage). Tout à fait rétabli, sauf une expression douloureuse et un léger vieillissement *inquiétant*" (I saw P.C. last night, out of a psychiatric hospital after six months [or more]). Completely recovered, apart from an anguished expression and some *disturbing* signs of old age) (emphasis in the original; my translation). In Emil Cioran, *Cahiers, 1957–1972*, preface by Simone Boué (Paris: Gallimard, 1997), 374. [T.N.]

9. See chapter 2, note 17 (pp. 194–95). [T.N.]

10. George Steiner, *Language and Silence* (New York: Atheneum, 1967), 24. [A.N.]

11. Will Vesper, editor-in-chief of the Nazi publication *Die Neue Literatür*, was the person who contested the authorship of Heine's famous poem "Lorelei." [A.N.]

12. Ian Wallace, "Literature—Transparent and Opaque," in *The Avant-Garde Tradition in Literature*, ed. Richard Kostelanetz (New York: Prometheus Books, 1992), 341–42. [A.N.]

13. Henri Michaux, *Dichtungen, Schriften*, 2 vols., trans. Paul Celan and Kurt Leonhard (Frankfurt am Main: S. Fischer, 1966). [T.N.]

14. Jean Starobinski described Celan's voice superbly, in a text originally published in Études Germaniques in Paris (Jul.–Sep. 1970) and reprinted in revised form in the special Celan issue of the Swiss journal *Revue des Belles Lettres* 2–3 (1972): "The absence of any security. Breathing through the grace of the unbreathable. Or, rather, as if the poem were born out of the brightness of a look, unsettled, of a rough sweetness . . . It seems to me that I can almost see, on the edges of words, the trace of the rupture that allowed them to become separate units, specks and clusters of specks, in search of new cohesion. Still, the piercing route, the obstinate melody of syllables, the magical distribution of timbre and accents. Could this melody be the remnant of an ancient harmony? The vibration, in memory, of the echo of a world in which the word was sovereign. Or does it celebrate, somehow, its own birth, on the eve of an invention that cannot avoid the melody, beyond all lacerations? Law of fluid undulation, of symmetrical contrasts: constrictive like the

geometry of a crystal, of breath, of tears. And when the word can no longer inhabit the world, the poet cannot live in his word either . . . The poem is entrusted to the voice, hence prey to transitoriness, left to drain, dragged towards its denouement, doomed to its own extinction but delaying it, anticipating it, playing with the ineluctability of death. Poems as victims . . . Victim exposed (rather than armed) by its own voice. Purity of the syllable which vibrates, defenseless, exposed to the endless hostility of the world, to the insidious assault of nothingness. Purity, like the sound of an overstretched chord which survives its own defeat, its own rupture . . . Voice inalterable, one might say, since everything has been lost; but, right afterward, falling prey to a renewed threat, coming from further away. A voice that speaks the language of Czernowitz: the German spoken by the Jews living there was destroyed by the masters from Germany. The voice of a survivor. . . ." Jean Starobinski based his text (titled *Lecture Publique*) on the notes he took after listening to Celan reading his poems. [A.N.]

15. Radu Boureanu (1906–97) was a Romanian poet, novelist, and translator. [T.N.]

16. Victor Felea (1923–93) was a Romanian poet, essayist, and literary critic. [T.N.]

17. In Romanian, in the original French text: I was sweltering in sorrow, tears in my soul. [T.N.]

18. Michael Hamburger, too, recognized the affinities between the two poets, remarking that "the 'inwardness' of [Celan's] poetry places it in a line of descent that runs from Hölderlin through Rilke to Expressionism." Michael Hamburger, introduction to *Paul Celan: Selected Poems*, trans. Michael Hamburger and Christopher Middleton (Harmondsworth: Penguin, 1972), 10. [T.N.]

19. Michael Hamburger, introduction to *Paul Celan: Selected Poems*, 10. [A.N.]

20. Celan, *Ansprache anläßlich der Entgegennahme des Literaturpreises der Freien und Hansestadt Bremen* (Stuttgart: Deutsche Verlags-Anstalt, 1958), 2; Celan, "Speech on the Occasion of Receiving the Literature Prize of the Free Hanseatic City of Bremen," in *Collected Prose*, trans. and intro. Rosmarie Waldrop (New York: Routledge, 2003), 34. Let us also recall Paul Celan's affirmation in his speech upon receiving the Büchner Prize in 1960: "The poem intends another, needs this other, needs an opposite. It goes toward it, bespeaks it. . . . The poem becomes—under what conditions—the poem of a person who still perceives, still turns towards phenomena, addressing and questioning them. The poem becomes conversation—often desperate conversation." Celan, "The Meridian," in *Collected Prose* (Routledge, 2003), 49–50. [T.N.]

21. Quoted in Picon, *L'Usage de la lecture*, 178. [A.N.]

22. Picon, *L'Usage de la lecture*, 182. Emphasis in the original. [A.N.]

23. Blanchot, himself a collaborator on *L'Éphémère*, stated in *L'espace littéraire* that language mimes death and that writing means entering the domain of "*on*," this impersonal pronoun being "that which seems very close the instant one dies." The literary space would be, therefore, a space of death. From this sophism Blanchot drew the conclusion that literature can do without writers. [A.N.]

24. Henri Meschonnic, "On appelle cela traduire Celan," 117–18. [A.N.]

25. *An Anthology of Concrete Poetry*, ed. Emmett Williams (New York: Something Else Press, 1967). [A.N.]

26. Alexandru Philippide, in an article published in *Luceafărul* (Apr. 7, 1973). [A.N.]

27. See Peter Horst Neumann, "*Atemwende*—ein neuer Gedichtband Paul Celans" (1967), in *Über Paul Celan*, ed. Meinecke, 198. [A.N.]

28. See Christoph Perels, "Das Gedicht im Exil" (1968), in *Über Paul Celan*, ed. Meinecke, 213. [A.N.]

29. The complete, untitled poem reads: "Klopf die / Lichtkeile weg: // das schwimmende Wort / hat der Dämmer" (Knock the / wedge of light away: // the swimming/buoyant word / has the dusk) (*Lichtzwang*, 1970); Paul Celan, *Die Gedichte: Kommentierte Gesamtausgabe in einem Band*, ed. Barbara Wiedemann (Frankfurt am Main: Suhrkamp, 2003), 285. [T.N.]

30. "Schwimmhäute zwischen den Worten" (*Lichtzwang*, 1970); Celan, *Die Gedichte*, ed. Barbara Wiedemann, 297. [A.N.]

31. "Für Éric" (*Schneepart*, 1971); Celan, *Die Gedichte*, ed. Wiedemann, 331. [T.N.]

32. See Rainer Gruenter, "Meister der Dunkelheit" (1960), in *Über Paul Celan*, ed. Meinecke, 52–54. [A.N.]

33. The Romanian word *răzbunare* (revenge) has special connotations, as Noica observed; see chapter 4 (pp. 100–101). [T.N.]

34. Henri Michaux, "Sur le chemin de la vie, Paul Celan," Études Germaniques 25(3) (Jul.–Sep. 1970): 250. [A.N.]

# Index

**Petre Solomon** was born in 1923 in Bucharest. Of Jewish descent, he attended courses at the Onescu College for Jewish students until 1944, when he left for Palestine. He returned to Bucharest in August 1946 and started to work at Cartea Rusă publishing house, where he met Paul Celan, who was already working there as a translator. He published several volumes of poetry, such as *Lumina zilei* (The Light of Day, 1954), *Între foc și cenușă* (Between Fire and Ashes, 1968), *Umbra necesară* (The Necessary Shadow, 1971), *Exerciții de candoare* (Exercises in Candour, 1974), *Culoarea anotimpurilor* (The Color of Seasons, 1977), or *Hotarul de hârtie* (The Paper Border, 1988). He was a highly appreciated translator, rendering in Romanian works by authors such as Milton, Shakespeare, Byron, Shelley, Victor Hugo, Baudelaire, Rimbaud, Celan, Balzac, Charles Dickens, Walter Scott, Herman Melville, Mark Twain, Joseph Conrad, Jack London, Joseph Kessel, Ray Bradbury, Graham Greene, Evelyn Waugh, and many others. He also published several monographs on John Milton, Mark Twain, Henry James, Arthur Rimbaud, and Paul Celan. Petre Solomon received the Writers' Union Prize for translations in 1981. He died on October 15, 1991.

**Emanuela Tegla** has a PhD in literature from the University of Ulster and has been working recently on postcolonial autobiography and the question of identity. She is the author of *J. M. Coetzee and the Ethics of Power. Unsettling Complicity, Complacency, and Confession* (2016) and *The Burden of the Self: Tim Parks, Salman Rushdie and Postmodernism* (2008). Her main research interests include ethics, morality, contemporary literature, and trauma studies.